Building Understanding
A Thematic Approach
to Reading Comprehension

Joan Baker-González

University of Puerto Rico - Mayaguez

Eileen K. Blau

University of Puerto Rico - Mayaguez

Longman

Building Understanding: A Thematic Approach to Reading Comprehension

Credits appear on page 237. Acknowledgments appear on page 238.

Pearson Education, 10 Bank Street, White Plains, NY 10606

Editorial director: Joanne Dresner
Acquisitions editor: Allen Ascher
Development editor: Françoise Leffler
Production editor: Liza Pleva
Text design: Pencil Point Studio
Cover design: Curt Belshe
Text art: Stephanie O'Shaughnessy/Ray Skibinski/Tom Sperling

Library of Congress Cataloging-in-Publication Data

Baker-González, Joan.
   Building understanding : a thematic approach to reading
comprehension / Joan Baker-González, Eileen K. Blau.
     p.   cm.
   ISBN 0-201-82528-7 (pbk.)
   1. English language—Textbooks for foreign speakers.   2. Reading
comprehension—Problems, exercises, etc.   3. Readers.   I. Blau,
Eileen K.   II. Title.
PE1128.B275   1995
428.6′4—dc20   94-31208
                                                              CIP

11 12 13 14 15 - CRS - 05 04 03 02 01

CONTENTS

UNIT 6: HUMANS AND OTHER ANIMALS 159

PREFACE

Building Understanding is a thematic or topical reader for young adult and adult ESL students at an intermediate to advanced level. Units One through Seven each consist of a set of five closely related readings on a topic of personal or world interest. The benefit of reading several selections on the same topic is that previous readings provide background knowledge and vocabulary for later readings. This makes it easier and easier to read about that topic. With increased knowledge of a topic, you have more to talk, think, and write about, as you acquire the language.

TEACHER'S INTRODUCTION

Description of the Text

There are seven main units in this book, preceded by a shorter introductory chapter about reading.

Each one of the main units is built around five authentic reading selections, of which the first three are nonfiction (magazine, or newspaper articles, textbook selections, brochures, personal essays, etc.). The fourth selection is a story, and the final selection is a poem or brief artistic piece. The background knowledge students gain from the early readings facilitates their comprehension and enjoyment of the stories and poems.

To benefit from a thematic reader, students must read several selections on a single topic. When making choices about what to include in a reading program, think in terms of whole units rather than single reading selections. Omission of a single selection or a selection and a poem, for example, would leave enough material for students to benefit from related readings, but choosing a single reading from a unit would not.

Unit Organization

The **Introductory Page** is a useful part of the unit. The title, focus questions, picture, and quote can all be used to activate background knowledge on the topic and create a purpose for reading, as well as to preview and make predictions about the content of the unit.

Each reading selection is accompanied by pre- and postreading exercises and activities that follow a uniform format. These exercises and activities encourage students to interact with the selection and each other. They also provide students with thinking tools they can use when reading on their own.

A **Before Reading** section activates the students' background knowledge and sometimes requires them to preview the text and make predictions about its content. After doing this exercise, the students should find the selection easier to read because they will have an idea of what to expect and will have a purpose for reading.

In reading the **Selection**, students should be encouraged to monitor their comprehension and to mark important ideas or difficulties as they read. They should, however, read straight through a selection on the first reading, trying to understand as much as they can without stopping. This is especially important when reading stories for enjoyment.

A **Comprehension Check** follows the reading selection to help students prepare for class activities. It is text-bound and focuses students' attention on what the text says as opposed to their opinions of it. Students should understand that it may take more than one reading to answer these questions. Many teachers will go over these questions in class, or they can be used as quiz items to check that students have prepared for class.

Sharing Your Thoughts offers a choice of discussion questions and interactive activities to be done in pairs, small groups, or as a whole class. These exercises move from those that depend more closely on the text to broader, related issues. At either level, students should defend and support their responses with specifics. One of the major goals of *Building Understanding* is to encourage students, whether in speaking or writing, to support general statements with meaningful specifics. We consider this important both for sharpening thinking skills and as an important foundation for writing.

The **Vocabulary** section begins with a *Content Vocabulary* exercise for all selections except the poems. This exercise is a brief summary of important aspects of the selection and is in cloze form; no vocabulary items are to be used more than once. Verbs that will be used in the active voice appear in the list in their basic form. Students must inflect the verb and are thus encouraged to pay attention to verb forms. Other vocabulary exercises focus on useful skills such as inferring the meaning of words from context, building meaning from known parts of the word, developing awareness of grammatical function to help understand meaning, and recognizing phrasal verbs and idiomatic expressions as units.

In addition to these exercises, teachers will, as always, find their own ways to handle the diverse vocabulary needs of their particular students. One strategy is to encourage students to ask about unknown vocabulary before getting into a discussion of the selection. In fact, some teachers may choose to do vocabulary exercises first despite the order in which they appear in the book. Another strategy is to encourage students to keep their own vocabulary lists (suggested in Student's Introduction, Vocabulary A). And finally, teachers should help students develop the confidence to skip unimportant words.

Text Analysis exercises analyze aspects of written discourse commonly used by North American writers. These exercises range from the overall organization of text and paragraphs to small writing conventions such as the use of quotation marks or citation of sources. *Text Organization* exercises ask students to determine the contribution of individual paragraphs or sets of paragraphs to the whole piece of writing. Note that often there is no single right answer to this type of exercise. Its purpose is to get students to pay closer attention to how paragraphs are focused and how writing is organized as an aid to reading comprehension and as a model for writing.

Writing Task exercises close the sequence of activities for each Reading Selection. Writing about reading enhances reading comprehension and language development. The process of writing clarifies and sometimes changes our ideas of the reading and is, therefore, as much a part of a reading program as it is a foundation for writing. It further aids language development because it is an opportunity to use language in which all students can participate, even the timid who might not respond orally. The writing sections are not meant to provide a full course in writing, but to give students frequent writing experience and exposure to the writing process. In the course of the book, students become acquainted with various steps in the process approach to writing, such as brainstorming and freewriting for ideas, peer review, and revision. Teachers who want to place greater emphasis on writing will probably do these steps more consistently than our occasional suggestions.

The writing section includes suggestions for a variety of types of writing, ranging from small tasks like writing definitions to writing complete compositions. It also includes personal, imaginative, and academic writing. Three general abilities, related primarily to academic writing, stand out as particularly important: supporting general statements, giving proper credit to people whose words or ideas are used, and integrating ideas from more than one source.

Many of the suggestions for writing and questions in "Sharing Your Thoughts" can be used as ideas for reading journals. You might also want to have students expand on their initial reactions to a reading selection after it has been discussed. Through writing about a text at different times, students learn that their understanding of the reading selection is clarified by the process of writing. In all cases, choose from suggestions according to the nature of your course and students' needs, interests, and work load.

A Final Look provides a choice of activities to achieve closure after reading five selections on a given topic. It includes *Discussion* and *Writing* sections. The first ***Discussion*** question is always to return to the introductory page to answer the focus questions, to reconsider the other material on the page, and to think about how points of view and knowledge have changed as a result of reading the unit.

Suggestions in the ***Writing*** section generally require integrating material from the readings in the unit and sometimes from other units as well. Again choose questions and activities from "A Final Look" according to your needs.

Basic Abilities of Efficient Readers

FOCUS

➤ Why is it important to read well?

➤ Why is it important to recognize our different purposes for reading?

➤ What are some basic abilities that efficient readers have developed?

> The man who has not the habit of reading is imprisoned in his immediate world, in respect to time and space. His life falls into a set routine; he is limited to contact and conversation with a few friends and acquaintances, and he sees only what happens in his immediate neighborhood. From this prison there is no escape. But the moment he takes up a book, he immediately enters a different world, and if it is a good book, he is immediately put in touch with one of the best talkers in the world.
>
> – Lin Yutang (1895–1976)
> *The Importance of Living*

This introduction to reading is an important foundation for all types of reading: the reading you do for English class, the reading you do for other classes, and the reading you do outside of school.

Before Reading

Work with a partner or in a small group. For numbers 1, 2, and 3 summarize your answers in a single list.

1. On the left side of a sheet of paper, list all the things you or your family members read in a typical week. List both the obvious things such as newspapers and the smaller things, perhaps less obvious, such as instructions on a package.
2. Discuss why you read each item, and write your reasons to the right.
3. Study your reasons for reading. List the different types of reading you do— for example, reading for information—and give at least one example for each type.
4. Share your feelings about the different types of reading. What do you enjoy reading? Why? If you don't enjoy reading some things, why not?
5. As a class, summarize the types of reading people do and give examples of each.

BASIC ABILITIES OF EFFICIENT READERS

1   As the Before Reading activity illustrated, people read a lot of different things for different reasons. Reading is especially important to students because it is a major part of the learning process. With the rate of change in the modern technological world, many people will be students for life, reading to keep up-to-date in their fields or to learn about new fields.

2   Since reading is so important, people need to become the most efficient readers possible. Fortunately, as a literate person, you have developed some or many of the abilities of efficient readers. But you may not have applied these to reading in English. Let's review the most fundamental abilities now.

3   Efficient readers use various abilities before, during, and after reading. Some of these apply to most types of reading; others are limited to a particular type of reading such as textbooks or professional articles.

BEFORE READING

4   When reading for pleasure, most people jump in and start reading without any preparation. They are usually satisfied with understanding most of what they read, as it would take away some of the pleasure if they interrupted their reading to be sure they understood everything. When reading more difficult material, however, or when reading academic or professional material for which they will be held accountable, efficient readers usually test the water before getting their feet wet.

5   First, efficient readers will preview the article or chapter to get a general idea of the content and organization of what they are going to read. According to educator and comedian Bill Cosby, when you **preview** you "read the entire first two paragraphs of whatever you've chosen. Next read only the first sentence of each successive

paragraph. Then read the entire last two paragraphs" (*How to Read Faster.* 1982, New York: International Paper.). Also, look carefully at the title and section headings, which can help you understand the main idea and see important sections of the piece. Look at pictures and charts, and read their captions. Exactly how you preview depends on the format of the material, but in general, good readers take advantage of any help they can get to learn something about the **topic**, or subject, of the reading and the organization of the material before they begin. Having an idea of what to expect makes reading easier and results in better comprehension.

6   Second, efficient readers think about their **background knowledge** of the topic. In other words, they think about what they already know about the topic. While reading, they use their background knowledge to help them understand new information and make intelligent guesses about the meaning of unknown words.

7   Third, efficient readers determine their purpose for reading and then read accordingly. They know they do not have to read everything at the same speed or with the same degree of care. For example, if they are looking for one specific detail, such as a telephone number or a price, they **scan** the material for that one detail, wasting no time on anything else. If they only need to understand the main idea of something, they **skim** it; that is, they read quickly, looking for key words and sentences to give them the general idea. When their lives or jobs depend on following instructions, they read very carefully, reread, and ask for help in understanding. Knowing when to scan, when to skim, and when to read slowly and carefully helps efficient readers handle the large amount of reading they have to or want to do.

DURING READING

8   Reading is an active process; the reader's mind is always working. Since readers cannot ask the writer questions, they use all possible clues in the text to figure out what the writer is

trying to communicate. Research shows that efficient readers form **hypotheses**, or tentative ideas, about what the text says and continuously check those ideas. If something they read contradicts their understanding of the text, they modify their ideas. This whole process is called **monitoring comprehension**, and efficient readers are good at it. They recognize when they don't understand something, and they use the words on the page, their background knowledge of the topic, and their general knowledge of the world to build the meaning.

9   Good readers know that it is not efficient to use a dictionary or ask another person for help each time they have a problem understanding something. They tackle vocabulary problems by following these steps.

Step 1: Locate the problem. Is it a single word, a multiword expression, or a whole idea? Could the problem be that you don't have cultural knowledge that is necessary for understanding? For instance:

In paragraph 8, is the word you need to know *figure* or *figure out*? If *figure* alone is the word, what will you do with *out*? *Figure out* must be one of the many multiword or phrasal verbs in English.

Step 2: Decide if the unknown word or expression is important or not. If it is not important, continue reading. For instance:

Is *clues* in paragraph 8 important or not? The paragraph says that readers decide on the meaning by using something (clues) in the text. The general meaning of *clues* must therefore be something like "information." You can understand the ideas of the paragraph without a more specific definition of *clues*. So you can decide that knowing the definition is NOT important, and you can keep reading.

Step 3: If you decide the word or expression is important, look first for a definition. For instance:

Monitoring comprehension (paragraph 8) is what efficient readers do. This phrase is important. It is defined in the previous sentences as the process of forming tentative ideas about the reading and checking them as you read.

Step 4: If there is no definition, examine the context (words and sentences surrounding the new word or phrase) and try to **infer**, or guess, the meaning from the context. For instance:

> What is the context for the word *tackle* in paragraph 9? What do good readers tackle? They tackle problems. What do you do with problems? You try to solve them, so *tackle* probably means something like "try to solve." As you keep reading the paragraph, you will see this definition makes sense.

Step 5: If you can't guess the meaning or understand the idea without it, then ask someone for help or consult a dictionary.

10 Sometimes the problem is larger than a word or phrase, for example, a new concept or idea or something that depends on cultural knowledge that you do not have. First, try rereading the relevant text several times. If you still cannot understand, consult another person or, later, a reference book in the library.

11 In addition to monitoring their comprehension, efficient readers also look for sentences that express the important ideas of the reading. They usually mark them in some way so they can be found easily later. Some readers also take notes as they read. Marking a text and note taking are especially important when you will be tested on the material or want to use it later in a report or term paper.

12 Finally, efficient readers have developed the ability to read in word groups, not word by word. For example:

> Finally, efficient readers   have developed the ability to read in word groups,   not word by word.

They can do this because they recognize most of the words in the text, and they know which words go together in meaningful groups. Since reading in word groups is your goal, you have a very good reason to work on improving your vocabulary and your knowledge of how words are organized in sentences.

AFTER READING

13 What readers do after reading also depends on their purpose. If they are reading for pleasure, they might think about their reactions to the reading, they might share ideas about the reading with a friend, or they might reread parts they especially enjoyed. If a teacher or boss is going to hold them accountable for knowing or using the information they read, they check their overall understanding of the material carefully. Here are three ways to check your understanding after reading a section of a text or a whole text.

1. Ask yourself questions such as
   - Why did the writer write this material?
   - What are the main or most important ideas that the writer wanted to communicate?
   - What are the major details related to these main ideas?
2. **Paraphrase** the most important ideas, that is, put them into your own words. This may not be easy, but it will help you remember and use the ideas in the future.
3. Explain the main ideas to another person.

If you cannot do these three things, you need to read some or all of the reading a second or third time. One mistaken idea that students sometimes have is that efficient readers can understand everything perfectly with one reading. This is just not true. You might need to reread something a number of times, the number depending on how difficult the text is, how important the reading is, and how much background information you have on the topic. If something is still not clear after you have made a thoughtful effort to understand, mark it and ask a friend or teacher for help.

14 After you understand what the text says, think more about its ideas and examples and evaluate them if possible. Ask yourself questions like these: Are the ideas clear? Do I agree with the writer's opinion? Whether I agree or disagree, does the writer provide convincing evidence? How do these ideas relate to my life or the lives of people I know? You may also want to write some of your reactions to what you read because writing can help you clarify your

thoughts, express them in English, and understand the reading selection better, too. Responding to what you read in these ways is very important. As the seventeenth-century English philosopher John Locke said, "Reading furnishes the mind only with materials for knowledge; it is thinking [that] makes what we read ours."

15   In conclusion, knowing about the skills and abilities of efficient readers can help you, but this knowledge will not make you a better reader any more than reading about swimming will make you a better swimmer. There is only one way to develop a skill and that is to practice it. So, take the plunge. Start reading and keep on reading even if you don't understand everything you read. When you are curious about something you don't understand, ask about it. You, too, can become an efficient reader in English.

Comprehension Check

Use these questions to check that you understood the reading.

1. How will efficient readers read differently for these purposes?
    a. You want to find a score on the sports page.
    b. You only want the general idea of a magazine article.
    c. You have to learn how to operate a machine for your job.
    d. You are passing the time of day on a long bus trip.
2. If good comprehension of academic material is required, what should you do before reading?
3. What steps should you follow in dealing with unknown vocabulary or multiword expressions when excellent comprehension is important?
4. What do efficient readers do while reading?
5. What can you do after you finish reading something to help you understand the reading?
6. How is written communication different from face-to-face oral communication?

Sharing Your Thoughts

*Work with a partner. Write his or her name on your paper, and then write the numbers 1–17 in a column on the left. Interview your partner to find out which of the things listed below he or she does when reading in his or her native language. Write **always, sometimes**, or **never** next to each number on your paper. After your partner interviews you, talk about each skill or strategy. Will it be easy or difficult to use it when you read in English? Could learning to use it help you?*

1. Adjust the way you read to fit your purpose.
2. Jump in and go with the flow when reading for pleasure.
3. Preview important material before reading.
4. Think about what you already know about the topic before reading.
5. Establish a purpose for reading.

6. Monitor or check understanding while reading.
7. Try to guess the meaning of unknown words from the context.
8. Use background knowledge or general knowledge to figure out meaning.
9. Use a dictionary only when a new word is important.
10. Look for definitions of new words in the text.
11. Mark important ideas while reading.
12. Check understanding by asking yourself questions.
13. Check understanding by paraphrasing ideas.
14. Check understanding by explaining ideas to another person.
15. Reread a selection or difficult parts of it.
16. Ask a friend or teacher for help when you don't understand.
17. Evaluate and react to ideas you read.

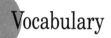

Vocabulary

A. Content Vocabulary

Complete the following statements about reading and efficient readers with words from the list. Change the form of verbs if the grammar of the sentence requires it. For this and every vocabulary exercise you do, add the words you want to remember to your own vocabulary list. You may choose to keep your vocabulary list in a small notebook that you carry with you and study whenever you have a moment, or you may prefer to put individual vocabulary items on small cards. You should include the word in its original sentence along with a **synonym** *(a word with the same meaning), a brief paraphrase, or a definition.*

agree	**captions**	**disagree**
figure out	**handle**	**held accountable**
literate	**mistaken**	**pleasure**
take advantage	**take the plunge**	**up-to-date**

1. Reading is important in the modern world. Everyone needs to be
_____, and people have to _____ large amounts of
reading.

2. Reading is particularly important to professionals because it helps them
keep _____ in their fields.

3. The purpose of previewing is to get an idea of what a selection is about.
Look at the _____ under the pictures and charts, read section
headings, follow Bill Cosby's instructions. In other words, _____
of all the help you can get before reading so that you will know what to
expect when you start to read.

4. Students and professionals will be _____ for understanding what they read, so they must reread the difficult parts. Remember it is a(n) _____ idea that efficient readers can understand perfectly with only one reading.

5. If you have a problem with a vocabulary item, use the context to try to _____ the meaning.

6. Be a thoughtful reader. Think about what you read. If you don't _____ with an idea, try to explain the reasons you _____ .

7. Reading can give you a lot of _____ if you become good at it, but it is a skill or ability that requires practice.

8. Patricia has been reading short stories in English for two semesters. Yesterday she borrowed a full-length novel from the library because she plans to _____ and start reading longer works of literature.

B. Recognizing Definitions

Good readers recognize when a word is defined in the text. For example, the word **scan** occurred in the context repeated below, and the words shown here in italics helped to define the word:

> For example, if they are *looking for one specific detail*, such as a telephone number or a price, they **scan** the material for that one detail, *wasting no time on anything else.*

Scan means to pass your eyes over the material fast, looking for specific details.

Underline the definitions of these words in the text and copy them below. What words, expressions, or punctuation tell you that you are reading a definition? (¶ means "paragraph")

DEFINITION

1. scan (¶7)　　　　　　　*read quickly, looking for one specific detail*
2. preview (¶5)　　　　　　_____
3. background knowledge (¶6)　_____
4. skim (¶7)　　　　　　　_____
5. hypotheses (¶8)　　　　　_____
6. monitoring comprehension (¶8)　_____
7. infer (¶9, Step 4)　　　　_____
8. paraphrase (¶13, Item 2)　　_____

Text Analysis

Text Organization

Writers often give the reader clues to important points by numbering them. Some of the numbering is very obvious as in the steps in paragraph 9. Other times words such as *first*, *second*, and *third* are used to mark consecutive important points. Use the numbering clues in the selection to help you answer this question: How do efficient readers prepare themselves before they begin academic reading?

Writing Task

Most people who are learning to express their thoughts in writing have two questions: What should I write about? and How much should I write? The writing suggestions in this book will give you some help with these decisions, but they are only suggestions; do not let them limit your creativity. Suggestions for length usually indicate the number of paragraphs you should try to write.

> A **paragraph** (¶) is a group of sentences all of which are related to one topic or idea. Paragraphs are usually marked by indenting the first line. They can be short or long, depending on the topic and how much a writer has to say about it. If you look at the readings in this book, you will find most paragraphs have between four and ten sentences.

1. Write a paragraph to answer one of these questions.
    - How do you feel when you have to read in English? Why do you feel this way?
    - Compare your ability to read in your native language and in English using some of the information from the Sharing Your Thoughts activity.
    - What do you need to work on to read more efficiently in English?
2. Reread the quote on this unit's introductory page. Write about a reading experience you have had which you felt opened a new world to you. What did you read? How did it affect you? Why do you think it had such an effect on you? Write about one page.

UNIT ONE
Friendship

A friend is a person with whom I may be sincere.
Before him I may think aloud.
— Ralph Waldo Emerson

FOCUS

➤ What are friends? What are the characteristics
of friendship?

➤ What function do friendships serve?
Do all friendships serve the same function?

➤ How do we make friends?

➤ How and why do friendships end?

1

SELECTION ONE

Before Reading

Psychologists Keith Davis and Michael J. Todd researched the characteristics of friendship and tested their model on 250 college students and community members. In the following excerpt from a 1985 article on their research that appeared in *Psychology Today*, Keith Davis presents the characteristics they found.

1. On your own, think about your friends. What are the characteristics of your relationships? What is a friend? To develop your ideas, complete these sentences:

- Friends always/usually/never _____ .
- A friend is a person who _____ .

Compare your ideas with a partner or in a group and make one list of the characteristics of friendship.

2. What do you think the word *fabric* means in the title of this selection?

3. Look at the format of this selection. What does it look like?

THE FABRIC OF FRIENDSHIP by Keith Davis

The original profile of friendship we developed included these essential characteristics beyond the fact that two people participate in a reciprocal relationship as equals:

1 ENJOYMENT: They enjoy each other's company most of the time, although there may be temporary states of anger, disappointment or mutual annoyance. ("I find whatever we do more enjoyable when Jim and I do it together." "He has the ability to make me laugh.")

2 ACCEPTANCE: They accept one another as they are, without trying to change or make the other into a new or different person. ("She's not always on me to do things that I don't want to do." "He appreciates my style.")

3 TRUST: They share mutual trust in the sense that each assumes that the other will act in light of his or her friend's best interest. ("Even when he is bugging me, I know that it's for my own good." "I just know that I can count on her; whatever she says, she will do." "He would never intentionally hurt me—except in a fit of extreme anger.")

4 RESPECT: They respect each other in the sense of assuming that each exercises good judgment in making life choices. ("She doesn't give advice unless asked, but then it is always good." "He will usually do what's right.")

5 MUTUAL ASSISTANCE: They are inclined to assist and support one another and, specifically, they can count on each other in times of need, trouble or personal distress. ("I feel like doing things that she needs to have done.")

6 CONFIDING: They share experiences and feelings with each other. ("He tells me things that no one else knows about him.")

7 UNDERSTANDING: They have a sense of what is important to each and why the friend does what he or she does. In such cases, friends are not routinely puzzled or mystified by each other's behavior. ("I know what makes her tick." "I can usually figure out what's wrong when he's troubled or moody.")

8 SPONTANEITY: Each feels free to be himself or herself in the relationship rather than feeling required to play a role, wear a mask or inhibit revealing personal traits. ("I feel completely comfortable around him.")

Comprehension Check

1. Which characteristics of friendship did you find easy to understand on the first reading? Which did you find more difficult?

2. Reread the selection and underline the key words that define each characteristic of friendship.

3. For each characteristic complete the sentence below using your own words. In doing this, you will be paraphrasing the definition you underlined.

   a. *Friends enjoy each other's company* means

   _____

   b. *Friends accept one another* means

   _____

   c. *Friends trust each other* means

   _____

   d. *Friends respect each other* means

   _____

   e. *Friends assist each other* means

   _____

   f. *Friends confide in each other* means

   _____

   g. *Friends understand each other* means

   _____

   h. *Friends are spontaneous with each other* means

   _____

Sharing Your Thoughts

1. Compare your sentences from Comprehension Check 3 above with those of a partner. Decide on the best paraphrase for each characteristic. Ask for help if there are any characteristics that you still do not understand.

2. Were the characteristics of friendship in the reading selection similar to those you listed in the Before Reading activity? What differences were there?

3. Which characteristics of friendship are the most important to you? Compare your choices with those of your classmates and discuss your reasons for your choices. How, if at all, do the men and women in the class differ in which characteristics they consider important?

4. The following quotes are from a book, *Among Friends*, by Letty Cottin Pogrebin. Which characteristic or characteristics does each quote refer to? Answer the same question for the quote on the introductory page. Are there any characteristics of friendship that should be added to the list in "The Fabric of Friendship"? If so, what are they?

   a. *A friend is someone who takes me as I am.*—Bruce, an appliance repairman

   b. *A friend is someone who knows all about me and still likes me.*—Betty, a librarian

   c. *A friend is someone who tells me the truth about me. I want to know when my work stinks or I'm being hurtful or stupid. I expect my friends to save me from myself.*—Bill, a carpenter

5. The author states that in friendship "two people participate in a reciprocal relationship as equals." Are friends always equals? Give examples to support your answer.

Vocabulary

A. Content Vocabulary

The following nouns are often used in descriptions of friendship. Each one of these nouns has a related verb. Write the related verb in the right column. Some of the verbs are used in the selection. If you are not sure of the verb form, use your dictionary.

Noun	Verb
acceptance	*accept*
assistance	
confiding	
enjoyment	
respect	
trust	
understanding	

Complete the following statements about friends with the correct word from the above list. In some cases you will use the noun; in others you will use the verb, depending on the grammar of the sentence. Add the words you want to remember to your vocabulary list.

1. It is fun to spend time with our friends; we _____ their company.

2. Friends can count on each other for _____ in times of need.

3. People are not confused or puzzled by their friends; on the contrary, they usually _____ what they do and why they do it.

4. To most people it is important to admire and think well of their friends. They want their friends to be people they can_____.

5. Friends don't try to change each other; _____ of people as they are is an important characteristic of friendship.

6. How can you be friends with someone you cannot count on, someone you cannot _____ ?

7. Close friends tell each other things that they would not tell most people; they _____ in each other.

B. Idioms and Phrasal Verbs

An **idiom** is an expression that has a special meaning that is not clear from the individual words in the expression. Idioms are not always in the dictionary, so before looking up an idiom, try to infer its meaning from the context.

> EXAMPLE:
> I can't do this alone. Can you ***give me a hand***?
> (Can you *help me*?)

Phrasal verbs, verbs that are made up of two or three words, are common in English. They are sometimes considered idioms because they may have a special meaning that you cannot figure out from the words they are made up of. For example, *figure out* does not mean the same as *figure + out*. Instead, it means *discover* or *determine*. It is best to consider idioms and phrasal verbs as single units rather than as several separate words.

The following statements are taken from the selection. Choose the better paraphrase for the idioms and phrasal verbs in italics. Use clues from the context in the selection to help you.

1. She's not always ***on me*** to do things that I don't want to do. (¶ 2)
   a. helping me
   b. telling me

2. Even when he is ***bugging me***, I know that it's for my own good. (¶ 3)
   a. bothering me
   b. laughing at me

3. I just know that I can ***count on her***; whatever she says, she will do. (¶ 3)
   a. depend on her
   b. remember her

4. I ***feel like doing*** things that she needs to have done. (¶ 5)
   a. am sentimental about doing
   b. have a desire to do

5. I know what ***makes her tick.*** (¶ 7)
   a. bothers her
   b. makes her do what she does

6. I can usually ***figure out*** what's wrong when he's troubled or moody. (¶ 7)
   a. discover
   b. forget

Text Analysis

Writing Conventions

In this selection, after each characteristic of friendship there are several statements in quotation marks. What are these statements? Why are they in quotation marks?

Writing Task

Think about one of your friends. Write a definition of *friend* and follow it with a few sentences that illustrate how your friend fits the definition.

SELECTION TWO

Before Reading

This selection is from a book called *Necessary Losses: The Loves, Illusions, Dependencies and Impossible Expectations That All of Us Have to Give Up in Order to Grow* by Judith Viorst.

1. Think about two or three of your friends. Consider the following questions and write a few sentences about each friend.
   - Why do you like them?
   - Why do you think they like you?
   - What do you do for each other?
2. Talk with a partner about what you discovered about your friends. Are they all the same kind of friend? That is, are your relationships with your various friends the same or different?
3. Preview the selection. What kinds of friends will you read about? How does the author make your preview easy?

All Kinds of Friends by Judith Viorst

1   *F*riends broaden our horizons. They serve as new models with whom we can identify. They allow us to be ourselves—and accept us that way. They enhance our self-esteem because they think we're okay, because we matter to them. And because they matter to us—for various reasons, at various levels of intensity—they enrich the quality of our emotional life.

2   In my discussions with several people about the people we call our friends, we established the following categories of friendship:

CONVENIENCE FRIENDS

3   These are the neighbor or office mate or member of our car pool[1] whose lives routinely intersect with ours. These are the people with whom we exchange small favors. They lend us their cups and silverware for a party. They drive our children to soccer when we are sick. They keep our cat for a week when we go on vacation. And, when we need a lift, they give us a ride to the garage to pick up the Honda. As we do for them.

4   But we don't, with convenience friends, ever come too close or tell too much: We maintain our public face and emotional distance. "Which means," says Elaine, "that I'll talk about being overweight but not about being depressed. Which means I'll admit being mad but not blind with rage. And which means I might say that we're pinched this month but never that I'm worried sick over money."

---

[1] car pool   several people who take turns driving so that each individual does not have to use his or her car all the time

5   But which doesn't mean that there isn't sufficient value to be found in these friendships of mutual aid, in convenience friends.

SPECIAL-INTEREST FRIENDS

6   These friendships depend on the sharing of some activity or concern. These are sports friends, work friends, yoga friends, nuclear-freeze[2] friends. We meet to participate jointly in knocking a ball across a net or saving the world.

7   "I'd say that what we're doing together is *doing* together, not being together," Suzanne says of their Tuesday-doubles[3] friends. "It's mainly a tennis relationship but we play together well." And as with convenience friends, we can, with special-interest friends, be regularly involved without being intimate.

HISTORICAL FRIENDS

8   With luck we also have a friend who knew us, as Grace's friend Bunny did, way back when ... when her family lived in that three-room flat[4] in Brooklyn, when her father was out of work for seven months, when her brother Allie got in that fight where they had to call the police, when her sister married the endodontist from Yonkers, and when, the morning after she lost her virginity, Bunny was the person she ran to tell.

9   The years have gone by, they have gone separate ways, they have little in common now, but they still are an intimate part of each other's past. And so, whenever Grace goes to Detroit, she always goes to visit this friend of her girlhood. Who knows how she looked before her teeth were straightened. Who knows how she talked before her voice got un-Brooklyned.[5] Who knows what she ate before she learned about artichokes. Who knew her when.

CROSSROADS FRIENDS

10   Like historical friends, our crossroads friends are important for what was— for the friendship we shared at a crucial, now past, time of life: a time, perhaps, when we roomed in college together; or served a stint in the U.S. Air Force together; or worked as eager young singles in Manhattan together; or went through pregnancy, child birth and those first difficult years of motherhood together.

---

[2] nuclear-freeze   stopping the proliferation of nuclear weapons

[3] doubles   tennis game with two players on each side

[4] flat   apartment (more common in British English)

[5] un-Brooklyned   lost her Brooklyn accent (Brooklyn, a part of New York City)

11   With historical friends and crossroads friends we forge links[6] strong enough to endure with not much more contact than once-a-year letters at Christmas, maintaining a special intimacy—dormant but always ready to be revived—on those rare but tender occasions when we meet.

CROSS-GENERATIONAL FRIENDS

12   Another tender intimacy—tender but unequal—exists in the friendships that form across generations, the friendships that one woman calls her daughter-mother and her mother-daughter relationships. Across the generations the younger enlivens the older, the older instructs the younger. Each role, as mentor or quester, as adult or child, offers gratifications of its own. And because we are unconnected by blood, our words of advice are accepted as wise, not intrusive, our childish lapses don't summon up warnings and groans. Without the risks, and without the ferocious investment, which are always a part of a real parent-child connection, we enjoy the rich disparities to be found among our cross-generational friends.

CLOSE FRIENDS

13   Emotionally and physically (by seeing each other, by mail, by talks on the phone) we maintain some ongoing friendships of deep intimacy. And although we may not expose as much—or the same kinds of things—to each of our closest friends, close friendships involve revealing aspects of our private self—of our private feelings and thoughts, of our private wishes and fears and fantasies and dreams.

14   Close friends contribute to our personal growth. They also contribute to our personal pleasure, making the music sound sweeter, the wine taste richer, the laughter ring louder because they are there. Friends furthermore take care—they come if we call them at two in the morning; they lend us their car, their bed, their money, their ear; and although no contracts are written, it is clear that intimate friendships involve important rights and obligations. Indeed, we will frequently turn—for reassurance, for comfort, for come-and-save-me help—not to our blood relations but to friends.

---

[6] **forge links**   make connections

Comprehension Check

1. What general purposes do friends serve according to Viorst? Do all friends serve these purposes for us?

2. Reread the selection and underline a sentence or key phrase that defines each category of friendship.

   EXAMPLE:

   convenience friends <u>the people with whom we exchange small favors</u> and <u>friendships of mutual aid</u>

   Paraphrase, or explain the meaning in your own words, of what you underlined.

3. Some friendships are more intimate or closer than others.
   Place each type of friendship into one of these three columns:

PRESENTLY INTIMATE	INTIMATE IN THE PAST	NOT INTIMATE
_____	_____	_____
_____	_____	_____
_____	_____	_____

Sharing Your Thoughts

1. Find a specific example in your life for each category of friend, if possible. Share these examples with your classmates, and tell them why the friend fits the category.

2. Do you think the author would agree or disagree with the following statements? Give evidence from the text to support your opinion.
   a. Convenience friends benefit from each other, but are not real friends.
   b. There is a high degree of trust between special-interest friends.
   c. Historical and crossroads friends are strong but inactive friendships.
   d. We confide equally in all our close friends.
   e. Friendships never change from one category to another.
   f. Close friends can sometimes be more important than relatives.

3. Do you agree or disagree with the above statements? Support your opinion with examples from your own experience.

4. What "rights and obligations" of being close friends could Viorst be referring to in paragraph 14?

5. How do you think Viorst would react to Davis's statement (Selection One) that friendships are reciprocal relationships between equals?

Vocabulary

A. Content Vocabulary

Complete the following statements about friendship with words from the list.
Use each word only once. Change the form of verbs if the grammar of the sentence
requires it. Add the words you want to remember to your vocabulary list.

allow	**share**	**close**
dormant	**enrich**	**exchange**
in common	**matter**	**broaden our horizons**

1. We have only a few intimate or _____ friends to whom we reveal our most private thoughts.

2. Some friendships are _____, waiting to be revived if old friends get together again.

3. With special-interest friends we _____ activities, but we do not usually have enough _____ to become lifelong friends.

4. With all types of friends, we _____ favors and help each other.

5. Friends don't try to change us; they _____ us to be ourselves.

6. Friends _____ our lives, not with money, but with feelings.

7. Friends _____; they bring new ideas into our lives.

8. Whatever kind of friend a person is, that friend is important to us; that friend _____ to us.

B. Word Analysis

> Words can have several parts.
> A **prefix** is a part that comes at the beginning of a word and changes the meaning of the basic word, for example, *un-* in the word *unhappy*.
> A **suffix** is a part that comes at the end of a word and changes its meaning or function, for example the suffix *-ly* in *happily* changes an adjective to an adverb.

Divide the following words into their meaningful parts. What prefix and / or suffix does it have? What is the basic word? How does the prefix or suffix change the meaning of the basic word? What other words do you know with the same prefix or suffix? Use a dictionary if necessary.

EXAMPLE:

friendship   friend   -ship

The suffix *–ship* changes the noun *friend* into another word with a related meaning: *Friendship* is the state or condition of being friends. Other words with the same suffix: *relationship, leadership, membership.*

1. broaden (¶1) _____

2. enrich (¶1) _____

3. regularly (¶7) _____

4. girlhood (¶9) _____

5. straighten (¶9) _____

6. motherhood (¶10) _____

7. unequal (¶12) _____

8. enliven (¶12) _____

9. unconnected (¶12) _____

10. frequently (¶14) _____

Text Analysis

A. Topic, Purpose, and Main Idea

Topic: The topic of a piece of writing is the subject, what it is about. The first paragraph or two of a selection usually introduces the topic.

1. What is the topic of this selection?

2. What does Viorst tell us in the first two paragraphs that this reading selection is going to do?

Purpose: Writers usually write for one or more of these general purposes:
  • to inform the reader about something
  • to persuade or convince the reader of something
  • to entertain the reader
  • to narrate an event
  • to satisfy the writer's own need to express his or her ideas

3. What do you think Viorst's purpose was in writing this selection?

> **Main Idea:** Especially when the purpose of a selection is to inform or persuade readers of an idea, the idea can often be expressed in a general statement, which is called the main idea. The main idea can be directly stated in the selection, but even when it is not directly stated, the reader should be able to figure it out.

4. Which is the best statement of the main idea in this selection?
   a. All friendships serve the same purpose.
   b. There are different types of friends that serve different purposes in our lives.
   c. Special-interest friends are people who do things together.

B. Text Organization

Writers organize writing in various ways to make it easy for the reader to follow their thinking and see connections and relationships easily. When the writer uses a **list**, as Viorst does, the order of items in the list should have some logic, for example, from most important to least important or vice versa. Which order did Viorst use?

Writing Task

Definitions can often be better understood if they are illustrated by specific examples. Reread Bill's definition of *friend* in Sharing Your Thoughts 4.c., p. 4. What specific examples does he put in his definition? You also found many specific examples in Viorst's writing.

Select one of Viorst's definitions of a particular type of friend. Support that definition with an example from your own experience. Two possible beginnings are suggested in the models below. Since you are using Viorst's definition, be sure to give her proper **credit**.

If you use her exact words, you must use quotation marks.

> DIRECT QUOTE:
>
> Viorst says, convenience friends are "the people with whom we exchange small favors." My neighbor and I are convenience friends. We . . .

If you paraphrase Viorst's definition, you must still give her credit by using an expression such as *according to*.

> BORROWED IDEA WITHOUT DIRECT QUOTE:
>
> According to Viorst, convenience friends are people who do each other favors. My neighbor and I . . .

SELECTION THREE

Before Reading

In his writing, Robert Fulghum expresses his thoughts on the ordinary things that have happened to him in the course of his varied life as father, neighbor, working cowboy, folksinger, IBM salesman, and minister, among others. This selection comes from his first book, *All I Need to Know I Learned in Kindergarten.*

1. Read the title. What could a barber have to do with friendship?
2. Because there is little to help you preview this type of writing and because this type of writing is primarily for enjoyment, just read from beginning to end without stopping. You can always reread parts of the text later.

The Barber

by Robert Fulghum

1   HAIR GROWS at the rate of about half an inch a month. I don't know where he got his facts, but Mr. Washington[1] came up with that one when we were comparing barbers. That means that about eight feet of hair had been cut off my head and face in the last sixteen years by my barber.

2   I hadn't thought much about it until I called to make my usual appointment and found that my barber had left to go into building maintenance. What? How could he *do* this? *My* barber. It felt like a death in the family. There was so much more to our relationship than sartorial[2] statistics.

3   We started out as categories to each other: "barber" and "customer." Then we became "redneck[3] ignorant barber" and "pinko[4] egghead[5] minister." Once a month we reviewed the world and our lives and explored our positions. We sparred over civil rights and Vietnam and a lot of elections. We became mirrors, confidants, confessors, therapists, and companions in an odd sort of way. We went through being thirty years old and then forty. We discussed and argued and joked, but always with a certain thoughtful deference. After all, I was his customer. And he was standing there with a razor in his hand.

---

[1] **Mr. Washington**   the writer's neighbor

[2] **sartorial**   related to tailors; barbers shape your hair like tailors shape clothes

[3] **redneck**   a rural, conservative person (an insult or putdown)

[4] **pinko**   outdated, insulting term that refers to leftist political ideas or person who has leftist political ideas

[5] **egghead**   an intellectual person (uncomplimentary; no longer commonly used)

4   I found out that his dad was a country policeman, that he grew up poor in a tiny town and had prejudices about Indians. He found out that I had the same small-town roots and grew up with prejudices about Blacks. Our kids were the same ages, and we suffered through the same stages of parenthood together. We shared wife stories and children stories and car troubles and lawn problems. I found out he gave his day off to giving free haircuts to old men in nursing homes. He found out a few good things about me, too, I suppose.

5   I never saw him outside the barber shop, never met his wife or children, never sat in his home or ate a meal with him. Yet he became a terribly important fixture in my life. Perhaps a lot more important than if we had been next-door neighbors. The quality of our relationship was partly created by a peculiar distance. There's a real sense of loss in his leaving. I feel like not having my hair cut anymore, though eight feet of hair might seem strange.

6   Without realizing it, we fill important places in each other's lives. It's that way with a minister and congregation. Or with the guy at the corner grocery, the mechanic at the local garage, the family doctor, teachers, neighbors, co-workers. Good people, who are always "there," who can be relied upon in small, important ways. People who teach us, bless us, encourage us, support us, uplift us in the dailiness of life. We never tell them. I don't know why, but we don't.

7   And, of course, we fill that role ourselves. There are those who depend on us, watch us, learn from us, take from us. And we never know. Don't sell yourself short. You may never have proof of your importance, but you are more important than you think.

8   It reminds me of an old Sufi[6] story of a good man who was granted one wish by God. The man said he would like to go about doing good without knowing about it. God granted his wish. And then God decided that it was such a good idea, he would grant that wish to all human beings. And so it has been to this day.

---

[6] Sufi   Moslem mystic sect in which teachers use stories to instruct their disciples

Comprehension Check

1. What did the author and his barber talk about over the years?
2. What stages did their friendship go through? Explain what they did for each other at each stage.
3. What did they find out about each other?
4. How important was this relationship to the writer? How do you know?
5. Which is the best statement of the main idea of this selection?
   a. People who come from different backgrounds can become close friends.
   b. We need people to provide services, and they need us as customers.
   c. People who come into contact in ways that seem unimportant can be important to each other.

Sharing Your Thoughts

1. Does this friendship fit into one of Viorst's categories? Explain. If it does not, what type of friendship is it?
2. The writer's friendship with the barber ended suddenly when the barber changed jobs. How did the writer feel? Discuss other ways friendships end and how people feel and act when friendships end.
3. Is this selection serious? Explain.
4. What message, if any, does this selection have for you in addition to the main idea you chose in Comprehension Check 5?
5. Working with a partner, list people whom you encounter on a regular basis, like a barber. How important are these relationships in your daily life? For whom, if anyone, do you play this role?

Vocabulary

A. Content Vocabulary

Complete the following statements about Fulghum's friendship with the barber with words from the list. Use each word once. Change the form of verbs if the grammar of the sentence requires it. Add the words you want to remember to your vocabulary list.

argue	**discuss**	**joke**	**loss**
odd	**realize**	**roles**	**stages**

1. The relationship between the author and the barber went through different _____; they started out as categories to each other and became friends of a(n) _____ sort.

2. Over the years, they played different _____ for each other; they were confidants, confessors, and therapists at different times.

3. They _____ many different topics, including the problems of parenthood and how to take care of a lawn.

4. Their discussions weren't always serious; they _____ and had a lot of fun together.

5. They sometimes _____ about politics because they didn't always agree on that topic.

6. Then one day the barber was gone, and the author felt a sense of _____ .

7. Author and barber were important to each other, although the author didn't _____ it until the barber changed jobs.

B. Idioms and Phrasal Verbs

Locate the following idioms and phrasal verbs in the selection. Check the context and choose the better paraphrase for each one.

1. **came up with** (¶1)
   a. climbed up to
   b. produced

2. **went through** (¶3)
   a. traveled
   b. experienced

3. **found out** (¶4)
   a. learned
   b. recovered something lost

4. **grew up** (¶4)
   a. spent his childhood
   b. got big

5. **relied upon** (¶6)
   a. depended on
   b. forgotten

6. **sell yourself short** (¶7)
   a. pay too much money
   b. think you are not important

Text Analysis

Text Organization

> Writers help readers by organizing the ideas they want to communicate into paragraphs. Each **paragraph** should contain sentences related to one idea. Some ideas require more than one paragraph to explain fully. Each paragraph, or group of paragraphs related to a single idea, should make a specific contribution to the whole piece of writing.

1. Reread "The Barber" and match each paragraph or set of paragraphs with its contribution to the whole piece of writing.

   PARAGRAPHS

   ____ ¶1–2

   ____ ¶3

   ____ ¶4

   ____ ¶5

   ____ ¶6–7

   ____ ¶8

   CONTRIBUTION

   a. shows what the writer and barber learned about each other

   b. describes the situation that started the writer thinking

   c. shows how important the barber was to the writer

   d. uses another story to explain the significance of this story

   e. shows how the relationship changed over time

   f. shows the meaning the writer sees in this incident

2. In this selection, Fulghum reflects on something that happened in his life. His organizational pattern can be called **anecdote** (story of a specific incident that really happened) plus interpretation. Which paragraphs correspond to the anecdote and which to the interpretation?

3. Is the main idea of this selection (Comprehension Check 5) stated explicitly? If so, where? If not, how can you figure it out? Does the text organization help you? If so, how?

Writing Task

Write about an experience you have had from which you learned something. Use the "anecdote plus interpretation" organizational pattern. Describe the experience and then tell what you learned from it. Write at least one paragraph to describe the experience and one paragraph to tell what you learned from it.

Before Reading

"The First Day of School" is a short story by William Saroyan. William Saroyan (1908–1981) was a prolific writer of novels, short stories, and plays, many based on his experience growing up as the son of Armenian immigrants in California. Saroyan is known for his exuberant style and his insight into human nature.

> One way to activate your background knowledge is to **freewrite** about a topic. Freewriting means to write whatever comes into your mind without worrying about correctness, organization, or style. Freewriting is usually done for a set period of time, for example five or ten minutes.

1. Freewrite on one of the topics below. The questions may help you get started.
   a. how children make friends
   - Where and how do children make friends?
   - Do children make friends in the same ways as adults?

   b. how you made friends when you started school
   - What friends did you make when you started school?
   - What did you have in common?
   - What were your first impressions of these people?

   Share ideas from your freewriting with your classmates.
2. "The First Day of School" is a short story about a little boy who is starting school. Why is school a logical place to make friends? What could happen in this story?

The First Day of School

by William Saroyan

HE WAS A LITTLE BOY NAMED JIM, the first and only child of Dr Louis Davy, 717 Mattei Building, and it was his first day at school. His father was French, a small heavy-set man of forty whose boyhood had been full of poverty and unhappiness and ambition. His mother was dead: she died when Jim was born, and the only woman
5 he knew intimately was Amy, the Swedish housekeeper.

It was Amy who dressed him in his Sunday clothes, and took him to school. Jim liked Amy, but he didn't like her for taking him to school. He told her so. All the way to school he told her so.

I don't like you, he said. I don't like you any more.

10   I like *you*, the housekeeper said.

Then why are you taking me to school? he said.

He had taken walks with Amy before, once all the way to the Court House Park for the Sunday afternoon band concert, but this walk to school was different.

What for? he said.

15   Everybody must go to school, the housekeeper said.

Did you go to school? he said.

No, said Amy.

Then why do I have to go? he said.

You will like it, said the housekeeper.

20   He walked on with her in silence, holding her hand. I don't like you, he said. I don't like you any more.

I like you, said Amy.

Then why are you taking me to school? he asked again. Why?

25   The housekeeper knew how frightened a little boy could be about going to school. You will like it, she said. I think you will sing songs and play games.

I don't want to, he said.

I will come and get you every afternoon, she said.

I don't like you, he told her again.

30   She felt very unhappy about the little boy going to school, but she knew that he would have to go.

The school building was very ugly to her and to the boy. She didn't like the way it made her feel, and going up the steps with him she wished he didn't have to go to school. The halls and rooms scared her, and him, and the smell of the place too. And

35 he didn't like Mr Barber, the principal.

Amy despised Mr Barber.

What is the name of your son? Mr Barber said.

This is Dr Louis Davy's son, said Amy. His name is Jim. I am Dr Davy's housekeeper.

40   James? said Mr Barber.

Not James, said Amy, just Jim.

All right, said Mr Barber. Any middle name?

No, said Amy. He is too small for a middle name. Just Jim Davy.

All right, said Mr Barber. We'll try him out in the first grade. If he doesn't get

45 along all right we'll try him out in kindergarten.

Dr Davy said to start him in the first grade, said Amy. Not kindergarten.

All right, said Mr Barber.

The housekeeper knew how frightened the little boy was, sitting on the chair, and she tried to let him know how much she loved him and how sorry she was about

50 everything. She wanted to say something fine to him about everything, but she couldn't say anything, and she was very proud of the nice way he got down from the chair and stood beside Mr Barber, waiting to go with him to a classroom.

On the way home she was so proud of him she began to cry.

Miss Binney, the teacher of the first grade, was an old lady who was all dried out.

55 The room was full of little boys and girls. School smelled strange and sad. He sat at a desk and listened carefully.

He heard some of the names: *Charles, Ernest, Alvin, Norman, Betty, Hannah, Juliet, Viola, Polly.*

He listened carefully and heard Miss Binney say, Hannah Winter, what *are* you
60 chewing? And he saw Hannah Winter blush. He liked Hannah Winter right from the beginning.

Gum, said Hannah.

Put it in the waste-basket, said Miss Binney.

He saw the little girl walk to the front of the class, take the gum from her mouth,
65 and drop it into the waste-basket.

And he heard Miss Binney say, Ernest Gaskin, what are *you* chewing?

Gum, said Ernest.

And he liked Ernest Gaskin too.

They met in the schoolyard and Ernest taught him a few jokes.
70 Amy was in the hall when school ended. She was sullen and angry at everybody until she saw the little boy. She was amazed that he wasn't changed, that he wasn't hurt, or perhaps utterly unalive, murdered. The school and everything about it frightened her very much. She took his hand and walked out of the building with him, feeling angry and proud.
75 Jim said, What comes after twenty-nine?

Thirty, said Amy.

Your face is dirty, he said.

His father was very quiet at the supper table.

What comes after twenty-nine? the boy said.
80 Thirty, said his father.

Your face is dirty, he said.

In the morning he asked his father for a nickel.

What do you want a nickel for? his father said.

Gum, he said.
85 His father gave him a nickel and on the way to school he stopped at Mrs Riley's store and bought a package of Spearmint.

Do you want a piece? he asked Amy.

Do you want to give me a piece? the housekeeper said.

Jim thought about it a moment, and then he said, Yes.

90 Do you like me? said the housekeeper.

I like you, said Jim. Do you like me?

Yes, said the housekeeper.

Do you like school?

Jim didn't know for sure, but he knew he liked the part about gum. And Hannah

95 Winter. And Ernest Gaskin.

I don't know, he said.

Do you sing? asked the housekeeper.

No, we don't sing, he said.

Do you play games? she said.

100 Not in the school, he said. In the yard we do.

He liked the part about gum very much.

Miss Binney said, Jim Davy, what are you *chewing*?

Ha ha ha, he thought.

Gum, he said.

105 He walked to the waste-paper basket and back to his seat, and Hannah Winter saw

him, and Ernest Gaskin too. That was the best part of school.

It began to grow too.

Ernest Gaskin, he shouted in the schoolyard, *what* are you *chewing*?

Raw elephant meat, said Ernest Gaskin. Jim Davy, what are *you* chewing?

110 Jim tried to think of something very funny to be chewing, but he couldn't.

Gum, he said, and Ernest Gaskin laughed louder than Jim laughed when Ernest

Gaskin said raw elephant meat.

It was funny no matter what you said.

Going back to the classroom Jim saw Hannah Winter in the hall.

115 Hannah Winter, he said, *what in the world* are you *chewing*?

The little girl was startled. She wanted to say something nice that would honestly

show how nice she felt about having Jim say her name and ask her the funny question,

making fun of school, but she couldn't think of anything that nice to say because they

were almost in the room and there wasn't time enough.

120 Tutti-frutti,[1] she said with desperate haste.

It seemed to Jim he had never before heard such a glorious word, and he kept

repeating the word to himself all day.

Amy Larson, he said, *what, are, you, chewing*?

He told his father all about it at the supper table.

125 He said, Once there was a hill. On the hill there was a mill. Under the mill there

was a walk. Under the walk there was a key. What is it?

I don't know, his father said. What is it?

Milwaukee,[2] said the boy.

The housekeeper was delighted.

130 Mill. Walk. Key, Jim said.

Tutti-frutti.

---

[1] **tutti-frutti**   mixed fruit flavor, as of ice cream or gum

[2] **Milwaukee**   largest city in the state of Wisconsin in the north central part of the United States (pronounced like mill + walk + key)

What's that? said his father.

Gum, he said. The kind Hannah Winter chews.

Who's Hannah Winter? said his father.

135 She's in my room, he said.

Oh, said his father.

After supper he sat on the floor with the small red and blue and yellow top that hummed while it spinned. It was all right, he guessed. It was still very sad, but the gum part of it was very funny and the Hannah Winter part very nice. Raw elephant

140 meat, he thought with great inward delight.

Raw elephant meat, he said aloud to his father who was reading the evening paper. His father folded the paper and sat on the floor beside him. The housekeeper saw them together on the floor and for some reason tears came to her eyes.

Comprehension Check

1. What do you learn about Jim's family?
2. How does Jim feel about starting school? How do you know?
3. How does Amy feel about Jim's starting school? How do you know?
4. How does Jim make friends at school?
5. What did Jim learn from the other children in school? What is the significance of what he learned from them?
6. What happens at the end of the story? What is Amy's reaction?

Sharing Your Thoughts

1. Look for details in the story that support your answers to the following questions:
   a. How do we know that Dr. Davy doesn't pay much attention to his son?
   b. Who is more afraid of the first day of school, Jim or Amy?
   c. Why doesn't Amy like Mr. Barber?
   d. What details give a realistic picture of first-grade children?
   e. Which character in the story changes most and how? In what ways does this character change?
2. How did you feel when you started school?
3. Do you remember the first friends you made at school? Why do you think you became friends? Are those reasons similar to the reasons Jim became friends with Hannah and Ernest?
4. Think about the friends you are making now. How are your current reasons for forming friendships similar to the reasons you had as a young child? How are they different?

Vocabulary

Content Vocabulary

Complete the following statements about the story with words from the list. Use each word only once. Two blanks with a noun or pronoun between are for the two parts of a phrasal verb. Change the form of verbs if the grammar of the sentence requires it. Add the words you want to remember to your vocabulary list.

amazed	**delighted**	**die**
frightened	**funny**	**get along**
on the way	**proud**	**try out**
way	**wish**	

1. Amy is the housekeeper who takes care of Jim because his mother _____ when he was born. Amy never went to school and seemed more _____ of the school than five-year-old Jim.

2. Amy didn't like the _____ the school made her feel, and she _____ that Jim didn't have to go to school at all.

3. She didn't like the principal either, but like a mother, she was _____ that Jim behaved well in his office.

4. Jim was only five, but his father wanted him in first grade, so the principal agreed to _____ him _____ in first grade. If he _____ okay, he could stay there. If not, he would go into kindergarten.

5. It didn't take Jim long to begin to make friends and learn some jokes from them. Soon everything the children did or said seemed _____ , especially chewing raw elephant meat.

6. Jim stopped at Mrs. Riley's store _____ to school and bought a package of spearmint gum because Miss Binney didn't allow the children to chew gum in class.

7. When Jim came out of school, Amy was _____ to see he was OK because she was sure something bad had happened to him.

8. She felt better that night and was _____ with the jokes that Jim told at the supper table.

Text Analysis

A. The Grammar-Meaning Connection.

A **pronoun** usually refers to something or someone mentioned elsewhere: *he, she, him, her,* for instance, refer to people. But it is not always clear what some pronouns refer to. The pronoun *it*, for instance, can refer to a concrete object or an abstract idea.

*What does **it** refer to in the following sentences?*

1. Line 106: **It** began to grow too.
2. Line 112: **It** was funny no matter what you said.
3. Line 137 & 138: **It** was all right, he guessed. **It** was still very sad, but the gum part of **it** was very funny…

B. Point of View

Stories can be told from different points of view. The **point of view** is the position from which we see something. In a story it depends on the narrator, the person telling the story. The narrator may be a character in the story, in which case you will notice the pronoun *I* in the text, and we say the point of view is that of the first-person narrator. If the narrator is not a character but a voice that appears to know everything about the story and characters, the point of view is often called that of the omniscient, or all-knowing, narrator.

1. What is the point of view in this story? Support your answer with evidence from the story.
2. How would you tell the same story from the point of view of each of the characters? For example, if you were telling this story from Dr. Davy's point of view, you might begin: "My little son started school today. I wanted him in the first grade even though he is only five…." Finish telling the story from Dr. Davy's point of view.
3. Tell the story from Amy's point of view or from Jim's.

Writing Task

Freewrite about people who are part of your early memories of school—classmates, teachers, or people who worked at a school. Choose one person and write at least a paragraph describing this person and what you remember about him or her.

SELECTION FIVE

Before Reading

The following poem is an English translation of a poem written in French by Marie-Thérèse Colimon, a Haitian writer and educator.

1. What does the title of this poem mean?
2. What does the punctuation in the poem indicate to you?
3. What do you think this poem might be about?

Encounter

by Marie-Thérèse Colimon

1 I'd say: "How are you?"
And you: "Fine, thanks."
I'd say: "We don't see you anymore."
And you: "I'm very busy."

2 A pause . . . I'd begin again very softly
"Tell me . . . " And you, not hearing
My mumbled words
Would go right on unsuspecting
Oh, (politely) you don't have your big straw hat anymore!
But . . . No, not anymore, I'd answer
And you, do you still like sugared almonds?
—Listen to that tune from the house opposite.

3 Then we would each go off across the city
Carrying in our hearts, full with silent sobs,
The bitter burden of unspoken words
And the empty pride of having kept our pain.

Comprehension Check

1. How many voices are there in this poem? Who are they and what do you learn about their relationship?
2. What are the topics of their conversation? Why do you think they talk about these things? How well are they communicating? What evidence can you find for your answer?

3. What are the "unspoken words"? What pain are they keeping inside?
4. Notice that the poem constantly uses *would* (and the related contraction *'d*). What does this tell us about the encounter?

Sharing Your Thoughts

1. Why does the speaker in the poem imagine this conversation? Have you ever imagined a conversation with someone who used to be your friend? What was your motivation or reason for imagining the conversation?
2. Compare the ending of the friendship in this poem and the ending of the friendship in Selection Three, p.14. What similarities and differences do you find?

Text Analysis

A. Text Organization

Poems are often divided into **stanzas**, or groups of lines, just as prose is divided into paragraphs. The space between stanzas shows the division. Like a paragraph in a work of prose, each stanza can serve a particular purpose or contribute something separate to the poem.

What are the three parts of this encounter as indicated by each of the three stanzas?

B. Writing Conventions

At first, this poem follows the usual convention for marking a person's exact words with quotation marks except that colons separate the quotation from the rest of the sentence instead of the more usual commas.

1. When does the poet stop using quotation marks?
2. Why do you think the poet stopped using quotation marks at that point? What effect does this have on the poem and the reader's impression of the encounter?

Writing Task

Think about a friendship that has ended or is not going well. Write a conversation you might have or would like to have with the person. Each speaker should speak at least three times.

A FINAL LOOK

Discussion

1. Work with a partner, in a small group, or as a whole class. Drawing on all five selections in this unit, discuss the focus questions and quote on the introductory page.

2. Why are friendships so important to people? Answer with information from any of the readings in this unit and from personal experience.

3. What does the following quotation say about how to make and keep friends? Do you agree with it? Why or why not?

   You can make more friends in two months by becoming interested in other people than you can in two years by trying to get other people interested in you.

   —Dale Carnegie

4. According to an Eastern proverb, a friend is someone who warns you. Do you think this is an important characteristic of friendship? Explain.

5. Some friendships go sour; others last. Why do some friendships last longer than others?

Writing

1. Write about someone you have met recently. Use these questions as a guide to writing one or two paragraphs.
   a. Who is the person and how did you meet?
   b. What attracted you to him or her? What were your first impressions?
   c. Do you think this person will become a close friend, some other kind of friend, or will the relationship end soon? Support your prediction with specific reasons that may be based on things you learned about friendship in this unit.

2. Write one or two paragraphs about how this unit has changed your thinking about friends or friendship. Be sure to make both your old idea and your new understanding clear. Refer to the selections that changed your views. Use the authors' names and put the titles in quotation marks. If you use the exact words of a writer, put them in quotation marks.

   EXAMPLE:

   Before I read "All Kinds of Friends" by Judith Viorst, I thought all my friends were close friends. Now I realize many of them are friends "at various levels of intensity." For example,…

UNIT TWO

Parents and Children

> I tell you there's a wall ten feet thick and ten miles high between parent and child.
>
> – George Bernard Shaw
> *Misalliance*

FOCUS

➤ How do parents influence their children's lives when the children are young? Consider both positive and negative influences.

➤ How does the way that parents treat their children affect the children's lives as adults?

➤ How do the parent-child relationship and the feelings of children toward their parents often change over time?

Before Reading

This selection is an article about a real family. It originally appeared in *Reader's Digest*.

1. At what stage in life do children most appreciate their parents?
2. What do you appreciate about your parents?
3. Read the title, the sentence under the title, and preview the article. Then answer these questions:
   - What kind of influence on the author did his mother have?
   - Is the point of view in this article that of a young child or an adult child?

MOTHER WAS REALLY SOMETHING

She challenged us to succeed— and then showed us the way

by Joseph N. Michelotti, M.D.

1 In June 1976, I graduated from Northwestern University Medical School in Chicago. When my name was called, I walked quickly across the stage and reached for my diploma. But before the medical-school dean handed me the certificate, he asked my parents, Anna and Carlo Michelotti, to stand. Surprised, they rose from their seats in the audience. They looked at each other and seemed puzzled.

2 The dean told the crowd that my parents, an immigrant Italian couple from a farm outside Chicago, had managed to send their six children to top colleges and graduate schools. (Three of us would become doctors, two were already lawyers and one was a physicist.) "It's remarkable," the dean said. Everyone cheered loudly.

3 Mama's face was radiant with pride. I knew that everything we had achieved or would achieve was because of my parents. When we were young children, my mother, especially, was our mentor. Not until I became an adult did I realize how special she was.

4 **DELIGHT IN DEVOTION.** My mother was born in a small town in northern Italy. She was three when her parents immigrated to this country in 1926. They lived on Chicago's South Side, where my grandfather worked making ice cream.

5 Mama thrived in the hectic urban environment. At 16, she graduated first in her high-school class, went on to secretarial school, and finally worked as an executive secretary for a railroad company.

6 She was beautiful too. When a local photographer used her pictures in his monthly window display, she was flattered. Her favorite portrait showed her sitting by Lake Michigan, her hair windblown, her gaze reaching toward the horizon. My mother always used to say that when you died, God gave you back your "best self." She'd show us that picture and say, "This is what I'm going to look like in heaven."

7 My parents were married in 1944. Dad was a quiet and intelligent man who was 17 when he left

Italy. Soon after, a hit-and-run accident left him with a permanent limp. Dad worked hard selling candy to Chicago office workers on their break. He had little formal schooling. His English was self-taught. Yet he eventually built a small, successful wholesale candy business. Dad was generous, handsome and deeply religious. Mama was devoted to him.

8   After she married, my mother quit her job and gave herself to her family. In 1950, with three small children, Dad moved the family to a farm 40 miles from Chicago. He worked the land and commuted to the city to run his business. Mama said good-bye to her parents and friends and traded her busy city neighborhood for a more isolated life. But she never complained. By 1958, our modest white farmhouse was filled with six children, and Mama was delighted.

9   **"THINK BIG."** My mother never studied books on parenting. Yet she knew how to raise children. She heightened our self-esteem and helped us reach our potential.

10   One fall day, I sat at the kitchen table while Mama peeled potatoes. She spied Dad out the window on his tractor and smiled. "Your father has accomplished so much," she said proudly. "He really is somebody."

11   My mother wanted each of us to be somebody too. "Your challenge is to be everything you can. Mine is to help," she always said.

12   She read to us every day and used homemade flash cards to teach us phonics. She bolstered our confidence, praising even our most ordinary accomplishments. When I was ten, I painted a stack of wooden crates and nailed them together to make a wobbly bookcase. "It's wonderful!" Mama exclaimed. "Just what we need." She used it for many years.

13   In the dining room are two paint-by-number pictures that my sister Gloria and brother Leo did as kids. Several years ago, Leo commented that the pictures weren't very good and offered to take them down. But Mama wouldn't hear of it. "They are there to remind you how much you could accomplish even as children," she said.

14   From the very beginning, she urged us to think big. One day, after visiting our grandparents on the South Side, she made Dad detour past the Prudential Building construction site. Mama explained that when finished, the 41-story building would be Chicago's tallest. "Maybe someday one of you can design a building like this," she said.

15   Her confidence in us was infectious. When my sister Carla was 12, she announced she was going to be a lawyer.

16   "You can do that," Mama said. "You can do anything you put your mind to."

17   **TOUR GUIDE.** To Mama, education was a key part of her blueprint[1] for success. Four of us went to a nearby, one-room schoolhouse. My mother made up for its shortcomings by getting us educational toys, talking to us about history, politics and current events, and helping with homework. The best part of getting a good report card[2] was her unstinting praise.

18   When I was in third grade, she urged our teacher to organize a field trip to Chicago museums. My mother helped the teacher rent a bus and plan the trip. She even served as tour guide, pointing out landmarks and recounting local history.

19   When it came time to think about college, there was never a question that we'd all go. Inspired by our parents' sacrifice, we studied hard to earn scholarships, and applied for grants and financial aid.[3] We also took jobs to earn money for school. Working in a grocery store, I learned the value of a dollar. "Work is a blessing," Mama always reminded us.

20   She never asked for anything for herself. "You don't have to buy me a birthday present," she said one time. "Instead write me a letter about yourself. Tell me about your life. Is anything worrying you? Are you happy?"

21   **"YOU HONOR US ALL."** My mother made family values and pride tangible. One time when I was a high-school junior, our school put on a production of *The Music Man*. My role was

---

[1] **blueprint**   architect's plan, used here to mean *plan*

[2] **report card**   report of child's grades in school sent to parents

[3] **financial aid**   scholarship, grant, or loan

totally insignificant. I played bass in the orchestra. "You don't have to come and see me," I told Mama. "I'm not doing anything important."

22 "Nonsense," she said. "Of course we're coming, and we're coming because you're in the program." The whole family showed up.

23 The next year when I was elected president of my high school's National Honor Society, my mother pulled Michael and Maria, my younger brother and sister, out of grade school and brought them to the ceremony. Other students' parents came to the event. But I was the only one with a brother and sister there.

24 "Everything you do reflects on the family," Mama explained. "If you succeed, you honor us all."

25 In the same way, she crowded us all around the kitchen table for breakfast and supper. She made sure we shared chores. She nurtured our religious faith, which kept our family close. Every Sunday, we filled a pew at church. At night, we knelt together in the living room and prayed.

26 My mother suggested games everyone could play and often joined in. I remember laughing as she marched around the dining-room table one evening, while John Philip Sousa[4] boomed from the record player. "Keep in step now," she called out to her parading children. "If you're gonna march or do anything else, you always want to do it the best you can."

27 **TIME FOR EVERYONE.** Success wasn't just making money, Mama always said. Success was doing something positive for others.

28 In 1977, when Leo received his Ph.D. in physics from the University of California at Irvine, my mother wrote him a long, warm letter. She praised his years of hard work and, typically, reminded him to use his education to help others. "To think, you have the knowledge to work for the betterment of mankind!" she stressed. "There is much good for you to accomplish."

29 Mama took time for everyone. One cold day, she saw the neighbors' three young children playing in our yard. They were shivering in thin, worn sweaters. Mama called the youngsters to our door,

where they stared greedily at a pot of steaming homemade soup she was making for supper. She hustled them in, fed them and rummaged through our closets for extra coats.

30 From that day, until the family moved a year later, Mama often brought stew, soup and pasta to their home. She telephoned the children in the morning to make sure they got up for school. Often, she walked them down the lane and waited with them for the bus. At Christmas, she even bought the children gifts.

31 My mother was the driving influence in my decision to become a physician. "Do good" she always said—and be there for others. I recall a long, difficult night when I was a resident at Northwestern Memorial Hospital. I hadn't slept much for days. Finally, one morning at around four o'clock, I dropped into a restless slumber. An hour later, I awoke with a jolt. I had dreamed my father died. Confused and exhausted, I called home in tears. "Everything is all right," my mother assured me. "Don't worry."

32 At six o'clock, the hospital security buzzed my room. I had visitors. Stumbling into the elevator, I wondered who had come to see me at that hour. There stood my parents. They had gotten up and driven into the city in the predawn darkness. "I just wanted to make sure you were okay," Mama said, sleepy-eyed and anxious.

33 **VIEW FROM ABOVE.** While my mother's spirit remained indomitable, her health turned poor. Early last year, she had major surgery. Complications developed. Eight days later, on January 31, 1990, Mama died suddenly. She was 66.

34 More than 200 people came to her funeral service. In his eulogy, Leo said, "Mama poured her life out for us, reserving nothing for herself, thinking of us always, of herself never."

35 Sitting in church, I could picture my mother in heaven, looking young and beautiful just as she did in her favorite photograph. But instead of gazing out over Lake Michigan, she would be looking down at us, her six children. And she would be bursting with pride.

36 But we're the proud ones—proud of her and all she accomplished. More than any of us, Mama was really somebody.

---

4 **John Philip Sousa** American bandmaster and composer of music for bands, primarily marches (1854–1932)

Comprehension Check

1. What are the important facts in the early lives of Anna and Carlo Michelotti? What were their early successes?
2. What kind of person was each parent? What talents did each have?
3. What kind of relationship did Anna and Carlo Michelotti have? What role did each play in the family?
4. What was family life like in the Michelotti family?
5. The author says his mother knew how to raise children (¶9). Reread the article and list the lessons this mother tried to teach her children and the things she thought were important.
6. As an adult, how does Joseph Michelotti feel about his mother and her influence on him?

Sharing Your Thoughts

1. What do you think Anna Michelotti meant by "work is a blessing" (¶19)?
2. What lessons are there to be learned from the Michelotti family?
3. Why do you think Joseph Michelotti wrote this article?
4. What lessons have you learned from your parents? Can you give a specific example of how they taught the lesson?
5. What do "success" and "being somebody" mean to you?

Vocabulary

A. Content Vocabulary

Complete the following statements about the Michelotti family with words from the list. Use each word only once. Change the form of verbs if the grammar of the sentence requires it.

achieve	chores	complain	manage
mentor	praise	proud	raise
reach	success		

1. After getting married, Anna Michelotti traded big city life in Chicago for a more isolated life in the country, but she never _____.

2. She really knew how to _____ children and dedicated her life to them.

3. She knew she should _____ her children's accomplishments, big or small.

4. She gave her children _____ to do so they shared the work of the family.

5. Mama was a guide or _____ for her children. She helped them _____ their potential. She taught them that _____ in life does not come from accumulating riches but from doing something for other people.

6. Anna and Carlo Michelotti worked hard and _____ to send their six children to top colleges and graduate schools. They were _____ of their children and all that they _____.

B. Grammatical Function

As was mentioned in the last unit, a **suffix** can change the function of a word (p.11).

    EXAMPLE: **accomplish** -ment
    a. There is much good for you *to accomplish*. (verb)
    b. She bolstered our confidence, praising our most ordinary *accomplishments*. (noun)

To read English well you must also recognize that some words can change function without adding a suffix.

    EXAMPLE: **praise**
    a. Mama knew she should *praise* her children's accomplishments. (verb)
    b. The best part of getting a good report card was Mama's unstinting *praise*. (noun)

Are the italicized words functioning as nouns, verbs, or adjectives? Write N, V, or A, as the case may be, next to each one.

1. Parents usually ***sacrifice*** _____ a lot for their children, but children don't always appreciate their parents' ***sacrifices*** _____.

2. In the Michelotti family, every child did his or her ***share*** _____ of the work. Mama taught her children to ***share*** _____ the chores.

3. Joseph Michelotti wrote this article as an ***adult*** _____. It is written from the point of view of an ***adult*** _____ child.

4. Mama **challenged** _____ her children to succeed. She said, "Your **challenge** _____ is to be everything you can."

5. Mama knew how to **parent** _____ ; she was a good **parent** _____ .

6. Joseph Michelotti went to a **top** _____ medical school. We do not know if he graduated at the **top** _____ of his class.

7. A photographer used Mama's **picture** _____ in a window display. After her death, Joseph **pictured** _____ his mother in heaven.

8. Carlo Michelotti had a **limp** _____ . He **limped** _____ because he had been hit by a car.

9. When the children succeeded, they brought **honor** _____ to the family; Mama said, "If you succeed, you **honor** _____ us all."

C. Inferring Meaning from Context

Reread paragraphs 8 and 29. Using the context of the paragraph in which they appear, can you infer the meaning of the words listed below? What words in the context help you figure out their meaning? Check your inferences with a dictionary if necessary.

PARAGRAPH 8:

quit _____

commuted _____

run _____

PARAGRAPH 29:

shivering _____

stared greedily _____

steaming _____

D. Word Analysis

> A word made up of two or more whole words is called a **compound word**. Some compounds are easy to identify because the parts are connected with hyphens (*day-to-day, mother-in-law*, etc.). In other compounds the parts are written as one word (*housekeeper, schoolyard*, etc.). In other cases, they are written as two words (*supper table, grocery store*, etc.). Recognizing the parts of the compound can help you understand its meaning.

Locate the following words in the selection. Check the context in which they each appear. Divide them into their meaningful parts. What is the meaning of the whole? What does each part contribute? What other words do you know that are formed the same way? Use a dictionary if necessary.

EXAMPLE:

self-esteem (¶9) = respect for yourself

self = relating to "me"   ***esteem*** = basic word, means respect

Other words formed the same way are: *self-taught* (¶7), *self-confidence, self-service, self-control, self-defense*.

1. medical-school (¶1) _____

2. ice cream (¶4) _____

3. railroad (¶5) _____

4. windblown (¶6) _____

5. hit-and-run accident (¶7) _____

6. farmhouse (¶8) _____

7. homemade (¶12, 29) _____

8. flash cards (¶12) _____

9. bookcase (¶12) _____

10. dining room (¶13) _____

11. paint-by-number (¶13) _____

12. homework (¶17) _____

13. report card (¶17) _____

14. record player (¶26) _____

15. sleepy-eyed (¶32) _____

Text Analysis

A. Text Organization

The way writers organize their writing relates to their purpose. When the writer's purpose is to explain or illustrate an idea (in this case that Mrs. Michelotti was really somebody), the writing is often organized according to the **IBC (Introduction–Body–Conclusion) pattern**. In the IBC pattern, there are three basic parts, each with its own functions:

INTRODUCTION
- gets the reader's interest
- states the topic
- states or suggests the writer's purpose for writing
- states or suggests the main idea

BODY
- presents ideas with supporting information, examples, and explanations to develop the main idea in detail

CONCLUSION
- provides a closing, or completion, to the article
- often summarizes or reviews important ideas in the body

1. Which paragraphs serve as an introduction to the article? How does the writer get the readers' interest? Which sentences state or suggest the reason Joseph Michelotti wrote this article?

2. Which paragraphs form the body? What does the writer do in the body of his article?

3. Which paragraphs serve as the conclusion? How does the conclusion provide a closing or completion to the article? What important ideas in the body of the article does the conclusion refer to? Does it repeat the earlier ideas exactly or does it make some change? Explain.

B. Supporting General Statements

Effective writers **support** their general statements with various kinds of more detailed material: facts and statistics, examples, reasons, and information or opinions from a knowledgeable person. In this selection, the author illustrates his general statements about his mother with facts about her and examples of things she did.

List the support that Joseph Michelotti provides for the following statements. Where is the support relative to the statement? What would the article be like without the support?

1. Mama challenged her children to succeed.
2. Mama bolstered her children's confidence.
3. Mama urged her children to think big.
4. Education was a key part of Mama's blueprint for success.
5. Mama never asked for things for herself.
6. Mama made family values and pride tangible.
7. Mama took time for everyone.

Writing Task

Think about how you could support the following statements. Write down several possibilities for each. Some examples have been given for the first one.

1. My father is my mentor.
   EXAMPLES OF HOW HE GUIDED ME:
   - He taught me how to resolve problems with friends. For example one time I ...
   - I worked for him during vacations and learned ...
     He showed me how to ...
   - He taught me how to take care of my possessions. For example ...
2. My mother is my best friend.
3. My grandmother/grandfather has been like a mother/father to me.

Write a paragraph beginning with one of the three general statements above or with your own statement about one of your family members. Complete the paragraph with specific examples to support the general statement.

SELECTION TWO

Before Reading

The following article was written by Enrique Hank López. The son of Mexican immigrants, Enrique Hank López grew up in Colorado. He taught at Harvard's Institute of Politics, was an international lawyer, and authored several books, including *The Harvard Mystique*. He published various articles, principally in *American Heritage* in the late 1960s and early 1970s.

1. Freewrite on typical problems between parents and children. These questions may help you get started.
   - What problems do parents and children you know have?
   - What problems can parents and children have when they are living in a new culture?

   Share ideas from your freewriting with your classmates.

2. Preview this selection and answer the following questions:
   a. Is the point of view one of a young child or an adult child?
   b. What bothers the writer about his father?

The Problem of Fathers and Sons

by Enrique Hank López

1 My father was an articulate, fascinating storyteller, but totally illiterate.

2 By the time I entered fourth grade, in Denver, Colo., I was a proud, proficient reader—and painfully aware of my father's inability to read a single word in either Spanish or English. Although I'd been told there were no schools in his native village of Bachimba, Chihuahua,[1] I found it hard to accept the fact that he didn't even know the alphabet.

3 Consequently, every night as I watched my mother read to him I would feel a surge of resentment and shame. Together they bent over La Prensa from San Antonio, Texas—the only available Spanish-language newspaper." "How can he be so dumb?" I would ask myself. "Even a little kid can read a damned newspaper."

4 Of course, there were many adults in our barrio[2] who couldn't read or write, but that was no comfort to me. Nor did it console me that my hero Pancho Villa[3] was also illiterate. After all, this was my own father, the man I considered to be smarter than anyone else, who could answer questions not even my mother could answer, who would take me around the ice factory where he worked and show me how all the machinery operated, who could make huge cakes of ice without any air bubbles, who could fix any machine or electrical appliance, who could tell me all those wonderful stories about Pancho Villa.

5 But he couldn't read. Not one damned word!

6 His ignorance was almost too much for me to bear. In fact, whenever I saw my mother reading to him—his head thrust forward like a dog waiting for a bone—I would walk out of the kitchen and sit on the back porch, my stomach churning with a swelling anger that could easily have turned to hatred. So bitter was my disappointment, so deep my embarrassment,

---

[1] Chihuahua   state in northern Mexico

[2] barrio   neighborhood (Spanish)

[3] Pancho Villa   one of the leaders of the Mexican Revolution of 1910, considered by some to be a champion of the people

that I never invited my friends into the house during that after-dinner hour when my mother habitually read to him. And if one of my friends had supped with us—which happened quite frequently—I would hastily herd them out of the kitchen when my mother reached for *La Prensa*.

7 Once, during a period of deepening frustration, I told my mother that we ought to teach him how to read and write. And when she said it was probably too late to teach him—that it might hurt his pride—I stomped out of the house and ran furiously down the back alley, finally staggering behind a trash can to vomit everything I'd eaten for supper.

8 Standing there in the dark, my hand still clutching the rim of the can, I simply couldn't believe that anyone as smart as my dad couldn't learn to read, couldn't learn to write "cat" or "dog" or even "it." Even I, who could barely understand the big words he used when he talked about Pancho Villa (*revolución, cacique, libertad, sabotaje, terreno*), even I, at the mere age of 10, could write big words in both English and Spanish. So why couldn't he?

9 Eventually, he did learn to write two words—his name and surname. Believing that he would feel less humble if he could sign his full name rather than a mere "X" on his weekly paycheck, my mother wrote "Jose López" on his Social Security card and taught him to copy it letter by letter. It was a slow, painstaking process and usually required two or three minutes as he drew each separate letter with solemn tight-lipped determination, pausing now and then as if to make sure they were in the proper sequence. Then he would carefully connect the letters with short hyphen-like lines, sometimes failing to close the gaps or overlapping the letters.

10 I was with him one Friday evening when he tried to cash his paycheck at a local furniture store owned by Frank Fenner, a red-faced German with a bulbous nose and squinty eyes. My father usually cashed his check at Alfredo Pacheco's corner grocery store, but that night Pacheco had closed the store to attend a cousin's funeral, so we had crossed the street to Fenner's place.

"You *cambiar* this?" asked my father, showing him the check.

"He wants you to cash it," I added, annoyed by my father's use of the word *cambiar*.

"Sure, Joe," said Fenner, "just sign your monicker[4] on the back of it."

"*Firme su nombre atras,*" I told my father, indicating that Fenner wanted him to sign it.

"Okay, I put my name," said my father, placing his Social Security card on the counter so he could copy the "Jose López" my mother had written for him.

11 With Fenner looking on, a smirk building on his face, my father began the ever-so-slow copying of each letter as I literally squirmed with shame and hot resentment. Halfway through "López," my father paused, nervously licked his lips, and glanced sheepishly at Fenner's leering face. "No write too good," he said. "My wife teach me."

12 Then, concentrating harder than before, he wrote the final *e* and *z* and slowly connected the nine letters with his jabby little scribbles. But Fenner was not satisfied. Glancing from the Social Security card to the check, he said, "I'm sorry, Joe, that ain't the same signature. I can't cash it."

"You bastard!"[5] I yelled. "You know who he is! And you just saw him signing it."

13 Then suddenly grabbing a can of furniture polish, I threw it at Fenner's head, but missed by at least 6 inches. As my father tried to restrain me, I twisted away and screamed at him, "Why don't you learn to write, goddamn it! Learn to write!"

14 He was trying to say something, his face blurred by my angry tears, but I couldn't hear him, for I was now backing and stumbling out of the store, my temples throbbing with the most awful humiliation I had ever felt. My throat dry and sour, I kept running and running down Larimer St. and then north on 30th St. toward Curtis Park, where I finally flung myself on the

---

4 **moniker**   name (slang)

5 **bastard**   literally, an illegitimate child; insult used for males

recently watered lawn and wept into a state of complete exhaustion.

15   Hours later, now guilt-ridden by what I had yelled at my dad, I came home and found him and my mother sitting at the kitchen table, a writing tablet between them, with the alphabet neatly penciled at the top of the page.
"Your mother's teaching me how to write," he said in Spanish, his voice so wistful that I could hardly bear to listen to him. "Then maybe you won't be so ashamed of me."

16   But for reasons too complex for me to understand at that time, he never learned to read or write. Somehow, the multisyllabic words he had always known and accurately used seemed confusing and totally beyond his grasp when they appeared in print or in my mother's handwriting. So after a while, he quit trying.

Comprehension Check

1. List the positive and negative feelings the boy has toward his father.
2. What happened when the boy's friends came to the house? Why?
3. How successful is the mother in teaching her husband to read and write?
4. What happened at the furniture store?
5. How did the boy and his father feel at the time of the incident and later that day? How do you know?

Sharing Your Thoughts

1. Why is this young boy so upset that his father cannot read or write? Would he feel the same if his mother were illiterate?
2. How do you think the mother felt about the situation?
3. What were the complex reasons that the father never learned to read or write? Wasn't he intelligent enough?
4. In what ways was this father a good role model?
5. How important is it for parents to be educated in order to raise children successfully?
6. What would you do to help this boy understand his father and his own feelings better?
7. Why do you think Enrique Hank López wrote this article? Evaluate each of the possible purposes below. Which one or two seem the most likely?
   a. to show that his father was not a successful parent
   b. to show that young children and parents have very different points of view on certain things
   c. to show why children need role models and why they are unhappy if they don't have them
   d. to illustrate his confused feelings about his father
8. Compare and contrast this son's feelings toward his parents with the feelings of the son in Selection One, p. 30. What similarities and differences do you find? To what do you attribute any differences?

Vocabulary

A. Content Vocabulary

Complete the following statements about father and son with words from the list. Use each word only once. Change the form of verbs if the grammar of the sentence requires it.

accurately	**articulate**	**aware**	**beyond his grasp**
fascinating	**humble**	**ignorance**	**illiterate**
painstaking	**quit**		

1. Hank López's father was a(n) _____ man; he could use many big words _____ when he spoke. He was a(n) _____ storyteller. People loved to listen to him tell stories.

2. Even though his wife tried to teach him to read, he could never learn. Reading was _____.

3. Hank was painfully _____ that his father was _____. To him, not being able to read and write was a sign of _____ that the child could not bear.

4. Mrs. López thought her husband would feel less _____ if he could at least write his name. He learned to do so, but it was a(n) _____ process. In the end, learning to read and write was so difficult for the father that he _____ trying.

B. Inferring Meaning from Context

Enrique Hank López expresses a number of negative feelings in the text. Use the context to help you match these feelings, which are given below in their adjective and noun forms, with their definitions (on next page).

_____ 1. ashamed; shame (¶3, ¶11)

_____ 2. disappointed; disappointment (¶6)

_____ 3. embarrassed; embarrassment (¶6)

_____ 4. frustrated; frustration (¶7)

_____ 5. annoyed; annoyance (¶10)

_____ 6. humiliated; humiliation (¶14)

_____ 7. guilt-ridden or guilty; guilt (¶15)

DEFINITIONS:

a. feeling dishonored because you or someone close to you is responsible for doing something that might be wrong

b. feeling humbled or small in the eyes of other people

c. feeling socially uncomfortable

d. feeling bad because you are responsible for a bad situation

e. feeling a little angry

f. feeling sad because what you wanted to be true, isn't true

g. feeling defeated or powerless, feeling you can't do anything to change a situation

Text Analysis

Text Organization

Reread the article and match each paragraph or set of paragraphs listed below with its contribution to the whole piece of writing. How is the article organized? How does the organization relate to the title and López's purpose in writing the article?

PARAGRAPHS		CONTRIBUTION
_____ ¶1–8	**a.**	presents the major anecdote or incident and its results
_____ ¶9	**b.**	gives a final comment on the situation
_____ ¶10–15	**c.**	presents the problem and the child's feelings about it
_____ ¶16	**d.**	provides the connecting link between problem and anecdote

Writing Task

1. Imagine you are the father or son. Write the thoughts in your mind immediately after the incident in the furniture store or ten years later. Write at least one paragraph.

2. Imagine you are the mother. Write a letter of about one page to a relative in Mexico describing your son's feeling about his father's illiteracy and how the situation makes you feel.

3. Write a conversation between the father and the mother when the father came home from the furniture store. Each person should speak at least five times in the conversation.

SELECTION THREE

Before Reading

In the introduction to the collection of thoughts from which this selection comes, *It Was on Fire When I Lay Down on It,* Robert Fulghum requests that we read his thoughts like we might read aloud a letter from a friend who is far away, "adding (our) own observations and explanations."

1. In what periods of a child's life do you think parents and children might have the most difficulties getting along?

2. Read the section headings. What do they suggest about the content of this selection?

Untitled   by Robert Fulghum

THIS IS 1963.

1   From deep in the canyoned aisles of a supermarket comes what sounds like a small-scale bus wreck followed by an air raid. If you followed the running box-boy armed with mop and broom, you would come upon a young father, his three-year-old son, an upturned shopping cart, and a good part of the pickles shelf—all in a heap on the floor.

2   The child, who sits on a plastic bag of ripe tomatoes, is experiencing what might nicely be described as "significant fluid loss." Tears, mixed with mucus from a runny nose, mixed with blood from a small forehead abrasion, mixed with saliva drooling from a mouth that is wide open and making a noise that would drive a dog under a bed. The kid has also wet his pants and will likely throw up before this little tragedy reaches bottom. He has that "stand back, here it comes" look of a child in a pre-*urp* condition. The small lake of pickle juice surrounding the child doesn't make rescue any easier for the supermarket 911 squad[1] arriving on the scene.

3   The child is not hurt. And the father has had some experience with the uselessness of the stop-crying-or-I'll-smack-you syndrome and has remained amazingly quiet in the face of the catastrophe.

4   The father is calm because he is thinking about running away from home. Now. Just walking away, getting into the car, driving away somewhere down South, changing his name, getting a job as a paperboy or a cook in an all-night diner. Something—anything—that doesn't involve contact with three-year-olds.

5   Oh sure, someday he may find all this amusing, but in the most private part of his heart he is sorry he has children, sorry he married, sorry he grew up, and,

---

[1] **911 squad**   rescue team; name comes from the nationwide telephone number (911) that people call in emergencies

above all, sorry that this particular son cannot be traded in for a model that works. He will not and cannot say these things to anybody, ever, but they are there and they are not funny.

6   The box-boy and the manager and the accumulated spectators are terribly sympathetic and consoling. Later, the father sits in his car in the parking lot holding the sobbing child in his arms until the child sleeps. He drives home and carries the child up to his crib and tucks him in. The father looks at the sleeping child for a long time. The father does not run away from home.

THIS IS 1976.

7   *S*ame man paces my living room, carelessly cursing and weeping by turns. In his hand is what's left of a letter that has been crumpled into a ball and then uncrumpled again several times. The letter is from his sixteen-year-old son (*same son*). The pride of his father's eye—or was until today's mail.

8   The son says he hates him and never wants to see him again. The son is going to run away from home. Because of his terrible father. The son thinks the father is a failure as a parent. The son thinks the father is a jerk.[2]

9   What the father thinks of the son right now is somewhat incoherent, but it isn't nice.

10   Outside the house it is a lovely day, the first day of spring. But inside the house it is more like *Apocalypse Now,*[3] the first day of one man's next stage of fathering. The old gray ghost of Oedipus[4] has just stomped through his life. Someday—some long day from now—he may laugh about even this. For the moment there is only anguish.

11   He really is a good man and a fine father. The evidence of that is overwhelming. And the son is quality goods as well. Just like his father, they say.

12   "Why did this happen to me?" the father shouts at the ceiling.

13   Well, he had a son. That's all it takes. And it doesn't do any good to explain about that right now. First you have to live through it. Wisdom comes later. Just have to stand there like a jackass[5] in a hailstorm and take it.

THIS IS 1988.

14   *S*ame man and same son. The son is twenty-eight now, married, with his own three-year-old son, home, career, and all the rest. The father is fifty.

15   Three mornings a week I see them out jogging together around 6:00 A.M. As they cross a busy street, I see the son look both ways, with a hand on his father's elbow to hold him back from the danger of oncoming cars, protecting him from harm. I hear them laughing as they run on up the hill into the morning. And when they sprint toward home, the son doesn't run ahead but runs alongside his father at his pace.

---

[2] **jerk** fool (slang)

[3] *Apocalypse Now* a movie about the Vietnam War; apocalypse refers to the destruction of the world as described in the Book of Revelation, the last book of the New Testament

[4] **Oedipus** tragic hero in Greek mythology; Oedipus was fated to kill his father and marry his mother; he left home forever and died in exile

[5] **jackass** donkey, considered a foolish animal

17   They love each other a lot. You can see it.

18   One of their favorite stories is about once upon a time[6] in a supermarket...

THIS IS NOW.

19   *A*nd this story is always. It's been lived thousands of times, over thousands of years, and literature is full of examples of tragic endings, including that of Oedipus. The sons leave, kick away and burn all bridges, never to be seen again. But sometimes (*more often than not, I suspect*) they come back in their own way and in their own time and take their own fathers in their arms. That ending is an old one, too. The father of the Prodigal Son[7] could tell you.

---

[6] **once upon a time**   conventional beginning for stories, especially when they are told orally to children

[7] **Prodigal Son**   from the New Testament, a son who comes home after wasting his inheritance and whose father accepts him in spite of what he has done

Comprehension Check

1963

1. Describe the scene in your own words. Where are the father and son and what has happened?

2. What liquids make up the child's "significant fluid loss"?

3. How does the father feel?

1976

4. What was the letter, and what did it say? How does the father feel? How do you know?

5. According to the author, why did this all happen to the father and what should he do about it?

1988

6. What do the father and son do together?

7. How do they feel about each other? How do you know?

NOW

8. What does Fulghum tell us in this section?

Sharing Your Thoughts

1. In addition to creating scenes in supermarkets, what other embarrassments can small children cause their parents?

2. Why do you think that the father felt he was sorry he had children at the time of the supermarket incident?

3. Why do you think the writer chose not to reveal the entire contents of the son's letter?

4. Why do some teenagers rebel against their parents in such obvious ways as this child did? What part can parents play in causing this rebellion? Do teenagers in other cultures rebel against their parents? If so, how?

5. The author did not give a title to this text. What title would you give it?

Vocabulary

A. Content Vocabulary

Complete the following statements about the father and son with words from the list. Use each word only once. Two blanks with a noun or pronoun between are for the two parts of a phrasal verb. Change the form of verbs if the grammar of the sentence requires it.

amusing	**be through**	**crumple**	**failure**
hate	**incoherent**	**run away**	**sobbing**
trade in	**tucked in**		

1. In 1963, the father was outwardly calm in the supermarket even though he didn't find the situation at all _____. In fact, he wanted to disappear, to _____.

2. Privately, he thought he would like to give away his _____ son, to _____ him _____ for a new model. Instead, he took his child home, put him in the crib, and _____ him _____.

3. He was obviously very emotional in 1976 when he _____ his son's letter and cursed in anger. His thoughts at that moment were _____; not even he could say what he was thinking.

4. The son was so angry in 1976 that he said he _____ his father; his father was a jerk and a _____ as a father.

5. The father couldn't understand why he had to go through such a crisis with his son. By 1988, father and son had _____ a lot together and had become good friends.

B. Idioms and Phrasal Verbs

> Reading English well requires recognizing **phrasal verbs** as meaningful units. The meaning of some phrasal verbs is quite literal and can be figured out.
>
> EXAMPLE:
> ### *drive away* (¶4)
>
> Others are more idiomatic.
>
> EXAMPLE:
> ### *run away* (¶4) means *escape*

Locate the following phrasal verbs in the selection. The verbs may be in an inflected form. Check the context and give a synonym or short paraphrase for each.

1. come upon (¶1) _____

2. throw up (¶2) _____

3. get into (¶4) _____

4. grow up (¶5) _____

5. kick away (¶19) _____

6. come back (¶19) _____

Text Analysis

A. The Grammar-Meaning Connection

Single and compound word modifiers precede the nouns they modify. Show that you understand the following phrases by paraphrasing their meaning.

EXAMPLE:
canyoned aisles of a supermarket ____*The aisles were like canyons.*____

1. small-scale bus wreck (¶1) _____

2. three-year-old son (¶1) _____

3. upturned shopping cart (¶1) _____

4. "stand back, here it comes" look (¶2) _____

5. pre-*urp* condition (¶2) _____

6. the stop-crying-or-I'll-smack-you syndrome (¶3) _____

7. the sobbing child (¶6) _____

8. the sleeping child (¶6) _____

B. Point of View

This selection, unlike the first two selections, is not written from a son's or a daughter's point of view. From whose point of view is it written? What helped you determine who the narrator is?

C. Tone

> Just as painters use different shades, or tones, of color, writers use words in ways that create different **tones**, or moods, in the work, for example, a serious tone, a light or playful tone, or a humorous tone. The tone indirectly reveals the writer's attitude toward the subject.

1. What is the tone of this selection? How does Fulghum feel about the problems between father and son? Does he treat them seriously? Is he light and playful? Is he trying to be humorous? Find evidence to support your answer.
2. This selection is by the same writer as "The Barber" in Unit One. Compare the tone of this selection with that of "The Barber" if you have read it. What, if any, similarities and differences do you find?

Writing Task

In 1976 the son wrote his father a letter that the father proceeded to crumple in anger. With a partner or in a small group discuss what you think happened between them. Imagine you are the son and write that letter to the father. It should be about one page.

SELECTION FOUR

Before Reading

David Michael Kaplan is an American writer and professor of writing. This story appeared in *Sudden Fiction International* where Kaplan is quoted as saying, "Reading a good short story is like coming into the theater to see the magic show. We have come to be astonished and delighted and mystified" (p. 322).

1. Note the punctuation in the title. Why is there a comma after the word *Love*? The first sentence of the story will give you a hint.

2. When would a mother write to a child under normal circumstances? Read the first two sentences of the story. Do you think these are normal circumstances? How do you know?

3. What can go wrong in parent-child relationships? What might happen in an extreme case?

Love, Your Only Mother

by David Michael Kaplan

1 I RECEIVED ANOTHER POSTCARD from you today, Mother, and I see by the blurred postmark that you're in Manning, North Dakota now and that you've dated the card 1961. In your last card you were in Nebraska, and it was 1962; you've lost some time, I see. I was a little girl, nine years old, in 1961. You'd left my father and me only two years before. Four months after leaving, you sent me—always me, never him—your first postcard, of a turnpike in the Midwest, postmarked Enid, Oklahoma. You called me "My little angel" and said that the sunflowers by the side of the road were tall and very pretty. You signed it, as you always have, "Your only mother." My father thought, of course, that you were in Enid, and he called the police there. But we quickly learned that postmarks meant nothing: you were never where you had been, had already passed through in the wanderings only you understand.

2 A postcard from my mother, I tell my husband, and he grunts.

3 Well, at least you know she's still alive, he says.

4 Yes.

5 This postcard shows a wheat field bending in the wind. The colors are badly printed: the wheat's too red, the sky too blue—except for where it touches the wheat, there becoming aquamarine, as if sky and field could somehow combine to form water. There's a farmhouse in the distance. People must live there, and for a moment I imagine you do, and I could walk through the red wheat field, knock on the door, and find you. It's a game I've always played, imagining you were hiding somewhere in the postcards you've sent. Your scrawled message, as always, is brief: "The beetles are so much larger this year. I know you must be enjoying them. Love, your only mother."

6   What craziness is it this time? my husband asks. I don't reply.

7   Instead, I think about your message, measure it against others. In the last postcard seven months ago, you said you'd left something for me in a safety deposit box in Ferndale. The postmark was Nebraska, and there's no Ferndale in Nebraska. In the card before that, you said you were making me a birthday cake that you'd send. Even though I've vowed I'd never do it again, I try to understand what you are telling me.

8   "Your only mother." I've mulled that signature over and over, wondering what you meant. Are you worried I'd forget *you*, my only mother? In favor of some other? My father, you know, never divorced you. It wouldn't be fair to her, he told me, since she might come back.

9   Yes, I said.

10 Or maybe you mean singularity: out of all the mothers I might have had, I have you. You exist for me alone. Distances, you imply, mean nothing. You might come back.

11 And it's true: somehow, you've always found me. When I was a child, the postcards came to the house, of course; but later, when I went to college, and then to the first of several apartments, and finally to this house of my own, with husband and daughter of my own, they still kept coming. How you did this I don't know, but you did. You pursued me, and no matter how far away, you always found me. In your way, I guess, you've been faithful.

12 I put this postcard in a box with all the others you've sent over the years—postcards from Sioux City, Jackson Falls, Horseshoe Bend, Truckee, Elm City, Spivey. Then I pull out the same atlas I've had since a child and look up Manning, North Dakota, and yes, there you are, between Dickinson and Killdeer, a blip on the red highway line.

13 She's in Manning, North Dakota, I tell my husband, just as I used to tell my friends, as if that were explanation enough for your absence. I'd point out where you were in the atlas, and they'd nod.

14 But in all those postcards, Mother, I imagined you: you were down among the trees in the mountain panorama, or just out of frame on that street in downtown Tupelo, or already through the door to The World's Greatest Reptile Farm. And I was there, too, hoping to find you and say to you, Come back, come back, there's only one street, one door, we didn't mean it, we didn't know, whatever was wrong will be different.

15 Several times I decided you were dead, even wished you were dead, but then another postcard would come, with another message to ponder. And I've always read them, even when my husband said not to, even if they've driven me to tears or rage or a blankness when I've no longer cared if you were dead or anyone were dead, including myself. I've been faithful, too, you see. I've always looked up where you were in the atlas, and put your postcards in the box. Sixty-three postcards, four hundred-odd lines of scrawl: our life together.

16 Why are you standing there like that? my daughter asks me.

17 I must have been away somewhere, I say. But I'm back.

18 Yes.

19 You see, Mother, I always come back. That's the distance that separates us.

20 But on summer evenings, when the windows are open to the dusk, I sometimes smell cities...wheat fields...oceans—strange smells from far away—all the places you've been to that I never will. I smell them as if they weren't pictures on a postcard, but real, as close as my outstretched hand. And sometimes in the middle

of the night, I'll sit bolt upright, my husband instantly awake and frightened, asking, What is it? What is it? And I'll say, She's here, she's here, and I am terrified that you are. And he'll say, No, no, she's not, she'll never come back, and he'll hold me until my terror passes. She's not here, he says gently, stroking my hair, she's not—except you are, my strange and only mother: like a buoy in a fog, your voice, dear Mother, seems to come from everywhere.

Comprehension Check

1. Who is the narrator of the story? Who is the narrator addressing?
2. Where does the mother send postcards from? Use an atlas to locate the towns. How far away are these places from each other? Are they big cities or small towns?
3. What does the daughter find curious about the messages and the signature on the cards?
4. What does the daughter tell other people about her mother?
5. What do we know about the family life of the narrator of this story as a child? Approximately how old is she now?
6. How does her husband feel about the postcards?
7. Reread the story and list what you know for sure occurred in the family. Write the questions that the story doesn't seem to answer.

Sharing Your Thoughts

1. Share with your classmates the unanswered questions you found in Comprehension Check 7 and try to answer them. Support your answers with evidence from the story. If you find no evidence, talk about what might be true.
2. Why does the daughter keep the postcards?
3. Why does the husband want his wife to forget about her mother?
4. How has this mother affected her daughter's life, both in childhood and in adulthood? Who or what is "like a buoy in the fog" (¶20)? What does this comparison add to our understanding of the daughter and her relationship with her mother?
5. What similarities and differences are there in the way different family members have reacted to the mother's desertion of the family? Do you think the reactions would have been the same if the father had left home? Explain.
6. What does this story say about parent-child relationships? How does it make you feel? Did Kaplan's story "astonish, delight, or mystify" you? Explain.
7. Compare and contrast "Love, Your Only Mother" to Selections One, Two, and Three. What similarities and differences in topic, characters, and message do you find?

Vocabulary

Content Vocabulary

Complete the following statements about the story with words from the list. Use each word only once. Change the form of verbs if the grammar of the sentence requires it.

bolt upright	**brief**	**come back**
faithful	**terrified**	**vow**
wander	**wonder**	

1. The mother in this story left home years ago. The many different postmarks on the mother's postcards to her daughter suggest that she has _____ from place to place over the years.

2. The messages on the postcards are always _____, never more than a few words.

3. The daughter seems preoccupied with the messages. She _____ what "your only mother" means. Once she _____ never to think about what the messages mean again, but she cannot get them out of her mind.

4. The daughter has mixed feelings about her mother. She saves the cards to show that she has remained _____ to her, but she also feels pursued by her.

5. At the end of the story the daughter dreams that her mother has _____. This thought frightens her, and she sits _____ in her bed. She is _____ that her mother is back.

Text Analysis

Details in Stories

> Writers of short stories must say and suggest a lot in a few words. Therefore, they select **details** carefully to communicate something important about a character or the situation. The meaning readers get from stories can depend on what details they notice.

1. In paragraph 1, note that the mother always sent the postcards to her daughter and not to the husband she left. What reasons could she have had? Does this detail help us understand the mother or the situation in any way? Find other examples of details in this story that raise questions, and discuss the questions they raise.

2. If you did not do it in Sharing Your Thoughts 1, use details in the story to calculate approximately how long the mother has been gone. How does this information affect your understanding of the daughter's thoughts and actions?

3. Study the many times a character mentions distance or leaving, being away, and coming back. Do all the examples refer to physical distance? Might the repeated references to distance have some relationship to the meaning of the story?

Writing Task

1. Write a letter of about one page to the mother from one of the following characters: a) the daughter, b) the son-in-law, c) the husband, or d) the granddaughter in which the writer explains his or her feelings about the mother's absence from the family. Use appropriate details from the story in the letter.

2. Write at least one paragraph describing your reaction to this story. Did you like it or not? Be specific about what you liked or didn't like. You might find other ideas for your reaction in the Sharing Your Thoughts questions.

3. Imagine the mother returns. Write a conversation between the mother and daughter. Each person should speak at least five times in the conversation.

SELECTION FIVE

Before Reading

Robert Hayden (1913–1980) was an African-American poet from Michigan who taught for many years at Fisk University in Nashville, Tennessee.

1. What are some of the difficulties people face in winter in a cold climate?
2. What might a winter Sunday be like for a father and son?

Those Winter Sundays

by Robert Hayden

1 Sundays too my father got up early
    and put his clothes on in the blueblack cold,
    then with cracked hands that ached
    from labor in the weekday weather made
    banked fires[1] blaze. No one ever thanked him.

2 I'd wake and hear the cold, splintering, breaking.
    When the rooms were warm, he'd call,
    and slowly I would rise and dress,
    fearing the chronic angers of that house,

3 Speaking indifferently to him,
    who has driven out the cold
    and polished my good shoes as well.
    What did I know, what did I know
    of love's austere and lonely offices?[2]

---

[1] **banked fires**   fires with wood piled in vertical rows

[2] **offices**   duties, responsibilities

Comprehension Check

1. Who is the speaker in this poem?
2. What did the father do for his child?
3. Is the speaker describing a single event? How do you know?
4. What does the speaker remember about life in his family?
5. What was the child's attitude toward what his father did for him or her?
6. What does the adult child appreciate that the young child could not?

Sharing Your Thoughts

1. Why do you think the child would get up "slowly"?
2. Why do you think the child spoke "indifferently" to his father?
3. How do you think the father felt about what he was doing for his family? What kind of man do you think he was?
4. What contrasts between cold and warmth do you find in this poem? What do they contribute to the meaning of the poem?
5. How does the poem make you feel? Which lines or words give you this feeling?
6. What does this poem say to you? Is it about parenting, childhood, growth, or love? Is it about differences in point of view? What lines suggest these interpretations?
7. Which previous selection(s) does this poem remind you of and why?

Text Analysis

A. Images

Writers, perhaps especially poets, use words imaginatively to create an **image** or a word picture that appeals to our senses (sight, hearing, smell, touch/feeling, and taste) and imaginations. Images can arouse different feelings in different readers.

1. Reread this poem and find images that appeal to each of your senses, if possible.
2. Which images appeal to more than one sense? Which senses?
3. Discuss the images. Do you think the images in the poem create a powerful picture and contribute to the effectiveness of the poem? Explain.

B. Text Organization

> Poems are divided not only into stanzas, but also into lines. Often the division into lines does not correspond to the division into ideas. Ideas may continue over several lines and may end in the middle of a line. The **punctuation** of the lines usually indicates where ideas continue from line to line and where they end.

Try reading this poem aloud. Read the punctuation as follows:

no punctuation— little or no pause as the meaning carries over to the next line

comma—slight pause to indicate a closely related idea follows

period or question mark—full stop, end of an idea

1. Where do thoughts end in this poem? Find examples of ideas that carry over from one line or one stanza to another.

2. What holds each stanza of this poem together? Who is the focus of the first stanza? Who is the focus of the second stanza? What happens in the third stanza? Which lines in the third stanza show the child's point of view and which show the adult's point of view?

Writing Task

1. Think of something specific one of your parents did for you when you were younger. Did you appreciate it? Did you thank your parent at the time? Write a letter of about one page to your parent to express the gratitude you feel today.

2. Think of something specific that your mother or father did in raising you that you will not do when raising your children. Write one or two paragraphs in which you explain what your parent did and why you will do things differently.

A FINAL LOOK

Discussion

1. Work with a partner, in a small group, or as a whole class. Drawing from all five selections in this unit and the quote on the introductory page, discuss the focus questions.

2. What kinds of walls between parents and children might Shaw be referring to in the quote on the introductory page? What examples of walls between parent and child did you see in these selections? Can you think of other examples of things that keep parents and children apart? Why do these walls exist? Are they permanent?

3. An anonymous parent once said, "Bear in mind that children of all ages have one thing in common—they close their eyes to advice and open their eyes to example." What kinds of examples did the parents in these selections provide? How important is a parent's example compared to a parent's words? Can children grow up well without a positive parental example? Explain.

4. Which of the parents portrayed in these selections do you admire most? Why? Which parents, if any, do you not admire? How would you feel if they were your parents? How would you deal with them?

5. Is it easy to be a parent? Are some people naturally good parents or is parenting something we can learn? Why aren't some adults able to do the job well? Explain your answers.

6. Discuss the roles of the father and the mother in these selections. How do they compare to parents' roles in your culture? In your family? Are these roles changing with time?

Writing

Choose one of the following beginnings, or write your own first sentence related to parents and children. Support your general statement with specific examples from your own experience and/or from the reading selections. Write one or two paragraphs.

1. My mother/father is like Mrs. Michelotti (or any other parent portrayed in these selections)...

2. I wish my parents were like..., but...

3. Being a parent is...

4. When I was younger, I thought my parents were..., but now...

When you use other people's ideas, give them proper credit by mentioning their names and using quotation marks if you quote their exact words (Writing Task, p. 13).

UNIT THREE

Coping with Stress

[Stress *comes from*] *any circumstances that threaten or are perceived to threaten our well-being and that thereby tax our coping abilities. The threat may be to our immediate physical safety, our long-range security, our self-esteem, our reputation, our peace of mind, or many other things that we value.*

— Wayne Weiten

FOCUS

➤ What is stress?

➤ What causes stress for you and for other people you know?

➤ How does stress affect people physically and emotionally?

➤ What kinds of people seem less likely to suffer from stress?

➤ How can people learn to handle stress well?

SELECTION ONE

Before Reading

This selection, adapted from an information sheet published by the U.S. Government Printing Office, was prepared by the National Institute of Mental Health, a division of the Department of Health and Human Services.

1. What do you do when you feel stress? Do you try to get rid of the feeling? If so, how?

2. Where would you be likely to find government information sheets of this type? What is the main purpose of this type of reading material?

Plain Talk about Handling Stress by Louis E. Kopolow, M.D.

1   *Y*ou need stress in your life! Does that surprise you? Perhaps so, but it is quite true. Without stress, life would be dull and unexciting. Stress adds flavor, challenge, and opportunity to life. Too much stress, however, can seriously affect your physical and mental well-being. A major challenge in this stress-filled world of today is to learn how to cope with stress so that it does not become too much.

2   What kinds of things can cause too much stress in our lives? We often think of major crises such as natural disasters, war, and death as main sources of stress. These are, of course, stressful events. However, according to psychologist, Wayne Weiten, on a day-to-day basis, it is the small things that cause stress: waiting in line, having car trouble, getting stuck in a traffic jam, having too many things to do in a limited time.

3   Interestingly, stress is unique and personal to each of us. So personal, in fact, that what may be relaxing to one person may be stressful to another. For example, if you are an executive who likes to keep busy all the time, "taking it easy" at the beach on a beautiful day may feel extremely frustrating, non-productive, and upsetting. You may be emotionally distressed from "doing nothing."

4   Hans Selye, M.D., a recognized expert in the field, has defined stress as a "non-specific response of the body to a demand." For the busy executive, the demand that causes stress might be to relax. For most of us, it is a demand to act. If we feel overwhelmed by the pressure to do too many things, we may

not be able to function at all. In this case, the stress that can be good for us becomes distress, or bad stress. When stress becomes prolonged or particularly frustrating, it can become harmful, causing physical illness.

Reacting to Stress

5 The body responds to stressful events by going through three stages: (1) alarm, (2) resistance, and (3) exhaustion. Let's take the example of a typical commuter in rush-hour traffic. If a car suddenly pulls out in front of him, his initial alarm reaction may include fear of an accident, anger at the driver who committed the action, and general frustration. His body may respond in the alarm stage by releasing hormones into the bloodstream which cause his face to flush, perspiration to form, his stomach to have a sinking feeling, and his arms and legs to tighten. The next stage is resistance, in which the body repairs damage caused by the stress. If the stress of driving continues with repeated close calls or traffic jams, however, his body will not have time to make repairs. He may become so conditioned to expect potential problems when he drives that he tightens up at the beginning of each commuting day. The third stage, exhaustion, occurs if the stress continues over a long period of time, and the body depletes its resources for fighting stress. A result may be illnesses such as insomnia, migraine headaches, backaches, ulcers, high blood pressure, and even heart disease.

6 While you can't live completely free of stress and distress, you can prevent some distress as well as minimize its impact. By recognizing the early signs of distress and then doing something about them, you can improve the quality of your life and perhaps even live longer.

Helping Yourself

7 When stress does occur, it is important to recognize and deal with it. Here are some suggestions for ways to handle stress. As you begin to understand more about how stress affects you as an individual, you will come up with your own ideas of helping to ease the tensions.

8 • **Try physical activity.** When you are nervous, angry, or upset, release the pressure through exercise or physical activity. Running, walking, playing tennis, or working in your garden are just some of the activities you might try. Physical exercise will relieve that "up tight" feeling, relax you, and turn the frowns into smiles. Remember, your body and your mind work together.

9 • **Share your stress.** It helps to talk to someone about your concerns and worries. Perhaps a friend, family member, teacher, or counselor can help you see your problem in a different light. If you feel your problem is serious, you might seek professional help from a psychologist, psychiatrist, social worker, or mental health counselor. Knowing when to ask for help may avoid more serious problems later.

10 • **Know your limits**. If a problem is beyond your control and cannot be changed at the moment, don't fight the situation. Learn to accept what is—for now—until such time when you can change it.

11 • **Take care of yourself.** You are special. Get enough rest and eat well. If you are irritable and tense from lack of sleep or if you are not eating correctly, you will have less ability to deal with stressful situations. If stress repeatedly keeps you from sleeping, you should ask your doctor for help.

12 • **Make time for fun.** Schedule time for both work and recreation. Play can be just as important to your well-being as work; you need a break from your daily routine to just relax and have fun.

13 • **Be a participant.** One way to keep from getting bored, sad, and lonely is to go where it's all happening. Sitting alone can make you feel frustrated. Instead of feeling sorry for yourself, get involved and become a participant. Offer your services in neighborhood or volunteer organizations. Help yourself by helping other people. Get involved in the world and the people around you, and you'll find they will be attracted to you. You will be on your way to making new friends and enjoying new activities.

14 • **Check off your tasks**. Trying to take care of everything at once can seem overwhelming, and, as a result, you may not accomplish anything. Instead, make a list of what tasks you have to do, then do one at a time, checking them off as they're completed. Give priority to the most important ones and do those first.

15 • **Must you always be right?** Do other people upset you—particularly when they don't do things your way? Try cooperation instead of confrontation; it's better than fighting and always being "right." A little give and take on both sides will reduce the strain and make you both feel more comfortable.

16 • **It's OK to cry**. A good cry can be a healthy way to bring relief to your anxiety, and it might even prevent a headache or other physical consequence. Take some deep breaths; they also release tension.

17 • **Create a quiet scene**. You can't always run away, but you can "dream the impossible dream." A quiet country scene painted mentally, or on canvas, can take you out of the turmoil of a stressful situation. Change the scene by reading a good book or playing beautiful music to create a sense of peace and tranquility.

18 • **Avoid self-medication**. Although you can use prescription or over-the-counter medications to relieve stress temporarily, they do not remove the conditions that caused the stress in the first place. Medications, in fact, may be habit-forming and also may reduce your efficiency, thus creating more stress than they take away. They should be taken only on the advice of your doctor.

19 The best strategy for avoiding stress is to learn how to relax. Unfortunately, many people try to relax at the same pace that they lead the rest of their lives. For a while, tune out your worries about time, productivity, and "doing right." You will find satisfaction in just *being*, without striving. Find activities that give you pleasure and that are good for your mental and physical well-being. Forget about always winning. Focus on relaxation, enjoyment, and health. Whatever method works for you, be good to yourself. If you don't let stress get out of hand, you can actually make it work for you instead of against you.

Comprehension Check

1. In what ways is stress good for you? When does good stress become bad stress, or distress? (Note that the word *stress* is usually used to refer to both good and bad stress.)

2. What three stages does the body go through in reacting to stress? In explaining the stages, use Dr. Kopolow's example, but put it in your own words.

3. Paraphrase each of Dr. Kopolow's suggestions. Which ones are mainly to help you avoid stress, and which ones are mainly to help you cope with it?

4. Which is the best statement of the main idea of this information sheet? Can you find a sentence in the selection that says the same thing as the one you choose?

   a. The best way to avoid stress is to relax.

   b. To handle stress in our lives, we must recognize its early signs.

   c. If we recognize stress in our lives and deal with it, we will live better.

Sharing Your Thoughts

1. Support or refute these statements first with evidence from the reading selection and then, if possible, with evidence from your experience.

   a. Most people have similar reactions to stressful events.

   b. Stress has physical effects only over a long period of time.

   c. Your objective in handling stress should be to eliminate it.

   d. Self-medication is a bad idea.

   e. It's easy to relax.

2. The suggestions for handling stress in this selection are all positive. People also react to stress in negative ways (e.g., smoking, doing nothing, giving up). List the things that cause stress in your life and how you react, both positively and negatively.

EXAMPLE:

CAUSE OF STRESS	NEGATIVE WAYS TO HANDLE	POSITIVE WAYS TO HANDLE
exams	*smoke*	*make study schedule*

As a group, compare your lists. What similarities and differences do you find?

3. In Comprehension Check 3 you categorized Dr. Kopolow's suggestions as helping a person cope with or avoid stress. They can also be categorized as different types of action. Categorize them in this way by grouping them under these headings:

- Taking care of your body
- Being socially involved
- Time management
- Handling attitudes and emotions

4. Give examples of what it means to "be good to yourself." Why do some people have to learn to be good to themselves? How do you like to be good to yourself?

Vocabulary

A. Content Vocabulary

Complete the following statements about stress with the correct word from the list. Use each word only once. Change the form of verbs if the grammar of the sentence requires it.

avoid	**challenge**	**impact**
irritable	**overwhelmed**	**respond**
signs	**sources**	**tension**

1. Stress has a(n) _____ on everyone's life. In some ways it is good; for example, it adds excitement and _____ to our lives. But when we experience too much _____ in our lives, we may be _____ and unable to cope.

2. The _____, or origins, of stress are different for different people, and people _____ differently to stressful events.

3. We cannot _____ stress, but when we see early _____ of it, such as feeling _____ and tired from lack of sleep, there are things we can do to keep from losing control of our lives.

B. Word Analysis

Locate the following words in the selection. Check the context in which they each appear. Divide them into their meaningful parts. What is the meaning of the whole? What does each part contribute? Use a dictionary if necessary.

1. unexciting (¶1) _____

2. well-being (¶1, 12, 19) _____

3. stress-filled world (¶1) _____

4. stressful (¶2, 3, 5) _____

5. harmful (¶4) _____

6. rush-hour traffic (¶5) _____

7. irritable (¶11) _____

8. give and take (¶15) _____

9. over-the-counter medication (¶18) _____

10. habit-forming (¶18) _____

C. Grammatical Function

The italicized words in the sentences below are all adjectives that come from verbs. Study the sentences. Then answer these questions: What do we describe when we use the –ing form of the adjective? and What do we describe when we use the –ed form?

1. Without stress, life would be **unexciting**.
2. Trying to take care of everything at once can be **overwhelming** and **distressing**.
3. If we feel **overwhelmed** by pressure, we may not be able to act.
4. But if we have too much stress, we will feel **distressed**.
5. What may be **relaxing** to one person may be stressful to another.
6. Some people feel **relaxed** after exercise; others feel **exhausted**.
7. Taking it easy may be **frustrating** to some people; they feel **frustrated** doing nothing.
8. Being inactive can be **boring**, but if you participate in activities, you will not feel **bored**.

D. Synonyms and Paraphrases

> Writers use **synonyms** (words with the same, or almost the same, meaning) or brief paraphrases to help the reader understand or to provide variety when they have to use a word a lot.

In the sentences below, replace the italicized words or expressions from the selection with synonyms or paraphrases that you also find in the selection.

1. Without stress our lives would be ***dull.***
2. A major challenge in this stress-filled world is to learn how to ***cope*** *with* stress.
3. We need to prevent good stress from becoming ***bad stress.***
4. A person who likes to keep busy all the time may find ***taking it easy*** at the beach extremely frustrating.
5. Physical exercise will relieve that ***"up tight"*** feeling.

Text Analysis

A. Informative Writing

The purpose of this selection is to inform. Which is the principal information Dr. Kopolow gives in this selection, **a**, **b**, *or* **c***? Check the first and last paragraphs to help you answer this question.*

a. the major signs of stress
b. the major causes of stress
c. things people can do to manage stress

> When a writer's purpose is **to inform**, the reader assumes the writer is presenting factual, that is real or true, statements and information. However, readers should not accept supposedly factual information blindly because facts can be misused in various ways.
>
> When writers use facts that readers cannot be expected to know or that are not accepted by people with knowledge of the topic, they should give the source. If no source is mentioned for facts, readers can presume the facts are general knowledge, or, they represent the knowledge of the author.

Locate the following statements of fact in the selection. Is a source given for each? If so, what is it? If not, is the fact general knowledge, is it information from Dr. Kopolow, or do you think a source should perhaps be given?

1. It's the small things that cause stress on a day-to-day basis. (¶2)
2. Stress is personal to each of us. (¶3)
3. The body responds to stress by going through three stages. (¶5)

B. Making Inferences

This article does not discuss the causes of stress, but they do not have to be stated explicitly in the text for the reader to understand what they are. Thinking readers can infer them from the suggestions of how to deal with stress. Follow the examples and infer causes of stress from each suggestion of how to deal with it.

EXAMPLES:

SUGGESTION	INFERRED CAUSE
Try physical activity.	not exercising
Share your stress.	not talking about problems

Writing Task

1. Write at least one paragraph giving advice to the person suffering from stress described below in **a** or **b**. Consider providing the person with reasons for the advice supported by factual information.

   a. Elena is a single mother with two small children, a six-year-old boy and an eight-year-old girl. She is a police officer. Since she is the only parent, she says she has almost no time for herself.

   b. Toshi is working full time as a store clerk and studying for his bachelor's degree at night. He has a wife and small baby. His wife is always complaining that they never have time for fun.

2. Freewrite about a stressful day or stressful days in your life. One of these questions may help you get started.

   • What is a typical stressful day in your life like?

   • Which is the most stressful day in your week? Why?

   • What time of day is most stressful for you? Why?

   Reread your writing. Look for and mark ideas you might want to write about in more detail on some other occasion. Keep your freewriting for possible use in the Writing Task, p. 77.

Before Reading

This selection is about the results of research conducted by Robert E. Thayer, professor of psychology at California State University, Long Beach; he is the author of *Biopsychology of Mood and Arousal*. The following article appeared in *Psychology Today* in 1988.

1. Preview the article carefully.
2. Can you state the main idea of the article from previewing alone? If so, state the main idea in your own words.
3. Where do the facts and examples used as support come from?

ENERGY WALKS

Don't touch that candy bar. A short walk gives you a longer energy boost and improves your mood.

by Robert E. Thayer

1   Recently, I met one of my students at a candy machine on our college campus. He told me he was about to attend a long and boring lecture and needed his favorite sweet to stay alert. I suggested that he join me for a brisk walk instead. When we returned, he thanked me for the tip. As he left for the lecture hall, he said he felt great.

2   Another one of my students suffered badly from test anxiety. She knew of my work on the psychology of mood and asked me for help because she had an important exam coming up. I suggested she take a 10-minute walk, moderately fast-paced but not exhausting, before the test. She took the advice and later reported that she "aced"[1] the exam.

3   I have been doing research for many years on the mood changes that occur with short, rapid walks. My latest findings clearly indicate that brisk walks increase people's feelings of energy, sometimes for several hours. They are a more effective (and less fattening) pick-me-up than a candy bar and can reduce tension and make personal problems appear less serious. These changes can be subtle, but repeated over time they become very apparent. Short walks may even make it easier to quit smoking.

4   I learned of these effects from several experiments with young or middle-aged people who were in fairly good shape. In an early experiment, I had a group of college students sit for a few minutes and rate their feelings of energy and tension using a short checklist. They then joined me for a moderately fast 10-minute walk around the campus. We returned and sat down, and within five minutes people completed the checklist again.

5   People felt more energetic and less tired following the walk. I later repeated this procedure with people who walked on a treadmill[2] in a

---

[1] **aced**   got an *A* grade

[2] **treadmill**   exercise equipment on which a person walks or runs without going anywhere

bare-walled room, to ensure that the mood shift was not due simply to a stroll through the attractive campus surroundings. Again, the energizing effect held true. Other aspects of this research made it clear that the mood change did not occur because people expected walking would make them feel better—it was the walk itself that was responsible. Cardiologist James Rippe has also found that walking—specifically a three-mile walk—reduces people's anxiety and tension, as well as their blood pressure.

6 My next step was to discover how long the energized mood lasted. This time, people walked on a number of occasions during a three-week period. Each time, they rated their energy and tension levels, then walked briskly for 10 minutes and repeated the ratings several times during the following two hours.

7 Twenty minutes after the walk, there were significant increases in energy and decreases in fatigue and tension. The effects lasted for at least an hour, impressive results when you consider that it took only 10 minutes of rapid walking to produce them. Even after two hours, the increased energy from walking was still present to a small degree.

8 As part of this experiment I compared walking to the effects of eating a sugar snack. I had people eat an average-sized candy bar instead of taking the walk. The immediate mood change from the candy bar was similar to the effect of walking: increased energy. But one hour after snacking, some negative changes began to show up: People felt more tired and a lot more tense (the tension was gone after two hours).

9 Other researchers have found that eating sugar can cause fatigue, perhaps because it leads to higher levels of the neurotransmitter serotonin in the brain, which acts as a sedative (see "Food for Thought," *Psychology Today*, April 1988). I found that the first reaction to sugar is enhanced energy, and fatigue seems to occur half an hour to an hour later. This might explain why people who ate candy bars subsequently felt tense. The sugar, after providing a short burst of energy, eventually

caused fatigue. People felt tired but were not able to sleep (it was during the day and they were busy), which made them tense. The people who walked enjoyed an energy boost, avoided the effects of a sugar sedative and didn't experience tension later on.

10 Short, rapid walks can also help make personal problems appear less serious and increase optimism. During the course of three weeks, one group of people repeatedly assessed the severity of a continuing personal problem, such as marital troubles or a stubborn weight problem. Another group rated their level of optimism. In addition to completing these ratings at fixed times each day, people in both groups took a brisk 10-minute walk.

11 After the walk, chronic personal problems appeared less serious. The walk also increased general optimism. These improvements were small and were not noticeable every day, but after three weeks the difference became obvious.

12 Walking produces some other interesting psychological effects, according to studies currently under way by various graduate students and myself. One especially important benefit may be for cigarette smokers who are trying to cut down or quit. Since people often smoke to increase their energy or reduce tension, we have asked smokers to take five-minute walks before they light up. So far the results are very impressive. Following a walk, smokers wait two times longer than non-walking smokers do between cigarettes during free-smoking periods. And those who report the greatest energy increases from the walk wait the longest to smoke the next cigarette.

13 Walking is, of course, very good physical exercise. Beyond that, it feels good to walk and at moderate walking speeds those good feelings occur right away. Try it after you have been sitting for a while. Keep your posture erect but otherwise relaxed, swing your arms freely and breathe naturally. You don't have to be a dedicated athlete to walk, nor do you need to invest a lot of time and money. Ten minutes should do it and the benefits—both mental and physical—should last a lot longer.

Comprehension Check

1. What kind of walking does Thayer recommend and for how long?
2. In what ways is walking better than eating a candy bar for energy?
3. What good effects does walking have in addition to increasing energy?

Sharing Your Thoughts

1. Find the essential information about this research. Use these questions as a guide:
    a. Who did the research? Where?
    b. Who were the subjects (people who participated in the study)?
    c. Paragraph 4 mentions "several experiments" that are discussed in paragraphs 4 to 9. Identify each experiment, and answer the following questions for each.
        *   What procedures were followed?
        *   What questions was Thayer trying to answer?
        *   What were the findings?
2. Could Thayer's findings be of use to smokers, people who get tension headaches, ulcers caused by bacteria, or people who get angry easily? For each, explain why or why not.
3. Have you ever tried walking to relieve stress? If so, what are its benefits? Compare it to other forms of physical exercise to relieve stress.

Vocabulary

A. Content Vocabulary

Complete the following statements about walking to relieve stress with words from the list. Use each word only once. Change the form of verbs if the grammar of the sentence requires it.

alert	anxiety	boost
brisk	fatigue	mood
pick-me-up	tip	

1. When you have an exam coming up, you want to be calm and _____,
    but you may be suffering from test _____ and _____.
    Feeling nervous and tired isn't going to help you ace the test.

2. A short, _____ walk can do a lot to calm your nerves and help you feel more energetic. It can put you in a more optimistic _____.

3. Walking is a better _____ than a sugar snack that provides only a brief _____ to our energy level. So take a(n) _____ from Robert Thayer and walk.

B. Idioms and Phrasal Verbs

Locate the following expressions in the selection. Check the context and give a synonym or short paraphrase for each.

1. coming up (¶2) _____

2. in fairly good shape (¶4) _____

3. held true (¶5) _____

4. show up (¶8) _____

5. under way (¶12) _____

6. cut down (¶12) _____

7. light up (¶12) _____

8. right away (¶13) _____

Text Analysis

A. Text Organization

Reread the article. Describe the contribution each paragraph or set of paragraphs makes to the whole piece of writing. Does the writer follow the IBC (Introduction–Body–Conclusion) organizational pattern?

PARAGRAPHS	CONTRIBUTION
¶1–3	_____
¶4–9	_____
¶10–12	_____
¶13	_____

B. Supporting General Statements

Writers, especially academic writers, sometimes add strength to their ideas or claims by citing the work or opinions of other people. Find two times that Thayer refers to the work of other researchers to support his findings. What idea about walking does their work support? Compare the information provided in the two citations. Which could be more useful to you at some time? Why?

Writing Task

A **summary** of a piece of writing presents the most important ideas and examples in a shortened form in the writer's own words. Writers often summarize information from an outside source when they refer to it in their work. Summarizing is also a valuable skill for you to develop. For example, by summarizing something you read, you can check your understanding of it, and your summary can then help you study for a test on the material.

1. Use the questions below as a guide to the important ideas in "Energy Walks," and write a one-paragraph summary of the article. Notice that in summarizing research, you should mention what was studied, when and by whom, how it was studied, and the main finding or findings.

   a. What has Robert Thayer been studying for many years?

   b. How does he find out the effects of walking on the subjects in his study? (First, he gives them a checklist... .)

   c. What has Thayer found are the effects of a good, brisk walk? How long do the effects last?

   d. What are some other benefits of walking?

2. Write two paragraphs about your physical activity in a typical day. In the first paragraph, describe the physical activity (walking, bike riding, sports, etc.) you engage in during the course of such a day. In the second paragraph, evaluate that physical activity: Is it enough? How does it make you feel? If it is not enough activity, what changes could you make in your daily routine to add more physical activity?

SELECTION THREE

Before Reading

This selection is an excerpt from an article that appeared in the *Harvard Medical School Health Letter* in 1989. The author, Dr. Raymond B. Flannery, Jr., is on the faculty of Harvard Medical School and a member of the Department of Psychiatry at Cambridge Hospital in Cambridge, Massachusetts.

1. How does Dr. Flannery's definition of stress compare to the definition on the introductory page?
2. What do you think a stress-resistant person is?
3. Look at the headings in the article. What are they? What do you expect to find in each section? What do they suggest might be the original form of this article?
4. How do you think this selection will be different from the previous selections on stress?

The Stress-Resistant Person

by Dr. Raymond B. Flannery, Jr.

A practical definition of stress is this: When the problems presented by everyday life exceed your resources for coping with them, you feel stressed.

Who are "stress-resistant" people?

1   I became interested in this question as a result of some personal experiences and observations. One Saturday evening, after I had myself spent a frazzling day working with "stressed-out" people in a walk-in clinic, I turned to a nurse who was also working there and said something like, "Everybody and his brother went through here today." She answered, "You know better than that. Some people *never* come here." I started to wonder what such people were like.

2   Around the same time, I began teaching night courses at a nearby college. I noticed that many of the adult students, who were holding down full-time jobs and starting their families—and who had just driven through some of the meanest rush-hour traffic in town—would come into the classroom looking lively and full of curiosity about what to expect that evening. Their lives were incredibly demanding, but they weren't stressed out. So I set about developing a research project to see whether I could find out the characteristics of people who cope effectively.

3   I wanted to learn whether such people had specific methods for coping and whether these skills could be learned by others who don't handle pressure as easily. The night-school students had some attributes that made them good subjects for such a project. Besides living inherently challenging lives, they represented a broad range of economic backgrounds, and there was a reasonable range of ages.

4   I have evaluated the ability to cope in several ways—principally by counting frequency of illnesses or by rating reports of physical symptoms, anxiety, and depression. For example, I have compared the coping styles of students with the most and the fewest episodes

of illness during a given time. I refer to the successful problem solvers as "stress-resistant persons."

Couldn't frequent illness be just another cause of stress?

5 No doubt it is. But some striking behavioral differences between the students at the extremes suggest that those who were sick least often also had effective ways of dealing with problems. The effective strategies fell into four main categories.

6 • Those who reported little illness tended to maintain reasonable personal control in their lives. If a problem came up, they would look for resources, perhaps do some reading or learning in another way, and then try a solution. If the first one didn't work, they would try another. People who reported being frequently ill were more likely to approach problems passively. To give some examples, they would leave it to a spouse to discipline the children or decide where they would go on a weekend evening; they would be uneasy about speaking to the boss when something was wrong at work.

7 • Those with the least illness were also personally committed to a goal of some kind. The goal might be completing a college career, being a better parent, advancing a community activity, or engaging in a hobby. But in any case, these people spent 4–6 hours out of the 168 in a week doing something that provided a sense of challenge and enhanced their sense of meaningful participation in life. I don't mean that everything went well for them during these hours, but rather that the activity had personal significance to them. People who were more prone to illness were quite likely to indicate that they were bored or were unable to find something that interested them.

8 • Certain choices in lifestyle also went along with a low rate of illness. (1) The low-illness people used a minimum of "substances"—things they regarded as drugs or drug-like, including nicotine and caffeine. In some cases, these choices may have reflected their general "take charge" attitude, but there are some obvious ways that a high intake of stimulants or intoxicants can reduce the ability to cope. (2) Some form of "active relaxation" took up at least 15 minutes of every day. This could range from the formal, such as meditation, to such informal activities as knitting or playing solitaire. When asked about relaxation, the people who were more vulnerable to stress were likely to reply, "I don't have time to relax." (3) About 80% of the low-illness group engaged in regular aerobic exercise,[1] whereas only 20% of the vulnerable group did so.

9 • The people with little illness tended to seek out other people, to be actively and empathically engaged with them. The vulnerable people tended to be more socially isolated.

How do you interpret these findings?

10 A convenient way of thinking about them is to consider the relative rapidity with which our species has entered what we call "modern life." After spending a few leisurely millions of years in bands, gathering and hunting, humans plunged into agriculture in the last 10,000 years or so, and then, within the last 250, yet again utterly transformed their lives, this time with the industrial revolution.[2]

11 No doubt much of contemporary life is less hazardous, and in that sense less stressful, than the world of people who were chased and eaten by lions and tigers and bears. Certainly we experience less physical trauma, less mortality in childbirth for both mother and infant, and less infectious disease. On the other hand, there are certain aspects of modern life that may not be attuned to the physiology of a species that evolved as gatherers and hunters.

---

[1] **aerobic exercise**   exercise, walking and running for example, that improves oxygen consumption by the body

[2] **industrial revolution**   the change from an agricultural to an industrial society in which cities developed

12 The hallmarks of contemporary urban life are that it is both sedentary and fast-paced. What we know of the gathering and hunting peoples, who represent the experience of humanity until very recent times, is that they are likely to engage in long walks several times a week, that they have frequent rest periods, and that a good deal of their activity goes on in the context of small, stable, intimate groups. The ritual or religious life of such a community also often imparts a strong sense of purpose to its activities.

13 We could speculate that stress-resistant persons have the knack of adapting certain stone-age habits to modern life. In any event, they are likely to maintain physical activity, to alternate activity with at least some time for relaxation, to exercise some reasonable personal control over their lives, and to be fairly strongly bonded to other people.

Comprehension Check

1. What did Dr. Flannery notice about people and their abilities to deal with challenging lives?
2. What was his research question? Locate it in the article.
3. How does he measure coping ability?
4. What are the four major strategies of stress-resistant people?
5. How has life changed in the last few centuries, and how does this relate to stress?
6. How are stress-resistant people similar to hunting and gathering people?

Sharing Your Thoughts

1. Think of people you know who seem to be stress-resistant. Which of the four strategies in Comprehension Check 4 do they use? Is there anything else that you think makes them stress-resistant?
2. Think of people you know who seem to be vulnerable to stress. What characteristics do they possess? What can those who are vulnerable to stress learn from stress-resistant people?
3. Which do you think is more stressful: modern life or the life of hunters and gatherers? Explain your answer. Which would be more stressful for you?
4. Compare the four strategies of stress-resistant people (Comprehension Check 4) to the suggestions made in Selections One and Two of this unit, pp. 60, 68. What similarities and differences do you find?

Vocabulary

A. Content Vocabulary

Complete the following statements about stress-resistant people with words from the list. Use each word only once. Change the form of verbs if the grammar of the sentence requires it.

anxiety	**attitude**	**committed**
demanding	**engage**	**seek out**
strategy	**vulnerable**	

1. Dr. Flannery wanted to find out about people who successfully cope with
   _____ lives. He wondered why some people were stress-resistant
   while others seemed much more _____ to stress.

2. He found that stress-resistant people are less likely to get sick, and they
   suffer less from _____ and depression.

3. They seem to be more resistant because they do many things that increase
   their involvement with people and with life. They _____ in
   a variety of activities, and they _____ other people. They are
   _____ to a goal.

4. Stress-resistant people often have a "take-charge" _____. If there
   is a problem to be solved, their _____ is to try to solve it.

B. Word Analysis

Locate the following words in the selection. Check the context in which they each appear. Divide them into their meaningful parts. What is the meaning of the whole? What does each part contribute? Use a dictionary if necessary.

1. stress-resistant people (title) _____

2. walk-in clinic (¶1) _____

3. full-time jobs (¶2) _____

4. night-school students (¶3) _____

5. problem solvers (¶4) _____

6. stone-age habits (¶13) _____

Text Analysis

Supporting General Statements

Writers commonly use **statistics** (numerical information or data) to support general statements. Knowing that numbers can be misinterpreted and are sometimes used just to impress, efficient readers do not accept statistics blindly. Most readers do not have the knowledge to make a complete evaluation of all statistics, but readers should require that writers use statistics to support some idea and indicate their source and date.

1. What statistics from his research does Flannery give to support the following ideas?
    a. Stress-resistant people are committed to a goal of some kind.
    b. Stress-resistant people are active people.
2. The headings suggest this article is based on an interview. In what kind of article might you expect Flannery to report more statistics?

Writing Task

1. What is one area of your life (for example, work or a personal relationship) in which you are vulnerable to stress? Write two paragraphs about your experience with stress in this area. In one paragraph describe and/or give details concerning the source of stress and how it is affecting your life. In a second paragraph discuss how you are handling the stress and if there are attributes of the stress-resistant person that could help you handle this stress more effectively.
2. Write a one-paragraph summary of "The Stress-Resistant Person" using the questions below as a guide. Refer to p. 72, to refresh your memory about writing summaries.
    a. What did Raymond B. Flannery become interested in? What did he want to find out?
    b. How did he define his group of stress-resistant people?
    c. What specific information did he get from them?
    d. What did Flannery find out about the lifestyles of the stress-resistant people?
    e. How does Flannery interpret his findings?

SELECTION FOUR

Before Reading

This story appeared in the *Saturday Review of Literature* in 1942. It appeared in a column entitled "Who Wrote This?" Mona Gardner heard the story in India, and it supposedly appeared in a magazine shortly before World War I, so it is an old story with mysterious origins.

1. This story takes place in India during the period when India was a British colony. Who do you think might be at the dinner party?

2. The stress that occurs in this story is different from the daily stress treated in the previous selections. The quote on the introductory page mentions that stress can come from a threat "to our immediate physical safety." What could threaten physical safety at a dinner party?

The Dinner Party

by Mona Gardner

1   THE COUNTRY IS INDIA. A colonial official and his wife are giving a large dinner party. They are seated with their guests—army officers and government attachés[1] and their wives, and a visiting American naturalist[2]—in their spacious dining room, which has a bare marble floor, open rafters and wide glass doors opening onto a veranda.

2   A spirited discussion springs up between a young girl who insists that women have outgrown the jumping-on-a-chair-at-the-sight-of-a-mouse era and a colonel who says that they haven't.

3   "A woman's unfailing reaction in any crisis," the colonel says, "is to scream. And while a man may feel like it, he has that ounce more of nerve control than a woman has. And that last ounce is what counts."

4   The American does not join in the argument but watches the other guests. As he looks, he sees a strange expression come over the face of the hostess. She is staring straight ahead, her muscles contracting slightly. With a slight gesture she summons the native boy standing behind her chair and whispers to him. The boy's eyes widen: he quickly leaves the room.

5   Of the guests, none except the American notices this or sees the boy place a bowl of milk on the veranda just outside the open doors.

---

[1] attachés   diplomatic officials

[2] naturalist   someone who studies animals and plants, a biologist

6   The American comes to with a start. In India, milk in a bowl means only one thing—bait for a snake. He realizes there must be a cobra in the room. He looks up at the rafters—the likeliest place—but they are bare. Three corners of the room are empty, and in the fourth the servants are waiting to serve the next course. There is only one place left—under the table.

7   His first impulse is to jump back and warn the others, but he knows the commotion would frighten the cobra into striking. He speaks quickly, the tone of his voice so arresting that it sobers everyone.

8   "I want to know just what control everyone at this table has. I will count to three hundred—that's five minutes—and not one of you is to move a muscle. Those who move will forfeit fifty rupees.[3] Ready!"

9   The twenty people sit like stone images while he counts. He is saying "…two hundred and eighty…" when, out of the corner of his eye, he sees the cobra emerge and make for the bowl of milk. Screams ring out as he jumps to slam the veranda doors safely shut.

10   "You were right, Colonel!" the host exclaims. "A man has just shown us an example of perfect control."

11   "Just a minute," the American says, turning to his hostess. "Mrs. Wynnes, how did you know that cobra was in the room?"

12   A faint smile lights up the woman's face as she replies: "Because it was crawling across my foot."

---

[3] rupee   monetary unit of India

Comprehension Check

1. What question were the dinner guests discussing? What opinions were expressed?
2. How does the American naturalist figure out what is happening?
3. What is clever about what he does?
4. How was the question of the dinner conversation resolved?

Sharing Your Thoughts

1. How did you feel as you read this story?

2. How, if at all, is this stressful situation different from everyday stress? Which kind of stress would you prefer to face? Explain your answer.

3. Who are the stress-resistant people in the story? What qualities and knowledge do they have that enable them to handle this stressful situation?

4. Do you think men and women differ in how they handle stress? If so, what do you think the differences are, and who do you think handles stress better?

5. What is the point of this story, or is it only meant to be entertaining? Explain.

Vocabulary

Content Vocabulary

Complete the following statements about the story with words from the list. Use each word only once. Change the form of verbs if the grammar of the sentence requires it.

bait	**commotion**	**crisis**
frighten	**outgrow**	**warning**

1. Having a cobra as an unexpected dinner guest would certainly _____ many people; even people who think they have _____ most of their fears might lose control.

2. Instead of _____ the other guests about the danger and causing a great _____, the American naturalist distracted the guests, giving the cobra time to find the _____ the hostess had directed a servant to place outside on the veranda.

3. Both the American and the hostess handled the _____ very well.

Text Analysis

Elements of Fiction

Short stories and novels have three principal elements: the **setting**, the **characters**, and the **plot**.

Setting: the place, time, and conditions under which a story takes place

Characters: the people in a story

Plot: the events that happen in a story

Story plots need **conflict** of some sort. The characters must struggle with some problem. The **climax** of the plot is the point at which the action reaches its highest emotional intensity. Most stories have a part after the climax, the **resolution**, which shows how things turn out in the end.

1. What is the setting of this story?
2. Who are the characters? What kind of people are they? What are their important personality traits?
3. What are the events in the plot? What is the conflict? Where does the plot reach its climax? Is there a part you would call the resolution?
4. Which of the elements—setting, characters, or plot—do you think is most important in this story, or are they almost equally important? Explain with reference to the story.

Writing Task

Write two or three paragraphs describing something frightening that happened to you or someone you know. Before beginning to write about the incident, write the question words *who, what, where, when, why, how,* and *how long* on a piece of paper. Make notes after each question word to be sure you include the necessary details and background information in your writing. Be sure to include details about how you and the other people felt in the situation. Exchange papers with a partner; read each other's writing and determine if there is enough detail for you to understand what happened. If not, revise accordingly. To **revise** means to change the content (ideas and support) to improve your writing.

SELECTION FIVE

Before Reading

Thich Nhat Hanh is a Vietnamese Zen Buddhist monk who lives in France. He is a poet, scholar, peace activist, and leader of retreats to help people learn the "art of mindful living." This selection is from one of his books, *Peace Is Every Step*.

Read the title of this selection. What could washing dishes have to do with stress?

Washing Dishes

by Thich Nhat Hanh

1   To my mind, the idea that doing dishes is unpleasant can occur only when you aren't doing them. Once you are standing in front of the sink with your sleeves rolled up and your hands in the warm water, it is really quite pleasant. I enjoy taking my time with each dish, being fully aware of the dish, the water, and each movement of my hands. I know that if I hurry in order to eat dessert sooner, the time of washing dishes will be unpleasant and not worth living. That would be a pity, for each minute, each second of life is a miracle. The dishes themselves and the fact that I am here washing them are miracles!

2   If I am incapable of washing dishes joyfully, if I want to finish them quickly so I can go and have dessert, I will be equally incapable of enjoying my dessert. With the fork in my hand, I will be thinking about what to do next, and the texture and the flavor of the dessert, together with the pleasure of eating it, will be lost. I will always be dragged into the future, never able to live in the present moment.

3   Each thought, each action in the sunlight of awareness becomes sacred. In this light, no boundary exists between the sacred and the profane. I must confess it takes me a bit longer to do the dishes, but I live fully in every moment, and I am happy. Washing the dishes is at the same time a means and an end— that is, not only do we do the dishes in order to have clean dishes, we also do the dishes just to do the dishes, to live fully in each moment while washing them.

Comprehension Check

1. How does Thich Nhat Hanh wash dishes?
2. How does the way he washes dishes illustrate his philosophy of life?
3. How can we turn necessary chores like washing dishes into something that can help us?

Sharing Your Thoughts

1. Check a dictionary for the meaning of *means* and *end* in the sentence, "Washing the dishes is at the same time a means and an end." What do you think the author means by this statement?
2. How do you think Thich Nhat Hanh would answer these questions?
    a. How do you cope with stress in your life?
    b. Why do some people have so much stress in their lives?
    c. How can we reduce the stress in our lives?
    d. What makes life worth living in your opinion?
3. How does Thich Nhat Hanh's philosophy of life compare to that of the authors of the other selections in this unit? What do you think their opinions of this selection would be?

Text Analysis

The Grammar-Meaning Connection

*The **adverbs** that Thich Nhat Hanh uses reveal something about his philosophy of life. Underline the adverbs in the sentences below. What, if anything, do they contribute to our understanding of his philosophy?*

1. I enjoy taking my time with each dish, being fully aware of the dish, the water, and each movement of my hands.
2. If I am incapable of washing dishes joyfully, if I want to finish them quickly so I can go and have dessert, I will be equally incapable of enjoying my dessert.

Writing Task

Write two to three paragraphs about how you do a routine chore, for example, how you clean your room, house, or apartment; wash your pet, bicycle, or car; paint something; or give a baby a bath. Indicate whether you find this chore relaxing. If so, why? If not, how could you make it more relaxing?

In one paragraph describe the chore. In the next paragraph describe your feelings about it, and in a possible third paragraph explain how you could make it more relaxing and stress-reducing.

A FINAL LOOK

Discussion

1. Work with a partner, in a small group, or as a whole class. Drawing from all five selections in this unit, and the quote on the introductory page, discuss the focus questions.

2. Change is one source of stress. Talk about a change you have had to make in your life such as changing schools, moving to a new culture, or starting a new job. What stress, if any, did it cause in your life?

3. Many people, including most students, feel stress because they have a lot of work to do and deadlines to meet. Some people get the work done on time; others don't. Why don't some people get their work done on time? What ideas do you have for managing time so the important things get done and there is time for relaxation, too?

4. Dangerous situations also create stress. What dangerous situations, if any, have you been in? Describe how you handled them.

5. A Chinese proverb says, "The longest journey begins with a single step," and an English one says, "Rome wasn't built in a day." What do these proverbs mean? How are they related to the topic of stress?

Writing

1. Write two or three paragraphs relating what you have learned about stress in this unit with relationships between friends or between parents and children. Write about one specific relationship. Does this relationship reduce stress, cause stress, or do both in your life? If it reduces stress, how does it do this? If the relationship causes stress, what are the reasons, and what could you do about it?

2. Write an information sheet on stress for some special group of people whose lives you are familiar with (for example, students, parents, secretaries, managers). Include the following parts:

   Introduction (one paragraph)
      Get the interest of your special audience, and state your main idea.
   Body (one or more paragraphs)
      Discuss where stress comes from in the lives of the people who will read your sheet (your audience) and how they can handle it.
   Conclusion (one paragraph)
      Remind your readers of the benefits of handling their stress well.

   If you use other people's ideas, be sure to give them proper credit (Writing Task, p. 13).

UNIT FOUR

Formation of Gender Roles

From earliest childhood, the girl learns that it is her job to take care of relationships. Year after year—with her dolls, siblings, baby-sitting charges, boyfriends—she learns to notice other people's needs, to empathize with their feelings and want to help them. While males are rewarded for developing independence, females are rewarded for getting along with others.

— Letty Cottin Pogrebin
Among Friends

FOCUS

➤ How do boys' and girls' daily lives differ?

➤ How are boys and girls treated differently by parents, teachers, and other adults?

➤ What do you think different treatment teaches boys and girls about they way they relate to other people?

➤ What might be some results later in life of the different treatment of the sexes during childhood?

SELECTION ONE

Before Reading

This excerpt is from the book, *You Just Don't Understand: Conversations between Men and Women*. Deborah Tannen writes about how men and women in North American culture communicate differently, explaining why they often have difficulty understanding each other. This selection focuses on how young children in the United States learn the male or female style of communicating.

1. In groups of all women and all men, talk about how you played in early childhood. Discuss the following questions:

   a. How much of your playtime did you spend with children of the same sex? the opposite sex? in mixed groups?

   b. Where did you play with these different play groups? What games did you play and what toys did you play with?

   c. Did you usually play in large groups or with one or two other friends?

   d. What did you talk about with your playmates?

   e. Did your play groups have leaders? If so, how were the leaders determined?

   f. Were some children in your play groups more popular than others? What made them popular and admired by others?

2. Summarize your group discussions as a class under these headings:

   HOW BOYS PLAY   HOW GIRLS PLAY   HOW MIXED GROUPS PLAY

It Begins at the Beginning   by Deborah Tannen

1   Even if they grow up in the same neighborhood, on the same block, or in the same house, girls and boys grow up in different worlds of words. Others talk to them differently and expect and accept different ways of talking from them. Most important, children learn how to talk, how to have conversations, not only from their parents but from their peers. After all, if their parents have a foreign or regional accent, children do not emulate it; they learn to speak with the pronunciation of the region where they grow up. Anthropologists Daniel Maltz and Ruth Borker summarize research showing that boys and girls have very different ways of talking to their friends. Although they often play together, boys and girls spend most of their time playing in same-sex groups. And, although some of the activities they play at are similar, their favorite games are different, and their ways of using language in their games are separated by a world of difference.

2   Boys tend to play outside, in large groups that are hierarchically structured. Their groups have a leader who tells others what to do and how to do it, and resists doing what other boys propose. It is by giving orders and making them stick that high status is negotiated. Another way boys achieve status is to take center stage by telling stories and jokes, and by sidetracking or challenging the stories and jokes of others. Boys' games have winners and losers and elaborate systems of rules that are frequently the subjects of arguments. Finally, boys are frequently heard to boast of their skill and argue about who is best at what.

3 Girls, on the other hand, play in small groups or in pairs; the center of a girl's social life is a best friend. Within the group, intimacy is key: Differentiation[1] is measured by relative closeness. In their most frequent games, such as jump rope and hopscotch, everyone gets a turn. Many of their activities (such as playing house) do not have winners or losers. Though some girls are certainly more skilled than others, girls are expected not to boast about it, or show that they think they are better than the others. Girls don't give orders; they express their preferences as suggestions, and suggestions are likely to be accepted. Whereas boys say, "Gimme that!" and "Get outta here!" girls say, "Let's do this," and "How about doing that?" Anything else is put down as "bossy." They don't grab center stage[2]—they don't want it—so they don't challenge each other directly. And much of the time, they simply sit together and talk. Girls are not accustomed to jockeying for status in an obvious way; they are more concerned that they be liked.

---

[1] **differentiation**   difference or distinction between things

[2] **center stage**   the focus of attention

Comprehension Check

1. Do children in the United States usually play in mixed gender groups or with other children of the same sex?

2. List the ways Tannen indicates that boys and girls play differently.

3. From the way they play, what seems to be important to boys? What seems to be important to girls?

4. Reread paragraph 1, and choose one of the ideas below that shows what Tannen is most interested in about children's play.

   a. the rules of their games

   b. the size of their play groups

   c. the way they talk when they play

Sharing Your Thoughts

1. What similarities do you find between what Tannen says about girls and the ideas in the quote on the introductory page?

2. How does the content of this selection compare to your prereading discussion of childhood play?

3. What kind of communication skills do little boys/girls in the United States learn through their play? What kinds of jobs require the skills that boys/girls are developing?

4. What do you think Tannen would discover about children's play if she did a similar study in your country? Give examples of similarities or differences.

5. How would you answer question 3 with reference to your culture?

6. What differences, if any, in communication style have you noticed between adult men and women? How could these differences relate to something that people learn as children?

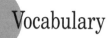

Vocabulary

A. Content Vocabulary

Complete the following statements about Tannen's findings with words from the list. Use each word only once. Change the form of verbs if the grammar of the sentence requires it.

accustomed	argue	boasting
concerned	grow up	hierarchically
intimacy	peers	resist
status		

1. Tannen says that even though boys and girls _____ in the same family, they play in different ways and learn different styles of communication, not only from their parents but from their _____ as well.

2. For example, boys tend to play outside in large groups, but girls are more _____ to playing indoors with one or two friends.

3. Boys' groups have a leader and followers; in other words, they are _____ structured. The leader tells the others what to do and _____ taking orders from anyone else. In contrast, girls' groups appear more democratically structured. Girls listen to the suggestions of others; they want to get along with their friends, not fight or _____ with them.

4. _____ is important in boys' groups; leaders often negotiate a high position in the group by telling stories and jokes and by _____ that they are the best. Girls, however, are _____ about having close friends to share secrets with. For them, _____ is important.

B. Vocabulary of Contrast

Locate these words and expressions of contrast in the Tannen selection or in the Content Vocabulary exercise above. Underline two groups of words to show what is contrasted. (Some contrasts involve more than one sentence.)

EXAMPLE:

although *(¶1)*   Although they *often play together,* boys and girls *spend most of their time in same-sex groups.*

1. even if (¶1) _____

2. although (¶1, last sentence) _____

3. though (¶3) _____

4. even though (Content Vocabulary 1) _____

5. whereas (¶3) _____

6. but (Content Vocabulary 2) _____

7. on the other hand (¶3) _____

8. in contrast (Content Vocabulary 3) _____

9. however (Content Vocabulary 4) _____

The above examples show two types of contrast. Some of the words and expressions show direct opposition; others focus on something that contrasts with what is expected. Which type do you find in 1–4? Which in 5–9?

Text Analysis

Text Organization

*When we **contrast** things, we show differences. Study the Tannen excerpt. What role does each paragraph play in the contrast?*

¶1: _____

¶2: _____

¶3: _____

Compare *the points in paragraph 2 with those in paragraph 3. What similarities, if any, do you notice between the paragraphs?*

Reread the Content Vocabulary exercise above. Fill in the blanks below based on the Content Vocabulary exercise.

Main idea in 1: ___*Boys and girls communicate in different ways.*___

Contrast in 2: ___*Examples for place of play, group size*___

    Boys ___*outside, large groups*___

    Girls ___*inside, one or two friends*___

Contrast in 3: examples for _____

    Boys _____

    Girls _____

Contrast in 4: examples for_____

    Boys _____

    Girls _____

What two ways of organizing contrasts are there?

Writing Task

With a group of classmates, brainstorm a list of differences you see between the men and women you know. To **brainstorm** means to think of and list ideas as they come to mind without evaluating them at the moment. For example, consider the way men and women communicate, the way they act in a certain situation, or their interests.

Write a paragraph contrasting men and women. Organize the points you want to make following either Tannen's organization or the one in the Content Vocabulary exercise. Begin with a general statement such as

- The men and women I know are really quite different. First,...
- There are three differences between men and women that I think are important. First,...

Complete the paragraph with specific examples to support the general statement.

SELECTION TWO

Before Reading

This article appeared in *Parade* magazine. It draws on research done in the early 1980s that is still relevant today. The principal researchers' recent findings were mentioned in 1994 news magazines.

1. What have you noticed, if anything, about the way teachers treat boys and girls in class?
2. Preview the article and answer these questions.
   a. In what country was the research conducted?
   b. What is the research about?
   c. What does *sex-biased* mean?

HIDDEN LESSONS

by Claire Safran

1   Our public-school teachers are targets once again of the researchers. This time, they have been charged with sex-biased instructional methods.

2   Drs. David and Myra Sadker of American University in Washington, D.C., last year sent observers to 100 classrooms in five states to sit in on teaching sessions. The Sadkers' researchers cited instances of boys being taught differently from girls in elementary schools, where women teachers far outnumber men, through secondary schools, where more than half the teachers are male.

3   The bias generally is unintentional and unconscious, says Myra Sadker, dean of the School of Education at American University. She notes: "We've met teachers who call themselves feminists. They show me their non-sexist textbooks and non-sexist bulletin boards. They insist there is equity in their classrooms. Then," she continues, "I videotape them as they're teaching—and they're amazed. If they hadn't seen themselves at work on film, they'd never have believed that they were treating boys and girls so differently."

4   Such videotaping of teachers is among the functions of 12 U.S. Department of Education Centers for Sex Equity in educational districts across the country.

5   From nursery school to beyond graduate school, studies show that teachers call on male students in class far more often than they call on female students. That difference in involvement in the learning process is crucial, say educators, who add that the students who are active in class are the ones who go on to higher achievement and a more positive attitude.

6   Many teachers unwittingly hinder girls from being active in class. Dr. Lisa Serbin of Concordia University in Montreal studied nursery schools in Suffolk County, N.Y. She tells how a teacher poured water into containers of different heights and widths, then told a little boy to try it—to learn for himself how water can change its shape without changing its amount.

7   "Can I do it?" a little girl asked.

8   "You'll have to wait your turn," the teacher replied, giving the pitcher to a second boy. The girl asked again, but it was time to put the materials away.

9   "You can help me to do that," the teacher offered.

10   Who gets to pour the water is important. Learning is connected to instruction and direction, and boys get more of that than girls do all through school. Why? Partly because teachers tend to question the students they expect will have the answers. Since girls traditionally don't do so well as boys in such "masculine" subjects as math and science, they're called on least in those classes. But girls are called on most in verbal and reading classes, where boys are expected to have the trouble. The trouble is in our culture, not in our chromosomes.[1] In Germany, everything academic is considered masculine. Most teachers are men, and girls have the reading problems. In Japan, there's no sex bias about reading, and neither sex has special problems with it.

11   In most U.S. schools, there are remedial classes for reading—the "boys' problem"—and boys quickly catch up to the girls. But there are very few remedial classes in math and science—the "girls' problems." Thus boys have the most skill in these subjects, which can lead to better-paying jobs later.

12   According to the National Assessment of Educational Progress, an organization in Denver that surveys both public and private schools nationally, girls get better math grades than boys do at age 9, but their scores decline as they progress while boys' math scores rise. Researchers say such things happen because boys are taught to take a more active part in learning than girls.

13   This differing of the educational process for the sexes starts at home. For example, in one study, preschool youngsters were shown a drawing of a house and asked, "How far can you go from your own house?" Most girls pointed to an area quite near the house and said that was how far their parents permitted them to go and how far they actually went. Most boys pointed to a much wider perimeter of permission and generally said they exceeded it.

14   In the classroom, unconscious sex bias takes various forms:

    •   Girls tend to be called on if they sit close to the teacher—first row—right under his or her nose. Boys tend to be called on wherever they sit. (*Girls' Lesson:* Be dependent—stay close to the teacher, and you'll be rewarded. *Boys' Lesson:* Be independent—sit anywhere; you'll be rewarded.)

    •   The Sadkers report this interchange. Fourth-grade teacher to a girl: "That's a neat paper. The margins are just right." To a boy: "That's a good analysis of the cause of the Civil War." (*Girl's Lesson:* Form, not content, is all that's expected of you. *Boy's Lesson:* Analytical thinking is what's expected of you.)

    •   Dr. Carol Dweck, professor of education at Harvard University, cites these comments by a teacher to students who have given incorrect answers. To a girl: "That's wrong." To a boy: "You'd know the right answer if you'd done your homework." (*Girl's Lesson:* The failure may be due to your own lack of ability. *Boy's Lesson:* You can do better if you make the effort.) Told that effort brings success, both sexes try—and succeed. Otherwise, both stop trying. Educators call this concept "attribution to effort."

15   Some teachers are learning to recognize—and then change—their methods. And small changes can make large differences. The Sadkers, for example, found that if teachers wait a few seconds after asking a question before they call on a student, more students will participate and their answers will be more complete.

16   Parents disturbed by sex bias in classrooms might first test themselves for it at home. Those who want to help combat teachers' sex bias might arrange to observe classes in their children's schools, and they might discuss sex bias at PTA[2] meetings. On this issue, awareness is the first step.

---

[1] **chromosome**   a part of animal or plant cells that carries hereditary information

[2] **PTA**   Parent–Teacher Association

Comprehension Check

1. What do teachers do without realizing it?
2. How did the research reveal that teachers do things differently from the way they think they do them?
3. How general was the sex bias in instructional methods? Did it occur only in elementary schools? Were women the only teachers who gave preference to boys?
4. How did teachers treat boys and girls differently? Give specific examples. Why is this important? What are the effects of this different treatment?
5. Who gets called on most in the United States in math and science classes? in verbal and reading classes? Why?
6. Which sex has more reading problems in the United States? in Germany? in Japan? What does this show about learning problems?
7. What evidence is there in the article that different treatment of boys and girls starts at home even before children go to school?

Sharing Your Thoughts

1. Support or refute the following statements first with evidence from the selection and then, if possible, with evidence from your personal experience.
   a. Teachers have the same expectations for boys and girls.
   b. Involvement in the learning process is important for students.
2. What effects, immediate and long-range, could these "hidden lessons" have on boys and on girls?
3. What do you think researchers would find if they studied classrooms in your country today?
4. If you are familiar with classrooms in the United States, what do you think the Sadkers would find if they repeated their study today?
5. What, if anything, are schools and teachers you know doing to involve males and females equally in learning?
6. Tannen showed readers something about how children learn to act in masculine and feminine ways. What, if anything, does this article contribute to our understanding of how we learn masculine and feminine roles?
7. Teachers who thought they were being non-sexist were, in fact, teaching in a sex-biased way. What are some other situations in which researchers might find that people act differently from the way they think they act?

Vocabulary

A. Content Vocabulary

Complete the following statements about sex bias in schools with words from the list. Use each word only once. Change the form of verbs if the grammar of the sentence requires it.

bias	**call on**	**catch up**
crucial	**decline**	**hindered**
rise	**treat**	

1. Researchers found that teachers _____ boys and girls differently.

2. The researchers observed that teachers _____ boys more frequently than girls, which is a form of sex _____.

3. American schools often provided special classes to help boys _____ to girls in reading, but girls didn't usually get extra help if they had problems with math. As you would expect, girls' math scores _____ while boys' math scores _____. Thus, girls are _____ from developing their math talents.

4. Studies show that how well boys and girls do is related to how well they are expected to do; this suggests that our expectations for people can make a(n) _____ difference in their lives.

B. Grammatical Function

Using a dictionary when necessary, fill in the blanks with words related to the word that is given.

	VERB	NOUN	ADJECTIVE	ADVERB
1.	_____	achievement		
2.		awareness	_____	
3.	_____	_____	_____	differently
4.	expect	_____		
5.	_____	_____	remedial	
6.	succeed	_____	_____	_____
7.	treat	_____		
8.	_____	_____	various	

Complete each of the following sentences with the word in parentheses or a related word from your chart, depending on which grammatical function the missing word should have. (Change the forms of verbs and nouns as necessary.)

1. Schools offer _____ classes to _____ the problems boys tend to have with reading.   (remedial)

2. Teachers are not _____ of their sex bias; seeing themselves on videotape increases their _____.   (awareness)

3. Many people have higher academic _____ for boys than for girls. They _____ boys, not girls, to excel in math.   (expect)

4. Both boys and girls can be _____ in math and reading class, as evidence from different cultures shows. Girls in Japan _____ in math class, so why not in other cultures as well?   (succeed)

5. People who do well in school, usually go on to _____ things in later life.   (achievement)

6. Talents _____ from person to person; everyone should try to develop a _____ of talents.   (various)

7. When teachers saw themselves on videotape, they were amazed at how biased their _____ of boys and girls was.   (treat)

8. They never would have believed they treated boys and girls so _____ if they hadn't seen it with their own eyes.   (differently)

C. Word Analysis

Locate the following words in the selection. Check the context in which they each appear. Divide each word into its meaningful parts. What is the meaning of the whole? What does each part contribute? Use a dictionary if necessary.

1. outnumber (¶2) _____

2. unintentional (¶3) _____

3. non-sexist (¶3) _____

4. better-paying jobs (¶11) _____

5. preschool (¶13) _____

6. otherwise (¶13) _____

Text Analysis

Supporting General Statements

> In this article Safran refers to studies done by various researchers. She and the researchers make general statements about U.S. teachers, a large group, based on evidence from a small number of U.S. teachers. This type of overall statement is called a **generalization**.
>
> Writers must support their generalizations with appropriate evidence. Most readers do not have the knowledge to make a complete evaluation of such supporting evidence, but they should at least notice whether the writer provides it. Efficient readers do not accept generalizations blindly.

What support does Safran give for the following generalizations about teachers and education in the United States? Considering that this is a short magazine article, do you think she has given enough support or would you like to have something clarified or supported with more examples?

1. The trouble [who has what learning difficulties] is in our culture, not in our chromosomes. (¶10)
2. In the classroom, unconscious sex bias takes various forms. (¶13)

Writing Task

Write a generalization about teachers, students, or schools you know.

EXAMPLES:

- When I was in elementary school, teachers favored girls not boys.
- Students today are not very interested in learning.
- Schools in my city/country are changing.

Write one or two paragraphs in which you provide evidence from your experience to illustrate the truth of your generalization. Exchange your first draft, the first version of your writing, with a partner. Read each other's writing and determine if there is enough support for the generalization. If not, revise accordingly.

SELECTION THREE

Before Reading

This selection is from *Psychology: Themes and Variations,* 2nd Ed., a college psychology textbook by Wayne Weiten. It is an excerpt from the chapter on "Human Development across the Life Span."

1. Discover some of your own ideas about gender differences, or differences between men and women, by sorting the following list of adjectives under two column headings: MASCULINE and FEMININE. Make a special column, if necessary, for words you cannot categorize.

   adventurous, aggressive, aware of the feelings of others, competent, decisive, easily influenced, emotional, gentle, logical, independent, passive, tactful, talkative, vain, knowledgeable about the world

   In a group or as a class, compare the way you sorted the adjectives.

   a. On which adjectives did you agree and on which did you disagree? Discuss your disagreements. What things that men or women do made you categorize the adjective as you did?

   b. Which adjectives were difficult to categorize? Why?

2. Preview this selection. Pay attention to the headings and try to answer these questions.

   a. What is the topic of this selection? What questions can you expect answers to?

   b. How do you expect it will be different from the first two selections?

3. Scan the selection again to locate the definitions of the following terms. Knowing what these terms mean will help you understand the selection.

   a. sex

   b. gender

   c. gender stereotypes

   d. gender differences

   e. socialization

   f. gender roles

4. You may find this textbook selection a little difficult. Discuss your purpose in reading it with your classmates and teacher. What final level of understanding do you want?

UNDERSTANDING GENDER DIFFERENCES   by Wayne Weiten

1 Answer the following "true" or "false."

❏ **1.** Females are more socially oriented than males.

❏ **2.** Males outperform females on spatial tasks.

❏ **3.** Females are more irrational than males.

❏ **4.** Males are less sensitive to nonverbal cues than females.

❏ **5.** Females are more emotional than males.

2 Are there genuine behavioral differences between the sexes similar to those mentioned above? If so, why do these differences exist? How do they develop? These are the complex and controversial questions that we'll explore.

Before proceeding further, we need to clarify how some key terms are used in this area of research. *Sex* **refers to the biologically based categories of female and male**. In contrast, *gender* **refers to culturally constructed distinctions between femininity and masculinity**. Individuals 3 are *born* female or male. However, they *become* feminine or masculine through complex developmental processes that take years to unfold.

The statements at the beginning reflect popular gender stereotypes in our society. *Gender stereotypes* **are widely held beliefs about females' and males' abilities, personality traits, and social behavior**. In North American society, the male stereotype is much more flattering, suggesting that men have virtually cornered the market on competence and rationality. After all, everyone knows that females are more dependent, emotional, irrational, submissive, and talkative than males. Right? Or is that not the case? Let's look at the research.

HOW DO THE SEXES DIFFER IN BEHAVIOR?

4 *Gender differences* **are actual disparities between the sexes in typical behavior or average ability**. Mountains of research, literally thousands of studies, exist on gender differences. It's difficult to sort through this huge body of research, but fortunately, many review articles on gender differences have been published in recent years. *Review articles* summarize and reconcile the findings of a large number of studies on a specific issue.

5 What does this research show? Are the stereotypes of males and females accurate? For the most part, no. The research indicates that genuine behavioral differences *do* exist between the sexes, but they are far fewer in number than stereotypes suggest. As you'll see, only two of the differences mentioned in our opening true-false questions (the even-numbered items) have been supported by the research.

6 ***Cognitive Abilities*** In the cognitive domain, several independently conducted reviews of hundreds of studies reveal three well-documented gender differences in mental abilities (Hyde, 1981; Linn & Petersen, 1986; Maccoby & Jacklin, 1974). First, on the average, females perform somewhat better than males on tests of *verbal ability*. Second, males show an advantage on tests of *mathematical ability*. Third, males tend to score high in *visual-spatial ability* more often than females do. For all three of these cognitive abilities, the gap between males and females doesn't open up until early adolescence. Moreover, these gender differences are rather small, and they appear to be shrinking (Linn & Hyde, 1989).

7 ***Social Behavior*** In regard to social behavior, research findings support the existence of three more gender differences. First, studies indicate

that males tend to be more *aggressive* than females, both verbally and physically (Eagly, 1987; Hyde, 1986). This disparity shows up early in childhood. Its continuation into adulthood is supported by the fact that men account for a grossly disproportionate number of the violent crimes in our society (Kenrick, 1987). Second, there are gender differences in *nonverbal communication*. The evidence indicates that females are more sensitive than males to subtle nonverbal cues (Hall, 1984). Females also smile and gaze at others more than males do (Hall & Halberstadt, 1986). Third, two separate reviews conclude that gender differences occur in *influenceability* (Becker, 1986; Eagly & Carli, 1981). That is, females appear to be slightly more susceptible to persuasion and conforming to group pressure than males are.

8 **Some Qualifications** Although there are some genuine gender differences in behavior, bear in mind that these are *group* differences that indicate nothing about individuals. Essentially, research results compare the "average man" with the "average woman." However, you are—and every individual is—unique. The average female and male are ultimately figments[1] of our imagination. Furthermore, the genuine group differences noted are relatively small.

9 To summarize, the behavioral differences between males and females are fewer and smaller than popular stereotypes suggest. Many supposed gender differences, including those in sociability, emotional reactivity, self-esteem, analytic ability, and dependence, have turned out to be more mythical than real (Maccoby & Jacklin, 1974).

ENVIRONMENTAL ORIGINS OF GENDER DIFFERENCES

10 **Socialization is the acquisition[2] of the norms[3] and behaviors expected of people in a particular society.** It includes all the efforts made by a society to ensure that its members learn to behave in a manner that's considered appropriate. The socialization process has traditionally included efforts to train children about gender roles. **Gender roles are expectations about what is appropriate behavior for each sex.** Investigators have identified three key processes involved in the socialization of gender roles: operant conditioning, observational learning, and self-socialization. First we'll examine these processes. Then we'll look at the principal sources of gender-role socialization: families, schools, and the media.

11 **Operant Conditioning** In part, gender roles are shaped by the power of reward and punishment—the key processes in *operant conditioning*. Parents, teachers, peers, and others often reinforce (usually with tacit approval) "gender appropriate" behavior and respond negatively to "gender inappropriate" behavior (Fagot, 1978). If you're a man, you might recall getting hurt as a young boy and being told that "men don't cry." If you succeeded in inhibiting your crying, you may have earned an approving smile or even something tangible like an ice cream cone. The reinforcement probably strengthened your tendency to "act like a man" and suppress emotional displays. If you're a woman, chances are your crying wasn't discouraged as gender-inappropriate.

12 Studies suggest that parents may use *punishment* more than *reward* in socializing gender roles (O'Leary, 1977). Many parents take gender-appropriate behavior for granted and don't go out of their way to reward it. But they may react negatively to gender-inappropriate behavior. Thus, a ten-year-old boy who enjoys playing with dollhouses may elicit strong disapproval from his parents.

13 **Observational Learning** As a young girl, did you imitate the behavior of your mother, your aunts, your older sister, and your female peers? As a young boy, did you imitate your father and other male role models? Such behaviors reflect *observational learning*, in which behavior is shaped by the observation of others' behavior and its consequences. In

---

[1] figments   creations

[2] acquisition   learning

[3] norm   standards or models

everyday language, observational learning results in *imitation*.

14   Children imitate both males and females, but most children tend to imitate same-sex role models more than opposite-sex role models (Perry & Bussey, 1979). Thus, imitation often leads young girls to play with dolls, dollhouses, and toy stoves. Young boys are more likely to tinker with toy trucks, miniature gas stations, or tool kits.

15   *Self-Socialization*   Children themselves are active agents in their own gender-role socialization. Several *cognitive theories* of gender-role development emphasize self-socialization (Bem, 1981; Kohlberg, 1966; Martin & Halverson, 1981). Self-socialization entails three steps. First, children learn to classify themselves as male or female and to recognize their sex as a permanent quality (around ages five to seven). Second, this self-categorization motivates them to value those characteristics and behaviors associated with their sex. Third, they strive to bring their behavior in line with what is considered gender-appropriate in their culture. In other words, children get involved in their own socialization, working diligently to discover the rules that are supposed to govern their behavior.

16   *Sources of Gender-Role Socialization*   There are three *main* sources of influence in gender-role socialization: families, schools, and the media. Of course, we are now in an era of transition in gender roles, so the generalizations that follow may say more about how you were socialized than about how children will be socialized in the future. We'll discuss this transition after describing the traditional picture.

17   FAMILIES.   A great deal of gender-role socialization takes place in the home (Huston, 1983). Fathers engage in more "rough-housing"[4] play with their sons than with their daughters, even in infancy. As children grow, boys and girls are encouraged to play with different types of toys. Substantial gender differences are found in toy preferences. Generally, boys have less leeway to play with "feminine" toys than girls do with "masculine" toys.

18   When children are old enough to help with household chores, the assignments tend to depend on sex. For example, girls wash dishes and boys mow the lawn. Likewise, the leisure activities that children are encouraged to engage in vary by sex. Johnny plays in Little League and Mary practices the piano. Given these patterns, it's not surprising that parents' traditional or nontraditional attitudes about gender roles have been shown to influence the gender roles acquired by their children (Repetti, 1984).

19   SCHOOLS.   Schools also contribute to the socialization of gender roles (Busch-Rossnagel & Vance, 1982; Etaugh & Harlow, 1975). Books that children use in learning to read influence their ideas about what is suitable behavior for males and females. Traditionally, males have been more likely to be portrayed as clever, heroic, and adventurous in these books, while females have been more likely to be shown doing domestic chores.

20   As youngsters progress through the school system, they are often channeled in career directions considered appropriate for their sex. For example, males have been more likely to be encouraged to study mathematics and to work toward becoming engineers or doctors. Females have often been encouraged to take classes in home economics and to work toward becoming nurses or homemakers.

21   MEDIA.   Television is another source of gender-role socialization. Television shows have traditionally depicted men and women in highly stereotypic ways (Basow, 1986). Women are often portrayed as submissive, passive, and emotional. Men are more likely to be portrayed as independent, assertive, and competent. Even commercials contribute to the socialization of gender roles. Women are routinely shown worrying about trivial matters such as a ring around their husband's shirt collar or the shine of their dishes.

22   One study strikingly demonstrates just how influential television can be. Many children's shows on public/educational television strive

---

4 rough-housing   playing in a rough, noisy, disorderly, way in which someone might get hurt

to promote nontraditional gender roles. Repetti (1984) found that children who watch a great deal of educational television tend to be less traditional in their views of gender roles than other children are. Thus, it appears that media content influences the gender roles acquired by children.

GENDER ROLES IN TRANSITION

23 Gender roles are in a period of transition in our society. Many women and men are rebelling against traditional role expectations based on sex. Many parents are trying to raise their children with fewer preconceived notions about how males and females "ought" to behave. Some social critics view this as a healthy trend because they believe that traditional roles have been too narrow and restrictive for both sexes (Bem, 1975; Fasteau, 1974; Goldberg, 1983). Such theorists argue that conventional sex roles lock people into rigid straitjackets[5] that prevent them from realizing their full potential. Other social critics, such as Gilder (1986), believe that changes in gender roles may harm intimate relationships between men and women and hurt the quality of family life. Thus, there's vigorous debate about the effects of evolving gender roles.

---

[5] **straitjackets**   things that prevent free development (from a garment used to tie the arms of potentially violent people)

Bibliography

Basow, S. A. (1986). *Gender stereotypes: Traditions and alternatives*. Pacific Grove, CA: Brooks/Cole.

Becker, B. J. (1986). Influence again: An examination of reviews and studies of gender differences in social influence. In J. S. Hyde & M. C. Linn (Eds.), *The psychology of gender: Advances through meta-analysis*. Baltimore: Johns Hopkins University Press.

Bem, S. L. (1975). Sex-role adaptability: One consequence of psychological androgyny. *Journal of Personality and Social Psychology, 31*, 634–643.

Bem, S. L. (1981). Gender schema theory: A cognitive account of sex typing. *Psychological Review*, 88, 354–364.

Busch-Rossnagel, N. A., & A. K. Vance. (1982). The impact of the schools on social and emotional development. In B. B. Wolman (Ed.), *Handbook of developmental psychology*. Englewood Cliffs, NJ: Prentice Hall.

Eagly, A. H. (1987). *Sex differences in social behavior: A social-role interpretation*. Hillsdale, NJ: Erlbaum.

Eagly, A. H., & L. L. Carli. (1981). Sex of researchers and sex-typed communications as determinants of sex differences in influenceability: A meta-analysis of social influence studies. *Psychological Bulletin*, 90, 424–435.

Etaugh, C. F., & H. Harlow. (1975). Behaviors of male and female teachers as related to behaviors and attitudes of elementary school children. *Journal of Genetic Psychology*, 127, 163–170.

Fagot, B. I. (1978). The influence of sex of child on parental reactions to toddler children. *Child Development*, 49, 459–465.

Fasteau, M. F. (1974). *The male machine*. New York: McGraw-Hill.

Gilder, G. (1986). *Men and marriage*. New York: Pelican.

Goldberg, H. (1983). *The new male-female relationship*. New York: Morrow.

Hall, J. A. (1984). *Non-verbal sex differences: Communication accuracy and expressive style*. Baltimore: Johns Hopkins University Press.

Hall, J. A., & A. G. Halberstadt. (1986). Smiling and gazing. In J. S. Hyde & M. C. Linn (Eds.), *The psychology of gender: Advances through meta-analysis*. Baltimore: Johns Hopkins University Press.

Huston, A. C. (1983). Sex-typing. In P. H. Mussen (Ed.), *Handbook of child psychology* (4th ed., Vol. 4). New York: Wiley.

Hyde, J. S. (1981). How large are cognitive gender differences? *American Psychologist*, 36, 892–901.

Hyde, J. S. (1986). *Understanding human sexuality* (3rd ed.). New York: McGraw-Hill.

Kenrick, D. T. (1987). Gender, genes, and the social environment. In P. C. Shaver & C. Hendrick (Eds.), *Review of personality and social psychology* (Vol. 8). Beverly Hills, CA: Sage Publications.

Kohlberg, L. (1966). A cognitive-developmental analysis of children's sex-role concepts and attitudes. In E. E. Maccoby (Ed.), *The development of sex differences*. Stanford, CA: Stanford University Press.

Linn, M. C., & A. C. Petersen. (1986). A meta-analysis of gender differences in spatial ability: Implications for mathematics and science achievement. In J. S. Hyde & M. C. Linn (Eds.), *The psychology of gender: Advances through meta-analysis*. Baltimore: Johns Hopkins University Press.

Linn, M. C., & J. S. Hyde. (1989). Gender Mathematics, & Science. *Educational Researcher*, 18(8), 17–19, 22–27.

Maccoby, E. E., & C. N. Jacklin. (1974). *The psychology of sex differences*. Stanford, CA: Stanford University Press.

Martin, C. L., & C. F. Halverson, Jr. (1981). A schematic processing model of sex typing and stereotyping in children. *Child Development*, 52, 1119–1134.

O'Leary, V. E. (1977). *Toward understanding women*. Pacific Grove, CA: Brooks/Cole.

Perry, D. G., & K. Bussey. (1979). The social learning theory of sex differences: Imitation is alive and well. *Journal of Personality and Social Psychology*, 37, 1699–1712.

Repetti, R. L. (1984). Determinants of children's sex-stereotyping: Parental sex-role traits and television viewing. *Personality and Social Psychology Bulletin*, 10 (3), 457–468.

Comprehension Check

1. What is the distinction between a gender stereotype and a gender difference?
2. What cognitive gender differences does research support?
3. What behavioral (social) differences does research support?
4. What do the research results say about individual people?
5. What is socialization? What are gender roles?
6. What are the three key processes through which children learn their gender roles? Give an example of how each works.
7. How do parents, schools, and the media each influence boys and girls to follow their respective traditional roles?

Sharing Your Thoughts

1. Support or refute the following statements first with evidence from the text and then with evidence from your personal experience.
   a. The male stereotype is more favorable than the female stereotype.
   b. Gender stereotypes are generally accurate.
   c. Parents treat their sons and daughters the same way.
   d. Children generally imitate role models of the same sex.
   e. People agree that gender roles should change.
2. In doing Before Reading 1, what stereotypes, if any, about males and females did you discover you might have?
3. Gender stereotypes, like other stereotypes, are beliefs based on overgeneralizations. Some men are aggressive, so people believe that all men are or should be aggressive and that no women are or should be aggressive. Why do people stereotype others in this way?
4. What are some of the bad consequences of believing gender stereotypes?
5. Many people have ethnic stereotypes, generalizations about people of a different cultural group. Do you think other people have stereotypes about your ethnic group? If so, how do you feel about this?
6. How do the research findings in this selection support or explain ideas in Selections One (p.86) and Two (p.91) ?
7. This selection is based mostly on research done in the United States. Which findings, if any, do you think would be different if the research had been done in your culture?

Vocabulary

A. Content Vocabulary

Complete the following statements about gender differences with words from the list. Use each word only once. Change the form of verbs if the grammar of the sentence requires it.

accurate	**appropriate**	**gap**
gender	**genuine**	**raise**
sex	**show up**	**sources**
support		

1. All of us are either males or females; that is our _____. The word _____, however, refers to our culture's ideas of *masculine* and *feminine*.

2. A lot of research has been done in an effort to answer the question: Are there _____ behavioral differences between men and women or are they mythical?

3. Research shows that the stereotypes about male-female differences are not very _____. Research _____ only six behavioral differences.

4. The average male and female differ in mathematical, visual-spatial, and verbal abilities. Interestingly, the _____ between males and females in these cognitive abilities does not _____ until adolescence, and it is small.

5. Children receive information about gender roles from three principal _____. Families, schools, and the media all play a role in teaching children what behavior is _____ for females and what is acceptable for males.

6. Some parents are trying to break with traditional ideas about gender and want to _____ their children in a less restricted way.

B. Idioms and Phrasal Verbs

Locate the following expressions in the selection, and figure out what they mean using the context in the selection to help you. Then, paraphrase the sentences in which they occur.

EXAMPLE:

The male stereotype is much more flattering, suggesting that men have virtually **cornered the market** on competence and rationality. (¶3)

MEANING: *have all of something*

PARAPHRASE: Beliefs about men are much more positive than beliefs about women. This suggests that only men can do things well and think in a logical way.

1. mountains of research (¶4) _____

2. bear in mind (¶8) _____

3. more mythical than real (¶9) _____

4. take...for granted (¶12) _____

5. go out of their way (¶12) _____

6. to bring...in line with (¶15) _____

C. Qualifying/Limiting Statements

What words in the following sentences show that the writer does not want to overgeneralize or exaggerate his statements? What happens to the meaning of the sentences when you remove those words?

EXAMPLE:

Females appear to be slightly more susceptible to persuasion and conforming to group pressure than males are.

The words that prevent overgeneralization or exaggeration are **appear to** and **slightly**. Without them, the statement is too strong. If at all, females are only a little more susceptible to persuasion.

1. First, on the average, females perform somewhat better than males on tests of verbal ability.
2. Most children tend to imitate same-sex role models.
3. Moreover, these gender differences are rather small.
4. Studies suggest that parents may use punishment more than reward in socializing gender roles.
5. Thus, imitation often leads young girls to play with dolls.
6. Young boys are more likely to tinker with toy trucks.

Text Analysis

A. Text Organization

> In organizing their text, academic writers often give the reader an idea of what is coming. Two common ways to do this are:
>
> **a.** to ask questions that they will then answer
> **b.** to use phrases that give the reader an idea of what is coming

1. Which paragraphs answer the questions Weiten asks in paragraph 1?

2. Find examples of statements or phrases that indicate what is coming next. What do they say about what is coming next?

   EXAMPLE:

   *Before proceeding further, we need **to clarify** how some **key terms** are used in this area of research.*

   > The reader knows that definitions are coming.

3. What other organizational help does Weiten give to make this material easier to read?

B. Writing Conventions

> Academic writers tell you where their information comes from, that is, they cite a **source**. The writer gives the reader enough information to be able to find the material cited. Different fields have different conventions for citing sources. In psychology and many other fields, writers indicate partial information about the source in parentheses in the text and give a complete bibliography at the end of the chapter or the book. The bibliography for this selection follows these conventions for presenting information about each type of source. Models appear on page 101.
>
> BOOK:
> author, date, book title, city, and publisher
>
> MAGAZINE OR JOURNAL ARTICLE:
> author, date, article title, magazine or journal title, volume number, page numbers
>
> ARTICLE IN A BOOK:
> author, date, article title, book's editor, book title, city, and publisher

1. Scan the selection and find a citation in the text. What information does it give? Where does the citation come in the text?

2. Answer these questions about the first three entries in the bibliography.

   a. Who is the author?

   b. What kind of information do you think you would fine in this source?

   c. Is it a journal article, an article in a book, or a whole book?

3. Why do academic writers provide this information?

4. Why would readers need the bibliographic information and how would they use it?

5. If you wanted to know more about how parents directly influence gender-role formation of their children, which sources in the bibliography would you try to get? If you wanted to know more about how schools and teachers influence children, which sources in the bibliography would you try to get?

Writing Task

1. Freewrite about how parents in your culture treat their male and female children. The following questions may help you get started.

   - What differences have you noticed in the way parents treat male and female children? Why do you think they make this difference?

   - Do you agree with the different treatment of males and females in your culture? Why or why not? Will you do the same when you are a parent? If not, what specific things will you do differently?

   Reread your writing. Look for and mark ideas you might want to write about in more detail on some other occasion. Keep your freewriting for possible use for the writing exercise in A Final Look.

2. Write one or two paragraphs about how this selection has changed your thinking. Begin with a general statement of what you learned or how your thinking changed. For example, *Before reading this selection, I used to think that.../I didn't know that...*Be sure to make both your old idea and your new understanding clear with detailed explanation and examples.

SELECTION FOUR

Before Reading

This satirical story was originally published in *Ms.* magazine. Lois Gould has written several novels, a book of essays, and numerous articles and book reviews. She has taught at various universities in the United States.

1. When we read for pleasure, we do not normally preview the selection, but since the title of this story is so uninformative, skim the first eight paragraphs to get an idea of what it is about.

2. As you skim the eight paragraphs, watch for words that suggest the tone. Do you think it will be serious or humorous?

NOTE: This story is long. If desired, it can be read in three parts: paragraphs 1 to 42, paragraphs 43 to 112, and paragraphs 113 to 147. The Comprehension Check questions have been divided into three corresponding parts.

X

by Lois Gould

1 ONCE UPON A TIME, a Baby named X was born. It was named X so that nobody could tell whether it was a boy or a girl.

2 Its parents could tell, of course, but they couldn't tell anybody else. They couldn't even tell Baby X—at least not until much, much later.

3 You see, it was all part of a very important Secret Scientific Xperiment, known officially as Project Baby X.

4 The Xperiment was going to cost Xactly 23 billion dollars and 72 cents. Which might seem like a lot for one Baby, even if it was an important Secret Scientific Xperimental Baby.

5 But when you remember the cost of strained carrots, stuffed bunnies, booster shots,[1] 28 shiny quarters from the tooth fairy[2]…you begin to see how it adds up.

6 Long before Baby X was born, the smartest scientists had to work out the secret details of the Xperiment, and to write the *Official Instruction Manual*, in secret code, for Baby X's parents, whoever they were.

7 These parents had to be selected very carefully. Thousands of people volunteered to take thousands of tests, with thousands of tricky questions.

8 Almost everybody failed because, it turned out, almost everybody wanted a boy or a girl, and not a Baby X at all.

9 Also, almost everybody thought a Baby X would be more trouble than a boy or a girl. (They were right, too.)

10 There were families with grandparents named Milton and Agatha, who wanted the baby named Milton or Agatha instead of X, even if it *was* an X.

11 There were aunts who wanted to knit tiny dresses and uncles who wanted to send tiny baseball mitts.

---

[1] **booster shot**   repeat vaccinations, after the original

[2] **tooth fairy**   imaginary creature that leaves a small amount of money in exchange for a child's baby teeth left under the pillow

12   Worst of all, there were families with other children who couldn't be trusted to keep a Secret. Not if they knew the Secret was worth 23 billion dollars and 72 cents—and all you had to do was take one little peek at Baby X in the bathtub to know what it was.

13   Finally, the scientists found the Joneses, who really wanted to raise an X more than any other kind of baby—no matter how much trouble it was.

14   The Joneses promised to take turns holding X, feeding X, and singing X to sleep.

15   And they promised never to hire any baby-sitters. The scientists knew that a baby-sitter would probably peek at X in the bathtub, too.

16   The day the Joneses brought their baby home, lots of friends and relatives came to see it. And the first thing they asked was what kind of a baby X was.

17   When the Joneses said, "It's an X!" nobody knew what to say.

18   They couldn't say, "Look at her cute little dimples!"

19   On the other hand, they couldn't say, "Look at his husky little biceps!"

20   And they didn't feel right about saying just plain "kitchy-coo."

21   The relatives all felt embarrassed about having an X in the family.

22   "People will think there's something wrong with it!" they whispered.

23   "Nonsense!" the Joneses said cheerfully. "What could possibly be wrong with this perfectly adorable X?"

24   Clearly, nothing at all was wrong. Nevertheless, the cousins who had sent a tiny football helmet would not come and visit any more. And the neighbors who sent a pink-flowered romper suit³ pulled their shades down when the Joneses passed their house.

25   The *Official Instruction Manual* had warned the new parents that this would happen, so they didn't fret about it. Besides, they were too busy learning how to bring up Baby X.

26   Ms. and Mr. Jones had to be Xtra careful. If they kept bouncing it up in the air and saying how *strong* and *active* it was, they'd be treating it more like a boy than an X. But if all they did was cuddle it and kiss it and tell it how *sweet* and *dainty* it was, they'd be treating it more like a girl than an X.

27   On page 1654 of the *Official Instruction Manual*, the scientists prescribed: "plenty of bouncing and plenty of cuddling, *both*. X ought to be strong and sweet and active. Forget about *dainty* altogether."

28   There were other problems, too. Toys, for instance. And clothes. On his first shopping trip, Mr. Jones told the store clerk, "I need some things for a new baby." The clerk smiled and said, "Well, now, is it a boy or a girl?" "It's an X," Mr. Jones said, smiling back. But the clerk got all red in the face and said huffily, "In *that* case, I'm afraid I can't help you, sir."

29   Mr. Jones wandered the aisles trying to find what X needed. But everything was in sections marked BOYS or GIRLS: "Boys' Pajamas" and "Girls' Underwear" and "Boys' Fire Engines" and "Girls' Housekeeping Sets." Mr. Jones went home without buying anything for X.

30   That night he and Ms. Jones consulted page 2326 of the *Official Instruction Manual*. It said firmly: "Buy plenty of everything!"

31   So they bought all kinds of toys. A boy doll that made pee-pee and cried "Pa-Pa." And a girl doll that talked in three languages and said, "I am the Pres-i-dent of Gen-er-al Mo-tors."

32   They bought a storybook about a brave princess who rescued a handsome prince from his tower, and another one about a sister and brother who grew up to be a baseball star and a ballet star, and you had to guess which.

---

³ romper suit   child's one-piece playsuit

33   The head scientists of Project Baby X checked all their purchases and told them to keep up the good work. They also reminded the Joneses to see page 4629 of the *Manual*, where it said, "Never make Baby X feel *embarrassed* or *ashamed* about what it wants to play with. And if X gets dirty climbing rocks, never say, " 'Nice little Xes don't get dirty climbing rocks.' "

34   Likewise, it said, "If X falls down and cries, never say, 'Brave little Xes don't cry.' Because, of course, nice little Xes *do* get dirty, and brave little Xes *do* cry. No matter how dirty X gets, or how hard it cries, don't worry. It's all part of the Xperiment."

35   Whenever the Joneses pushed Baby X's stroller in the park, smiling strangers would come over and coo: "Is that a boy or a girl?" The Joneses would smile back and say, "It's an X." The strangers would stop smiling then and often snarl something nasty—as if the Joneses had said something nasty to *them*.

36   Once a little girl grabbed X's shovel in the sandbox, and zonked X on the head with it. "Now, now, Tracy," the mother began to scold, "little girls mustn't hit little—" and she turned to ask X, "Are you a little boy or a little girl, dear?"

37   Mr. Jones, who was sitting near the sandbox, held his breath and crossed his fingers.

38   X smiled politely, even though X's head had never been zonked so hard in its life. "I'm a little X," said X.

39   "You're a *what*?" the lady exclaimed angrily. "You're a little b-r-a-t, you mean!"

40   "But little girls mustn't hit little Xes, either!" said X, retrieving the shovel with another polite smile. "What good's hitting, anyway?"

41   X's father finally X-haled, uncrossed his fingers, and grinned.

42   And at their next secret Project Baby X meeting, the scientists grinned, too. Baby X was doing fine.

43   But then it was time for X to start school. The Joneses were really worried about this, because school was even more full of rules for boys and girls, and there were no rules for Xes.

44   Teachers would tell boys to form a line, and girls to form another line.

45   There would be boys' games and girls' games, and boys' secrets and girls' secrets.

46   The school library would have a list of recommended books for girls, and a different list for boys.

47   There would even be a bathroom marked BOYS and another one marked GIRLS.

48   Pretty soon boys and girls would hardly talk to each other. What would happen to poor little X?

49   The Joneses spent weeks consulting their *Instruction Manual*.

50   There were 249 and one-half pages of advice under "First Day of School." Then they were all summoned to an Urgent Xtra Special Conference with the smart scientists of Project Baby X.

51   The scientists had to make sure that X's mother had taught X how to throw and catch a ball properly, and that X's father had been sure to teach X what to serve at a doll's tea party.

52   X had to know how to shoot marbles and jump rope and, most of all, what to say when the Other Children asked whether X was a Boy or a Girl.

53   Finally, X was ready.

54   X's teacher had promised that the class could line up alphabetically, instead of forming separate lines for boys and girls. And X had permission to use the principal's bathroom, because it wasn't marked anything except BATHROOM. But nobody could help X with the biggest problem of all—Other Children.

55   Nobody in X's class had ever known an X. Nobody had even heard grown-ups say, "Some of my best friends are[4] Xes."

56   What would other children think? Would they make Xist jokes? Or would they make friends?

57   You couldn't tell what X was by its clothes. Overalls don't even button right to left, like girls' clothes, or left to right, like boys' clothes.

58   And did X have a girl's short haircut or a boy's long haircut?

59   As for the games X liked, either X played ball very well for a girl, or else played house very well for a boy.

60   The children tried to find out by asking X tricky questions, like, "Who's your favorite sports star?" X had two favorite sports stars: a girl jockey named Robyn Smith and a boy archery champion named Robin Hood.

61   Then they asked, "What's your favorite TV show?" And X said: "Lassie," which stars a girl dog played by a boy dog.

62   When X said its favorite toy was a doll, everyone decided that X must be a girl. But then X said the doll was really a robot, and that X had computerized it, and that it was programmed to bake fudge and then clean up the kitchen.

63   After X told them that, they gave up guessing what X was. All they knew was they'd sure like to see X's doll.

64   After school, X wanted to play with the other children. "How about shooting baskets in the gym?" X asked the girls. But all they did was make faces and giggle behind X's back.

65   "Boy, is *he* weird," whispered Jim to Joe.

66   "How about weaving some baskets in the arts and crafts room?" X asked the boys. But they all made faces and giggled behind X's back, too.

67   "Boy, is *she* weird," whispered Susie to Peggy.

68   That night, Ms. and Mr. Jones asked X how things had gone at school. X tried to smile, but there were two big tears in its eyes. "The lessons are okay," X began, "but..."

---

[4] **some of my best friends are**   comment heard from some people who are trying to cover up their prejudice toward another group

69 "But?" said Ms. Jones.

70 "The Other Children hate me," X whispered.

71 "Hate you?" said Mr. Jones.

72 X nodded, which made the two big tears roll down and splash on its overalls.

73 Once more, the Joneses reached for their *Instruction Manual*. Under "Other Children," it said:

74 "What did you Xpect? Other Children have to obey silly boy-girl rules, because their parents taught them to. Lucky X—you don't have rules at all! All you have to do is be yourself.

75 "P.S. We're not saying it'll be easy."

76 X liked being itself. But X cried a lot that night. So X's father held X tight, and cried a little, too. X's mother cheered them up with an Xciting story about an enchanted prince called Sleeping Handsome, who woke up when Princess Charming kissed him.

77 The next morning, they all felt much better, and little X went back to school with a brave smile and a clean pair of red and white checked overalls.

78 There was a seven-letter-word spelling bee in class that day. And a seven-lap boys' relay race in the gym. And a seven-layer-cake baking contest in the girls' kitchen corner.

79 X won the spelling bee. X also won the relay race.

80 And X almost won the baking contest, Xcept it forgot to light the oven. (Remember, nobody's perfect.)

81 One of the Other Children noticed something else, too. He said: "X doesn't care about winning. X just thinks it's fun playing boys' stuff *and* girls' stuff ."

82 "Come to think of it," said another one of the Other Children, "X is having twice as much fun as we are!"

83 After school that day, the girl who beat X in the baking contest gave X a big slice of her winning cake.

84 And the boy X beat in the relay race asked X to race him home.

85 From then on, some really funny things began to happen.

86 Susie, who sat next to X, refused to wear pink dresses to school any more. She wanted red and white checked overalls—just like X's.

87 Overalls, she told her parents, were better for climbing monkey bars.

88 Then Jim, the class football nut, started wheeling his little sister's doll carriage around the football field.

89 He'd put on his entire football uniform, except for the helmet.

90 Then he'd put the helmet *in* the carriage, lovingly tucked under an old set of shoulder pads.

91 *Then* he'd jog around the field, pushing the carriage and singing "Rockabye Baby" to his helmet.

92 He said X did the same thing, so it must be okay. After all, X was now the team's star quarterback.[5]

93 Susie's parents were horrified by her behavior, and Jim's parents were worried sick about his.

94 But the worst came when the twins, Joe and Peggy, decided to share everything with each other.

95 Peggy used Joe's hockey skates, and his microscope, and took half his newspaper route.

96 Joe used Peggy's needlepoint kit, and her cookbooks, and took two of her three baby-sitting jobs.

---

[5] **quarterback** in American football, leader of the offensive team

97   Peggy ran the lawn mower, and Joe ran the vacuum cleaner.

98   Their parents weren't one bit pleased with Peggy's science experiments, or with Joe's terrific needlepoint pillows.

99   They didn't care that Peggy mowed the lawn better, and that Joe vacuumed the carpet better.

100   In fact, they were furious. It's all that little X's fault, they agreed. X doesn't know what it is, or what it's supposed to be! So X wants to mix everybody else up, too!

101   Peggy and Joe were forbidden to play with X any more. So was Susie, and then Jim, and then *all* the Other Children.

102   But it was too late: the Other Children stayed mixed-up and happy and free, and refused to go back to the way they'd been before X.

103   Finally, the parents held an emergency meeting to discuss "The X Problem."

104   They sent a report to the principal stating that X was a "bad influence," and demanding immediate action.

105   The Joneses, they said, should be *forced* to tell whether X was a boy or a girl. And X should be *forced* to behave like whichever it was.

106   If the Joneses refused to tell, the parents said, then X must take an Xamination. An Impartial Team of Xperts would Xtract the secret. Then X would start obeying all the old rules. Or else.

107   And if X turned out to be some kind of mixed-up misfit, then X must be Xpelled from school. Immediately! So that no little Xes would ever come to school again.

108   The principal was very upset. X, a bad influence? A mixed-up misfit? But X was an Xcellent student! X set a fine Xample! X was Xtraordinary!

109   X was president of the student council. X had won first prize in the art show, honorable mention in the science fair, and six events on field day,[6] including the potato race.

110   *Nevertheless*, insisted the parents, X is a Problem Child. X is the Biggest Problem Child we have ever seen!

111   So the principal reluctantly notified X's parents and the Joneses reported this to the Project X scientists, who referred them to page 85769 of the *Instruction Manual*. "Sooner or later," it said, "X will have to be Xamined by an Impartial Team of Xperts.

112   "This may be the only way any of us will know for sure whether X is mixed up—or everyone else is."

113   At Xactly 9 o'clock the next day, X reported to the school health office. The principal, along with a committee from the Parents' Association, X's teacher, X's classmates, and Ms. and Mr. Jones, waited in the hall outside.

114   Inside, the Xperts had set up their famous testing machine: the Superpsychiamedicosocioculturometer.

115   Nobody knew Xactly how the machine worked, but everybody knew that this examination would reveal Xactly what everyone wanted to know about X, but were afraid to ask.

116   It was terribly quiet in the hall. Almost spooky. They could hear very strange noises from the room.

117   There were buzzes.

118   And a beep or two.

119   And several bells.

---

[6] **field day** *school sports day*

120 An occasional light flashed under the door. Was it an X-ray?

121 Through it all, you could hear the Xperts' voices, asking questions, and X's voice, answering answers.

122 I wouldn't like to be in X's overalls right now, the children thought.

123 At last, the door opened. Everyone crowded around to hear the results. X didn't look any different; in fact, X was smiling. But the Impartial Team of Xperts looked terrible. They looked as if they were crying!

124 "What happened?" everyone began shouting.

125 "*Sssh*," ssshed the principal. "The Xperts are trying to speak."

126 Wiping his eyes and clearing his throat, one Xpert began: "In our opinion," he whispered—you could tell he must be very upset—"in our opinion, young X here—"

127 "Yes? Yes?" shouted a parent.

128 "Young X," said the other Xpert, frowning, "is just about the *least* mixed-up child we've ever Xamined!" Behind the closed door, the Superpsychiamedicosocioculturometer made a noise like a contented hum.

129 "Yay for X!" yelled one of the children. And then the others began yelling, too. Clapping and cheering and jumping up and down.

130 "SSSH!" SSShed the principal, but nobody did.

131 The Parents' Committee was angry and bewildered. How *could* X have passed the whole Xamination?

132 Didn't X have an *identity* problem? Wasn't X mixed up at *all*? Wasn't X *any* kind of a misfit?

133 How could it *not* be, when it didn't even *know* what it was?

134 "Don't you see?" asked the Xperts. "X isn't one bit mixed up! As for being a misfit—ridiculous! X knows perfectly well what it is! Don't you, X? The Xperts winked. X winked back.

135 "But what *is* X?" shrieked Peggy and Joe's parents. "*We* still want to know what it is!"

136 "Ah, yes," said the Xperts, winking again. "Well, don't worry. You'll all know one of these days. And you won't need us to tell you."

137 "What? What do they mean?" Jim's parents grumbled suspiciously.

138 Susie and Peggy and Joe all answered at once. "They mean that by the time it matters which sex X is, it won't be a secret any more!"

139 With that, the Xperts reached out to hug Ms. and Mr. Jones. "If we ever have an X of our own," they whispered, "we sure hope you'll lend us your instruction manual."

140 Needless to say, the Joneses were very happy. The Project Baby X scientists were rather pleased, too. So were Susie, Jim, Peggy, Joe, and all the Other Children. Even the parents promised not to make any trouble.

141 Later that day, all X's friends put on their red and white checked overalls and went over to see X.

142 They found X in the backyard, playing with a very tiny baby that none of them had ever seen before.

143 The baby was wearing very tiny red and white checked overalls.

144 "How do you like our new baby?" X asked the Other Children proudly.

145 "It's got cute dimples," said Jim. "It's got husky biceps, too," said Susie.

146 "What kind of baby is it?" asked Joe and Peggy.

147 X frowned at them. "Can't you tell?" Then X broke into a big, mischievous grin. "*It's a Y*!

Comprehension Check

Part 1, Paragraphs 1–42

1. What type of parents were suitable for Project Baby X?
2. How does the *Official Instruction Manual* recommend treating Baby X: according to male stereotypes, according to female stereotypes, combining both, or trying to avoid all stereotypes?
3. Why were relatives and strangers upset that the Joneses would not tell them X's sex?

Part 2, Paragraphs 43–112

4. What problems would school bring? How was X prepared for school?
5. How did the other children treat X in the beginning?
6. How did their behavior toward X change? Why?
7. How did their own behavior change as a result of having X in the class?
8. How did parents react to their children's changed behavior?
9. What was the principal's opinion of X?

Part 3, Paragraphs 113–147

10. What is the "Superpsychiamedicosocioculturometer" supposed to measure? Can you divide the word into meaningful parts? What does each contribute?
11. How did X do on the test?
12. How did the kids react to the test results?
13. How did the parents react to the test results?
14. How does the story end?

Sharing Your Thoughts

1. What are some examples from the story of ways parents and schools influence gender-role socialization?
2. Why do you think X did so well on the test?
3. What is the purpose of raising children in a nonsexist way? How does the story suggest it can be done? Is it a good idea? Why or why not?
4. What type of adult do you think X grew up to be?
5. Why do you think Gould wrote this story? To entertain readers? To make some point about life in her culture? If so, what point or points was she trying to make? Explain your answers to these questions with specific references to the story.
6. How do you think you would be different if you had been raised as an X? Would that be good or bad?
7. Would you try to raise a child of yours as an X? Why or why not?

Vocabulary

A. Content Vocabulary

Complete the following statements about the story with words from the list. Use each word only once. Change the form of verbs if the grammar of the sentence requires it.

cheer up	**consult**	**give up**
imitate	**influence**	**mixed up**
no matter	**plenty of**	**promise**
treat	**weird**	

1. The Joneses wanted to raise an X _____ how much trouble it was. They _____ to follow the *Instruction Manual* carefully and to _____ it when they didn't know what to do.

2. The *Manual* told them to _____ X like a boy and like a girl, giving it _____ gentle female-like treatment as well as rougher male-like treatment.

3. At school, some children were nasty to X in the beginning. They said X was really strange or _____ because it did things differently. At home, X was sad, and the Joneses tried to _____ X _____ by reading a story.

4. Although things were sometimes difficult, neither X nor the Joneses would _____. After a while, children accepted and even started to _____ X because they realized that X was free to be itself and had the best of both worlds.

5. The other children's parents, however, were not happy. They thought X was a bad _____ on their children. An evaluation revealed that X was not at all _____, but a very well-adjusted child.

B. Connotations

A **connotation** is a meaning or an idea suggested by words in addition to the literal meaning found in the dictionary. For example, the dictionary tells us a *rat* is a long-tailed rodent, similar to a mouse but bigger. For many people *rat* suggests something dirty; it has a negative connotation. Connotations of words can vary from person to person and culture to culture.

In any culture, some words are considered more appropriate for describing males, others are more appropriate for describing females, while most words are neutral and don't have either a masculine or a feminine connotation.

Locate the adjectives below in the story. Use the context, and a dictionary if necessary, to categorize them as masculine, feminine, or neutral.

active (¶26, ¶27) _____   brave (¶32, ¶34) _____

cute (¶18) _____   dainty (¶26, ¶27) _____

handsome (¶32, ¶76) _____   husky (¶19) _____

nice (¶33, ¶34) _____   strong (¶26, ¶27) _____

sweet (¶26, ¶27) _____   tiny (¶142) _____

Are they all used with the expected connotation? If not, which are not and why?

Text Analysis

Tone

Writing that combines a humorous tone with criticism is called **satire**. Satire can be quite gentle or very biting. In either case, the writer wants to call attention to the failings of people or their institutions.

1. Two ways to create humor are to exaggerate something and to reverse, or contradict, what is expected. What specific examples of humor can you find in "X"? What is exaggerated, reversed, or unexpected?
2. What failings of Americans or people in general does this story call attention to? What could Gould be criticizing?

Writing Task

Earlier you speculated on why Gould wrote this story. Unless you have the opportunity to talk with writers of stories, you can never be sure about their purpose or message. But you can decide what the story says to you through its characters and events.

Write one or two paragraphs explaining what the story "X" means to you. Support your opinion with specific references to details in the story. Give enough details so that a person who has never read the story will be able to understand what you are talking about. If you quote exact words from the story, remember to use quotations marks.

SELECTION FIVE

Before Reading

This poem, a translation from Dutch, appeared in *The Literary Review*. Ini Statia grew up in the ABC islands (Aruba, Bonaire, Curaçao) and studied Dutch language and literature in the Netherlands.

1. This selection differs from the first four in this unit in one basic way that is revealed by the title. What is this difference?

2. Scan the poem to see what words are repeated. What do you think the poem might be about?

Black Woman

by Ini Statia

1 You are afraid
to show your
hatred and pain
because then you are frustrated
5 You are afraid
to react and to show your teeth
because then you have a complex[1]
You are afraid
to shout out your weakness
10 because then you are too emotional
You are afraid
to show your solidarity
because then you favour cliques[2]
You are afraid
15 to show your anger
and to refuse to serve
because then you are proud
You are afraid
to show intelligence

---

[1] **complex** group of unconscious wishes, fears, or feelings; for example, an inferiority or superiority complex

[2] **cliques** closely united, usually small groups of people who do not allow others to easily join the group

20 because then you are too serious
But you must:
show your solidarity with:
the black man
the worker
25 the white woman
because they too are oppressed
meanwhile you forget to
show solidarity with yourself
and your sisters
30 You are afraid of the truth
You are afraid of your own
strength
You are afraid to organize yourself
because then you'll have to do
35 everything
You're afraid of
And so you shrink totally into
one rigid smile
and you manage to be
40 only beautiful, sweet and sexy
so you don't even know anymore
that you're only a shadow
moving along paths others
designed for you

Comprehension Check

1. Who is the speaker in the poem addressing as *you*?
2. What six specific fears does the woman in the poem have? What do these fears have in common?
3. Why doesn't the woman show her true feelings? What would be the consequences of being herself?
4. What do black women, black men, and white women have in common?
5. Why is the speaker in the poem critical of the woman? What should the woman do that she doesn't do?
6. What could be the "paths others designed for [this woman]"?

Sharing Your Thoughts

1. Who, in your opinion, are the people who might criticize this woman? Why is she so concerned about their possible comments? Do her critics really exist?

2. Could this woman's childhood have contributed to making her a "shadow" of her true self? Refer to the first four selections in this unit to help explain why this woman might be the way she is.

3. What could the woman be that she isn't at the moment?

4. Do you think this poem applies to women in general or just to black women? Explain.

5. Who do you think is speaking in this poem: a man or a woman? a person who is black or a person who is not black? Or do you think the speaker could be anyone at all? Explain.

6. Do you ever feel you are "moving along paths others designed for you"? If so, in what ways?

Text Analysis

Text Organization

1. Although this poem does not have stanzas, it could logically be divided into three major sections.
   a. What are these three sections?
   b. What does the poet do in each?

2. What repeats in this poem? What does the repetition contribute, if anything, to the meaning or feeling of the poem?

Writing Task

1. In the poem, someone is talking to the black woman. Imagine you are that black woman. What would you like to say back to the speaker? Write a note or letter to the speaker from the black woman.

2. Imagine you are the woman in the poem. Write a letter to a close friend or family member telling that person about areas of your life you are dissatisfied with.

3. Write a paragraph or two in which you give the woman advice about changing her life.

A FINAL LOOK

Discussion

1. Work with a partner, in a small group, or as a whole class. Drawing from all five selections in this unit, and the quote on the introductory page, discuss the focus questions.

2. What factors influencing the formation of gender roles are mentioned in this unit? Are there others you can add to the list?

3. What are the expectations for boys and girls, and men and women, in your culture? Are these expectations changing? If so, in what ways? If not, why not?

4. What differences have you noticed between men's and women's behavior in your culture or in the culture you live in now? Do you think the differences go back to something learned in childhood? Explain.

5. Excluding biological differences, can you think of any area in which men and women could never be truly equal? If so, what area and why could they never be equal?

6. If you could break only one stereotype in raising a son or a daughter, what would it be? Why and how would you try to break it?

7. How could men and women each benefit by adopting some of the characteristics we usually associate with the opposite sex?

Writing

1. Alexa Canady, the first black woman neurosurgeon in the United States, is quoted in *U.S. News and World Report*, February 13, 1989, as saying:

   I used to tease my parents by saying, You're raising me to be the person that you don't want my brothers to marry. People are just not very ambitious for women still. Your son you want to be the best he can be. Your daughter you want to be happy.

   Write a reaction to this quote in which you answer some of these questions:

   • How do you think her parents raised her?

   • How were her parents different from most parents of their generation in her opinion?

   • Do you agree that most people have different ambitions for sons and daughters? Explain.

2. Write several paragraphs about the pressures you face as a male or a female. What expectations do you feel you have to live up to as a male or a female in your culture? Do these expectations motivate you, or are they a source of stress for you? Illustrate with concrete examples

UNIT FIVE

Cultures in Contact

The barriers that cultural differences pose may be more formidable than those presented by even the harshest physical environment.

– Tom J. Lewis and Robert E. Jungman
On Being Foreign, Culture Shock in Short Fiction

FOCUS

➤ What does culture include?

➤ How do we learn it?

➤ How does our culture affect our lives?

➤ How do people feel when they visit a different culture? when they live in a different culture?

➤ What problems and what benefits are possible when people from different cultures come into contact?

SELECTION ONE

Before Reading

This selection is an excerpt from a college anthropology textbook, *Anthropology: The Exploration of Human Diversity*, Fifth Edition. The author is a professor at the University of Michigan.

1. Read the poem, "Reflection," by Shel Silverstein. What do you think the poem means? How do you think it relates to culture?

REFLECTION

Each time I see the Upside-Down Man
Standing in the water,
I look at him and start to laugh,
Although I shouldn't oughtter.*
For maybe in another world
Another time
Another town,
Maybe HE is right side up
And I am upside down.

2. All of the following are food to people in some parts of the world. Alone, rank these foods from those you think would be the easiest for you to learn to eat to those you think would be the most difficult.

snake	giant waterbugs
horsemeat	dog
ants	octopus
rose petals	eels
grasshoppers	chicken cooked in its own blood
blood sausage	

Compare lists in a group or as a class. Is there anything that members of your group agree would be very difficult to eat? Why would you find it difficult to eat?

3. What do anthropologists study? What do students learn in an anthropology course? Freewrite about what you think culture is and what you think this selection will include. Share your ideas with your classmates.

---

* **oughtter**   a distortion of *ought to*, to rhyme with *water*; repeats the meaning of *should*

CULTURE

by Conrad Phillip Kottak

1 "Culture…is that complex whole which includes knowledge, belief, arts, morals, law, custom, and any other capabilities and habits acquired by man as a member of society" (Tylor 1871/1958, p. 1). The crucial phrase here is "acquired by man as a member of society." Tylor's definition focuses on beliefs and behavior that people acquire not through biological heredity but by growing up in a particular society where they are exposed to a specific cultural tradition. Enculturation is the process by which a child learns his or her culture.

2 Every person begins immediately, through a process of conscious and unconscious learning and interaction with others, to internalize, or incorporate, a cultural tradition through the process of enculturation. Sometimes culture is taught directly, as when parents tell their children to "say thank you" when someone gives them something or does them a favor.

3 Culture is also transmitted through observation. Children pay attention to the things that go on around them. They modify their behavior not just because other people tell them to but as a result of their own observations and growing awareness of what their culture considers right and wrong. Culture is also absorbed unconsciously. North Americans acquire their culture's notions about how far apart people should stand when they talk not by being told to maintain a certain distance but through a gradual process of observation, experience, and conscious and unconscious behavior modification. No one tells Latins to stand closer together than North Americans do, but they learn to do so anyway as part of their cultural tradition.

4 Despite characteristic American notions that people should "make up their own minds" and "have a right to their opinion," little of what we think is original or unique. We share our opinions and beliefs with many other people. Illustrating the power of shared cultural background, we are most likely to agree with and feel comfortable with people who are socially, economically, and culturally similar to ourselves. This is one reason why Americans abroad tend to socialize with each other, just as French and British colonials did in their overseas empires. Birds of a feather flock together, but for people the familiar plumage is culture.

CULTURE SEIZES NATURE

5 Culture imposes itself on nature. I once arrived at a summer camp at 5 P.M. I was hot and wanted to swim in the lake. However, I read the camp rules and learned that no swimming was permitted after five. A cultural system had seized the lake, which is part of nature. Natural lakes don't close at five, but cultural lakes do.

6 Culture takes the natural biological urges we share with other animals and teaches us how to express them in particular ways. People have to eat, but culture teaches us what, when, and how. In many cultures people have their main meal at noon, but Americans prefer a large dinner. English people eat fish for breakfast, but Americans prefer hot cakes and cold cereals. Brazilians put hot milk into strong coffee, whereas Americans pour cold milk into a weaker brew. Midwesterners dine at five or six, Spaniards at ten. Europeans eat with the fork in the left hand and the knife in the right. Meat cut by the knife is immediately conveyed to the mouth with the fork, which Americans switch to the right hand before eating.

7 For the Betsileo of Madagascar, there is no way of saying "to eat" without saying "to eat rice," their favorite and staple food. So strong is their preference for rice that they garnish it with beans, potatoes, and other starches. Eels cooked in their own grease are a delicacy for the Betsileos' honored visitors, a category in which

I feared being included because of my cultural aversion to eel meat (although I did tolerate grasshoppers cooked in peanut oil; they tasted like peanuts). In northeastern Brazil I grew to like chicken cooked in its own blood, a favorite there.

8 Like the lake at summer camp, human nature is appropriated by cultural systems and molded in hundreds of directions. All people must eliminate wastes from their bodies. However, some cultures teach people to defecate standing up, while others tell them to do it sitting down… Peasant women in the Peruvian highlands squat in the streets and urinate into gutters. They get all the privacy they need from their massive skirts. All these habits are parts of cultural traditions that have converted natural acts into cultural customs.

9 Cultures vary tremendously in their beliefs and practices. By focusing on and trying to explain alternative customs, anthropology forces us to reappraise our familiar ways of thinking. In a world full of cultural diversity, [our own[1]] culture is just one cultural variant, no more natural than the others.

[1] Tylor E.B. (1871/1958). *Primitive Culture*. New York: Harper Torchbooks.

Comprehension Check

1. What is culture? What is enculturation?
2. List three ways that we learn our culture and give an example of each.
3. What two areas does the author mention in which culture imposes itself on nature?
4. What is the value of learning about other cultures?

Sharing Your Thoughts

1. Which of the customs in paragraphs 6 to 8 seem odd to you? Which ones would be easy to adapt to and which would be more difficult? Explain.
2. Some of the areas in which cultures differ include the amount of importance given to punctuality, the situations that require apologies and/or excuses, what favors to do, and how and when to extend invitations and how to interpret how sincere they are. In what other areas do cultures differ? Give examples of cultural differences in these areas.
3. Do you think we obtain most of our culture unconsciously or consciously? Give examples to support your answer.
4. Why do you think people believe their own culture is more natural than others?
5. Do you think children adapt to a new culture more easily than adults? Give examples to support your answer.
6. What does "birds of a feather flock together" mean (¶4)? Do you think it is true? Why or why not? Give examples from your own experience to support your answer.

Vocabulary

A. Content Vocabulary

Complete the following statements about culture with the correct word from the list. Use each word only once. Change the form of verbs if the grammar of the sentence requires it.

acquire	**aversion**	**aware**
background	**conform**	**familiar**
notions	**share**	

1. We _____ the culture of the group in which we are raised. As we grow up, we modify our behavior to _____ to what people around us do.

2. Until we come into contact with other cultures, the _____ of our own culture about eating, communicating, and so forth are so _____ to us that we take them for granted.

3. In fact, if we do not have contact with people from other cultures, we may not be fully _____ that all cultures do not _____ the same ideas, preferences, and beliefs.

4. When we first learn about some of the customs of other people, we may have a(n) _____ to them because we are not used to them.

5. It takes time to get used to other ways of doing things, so people from the same cultural _____ often stick together.

B. Word Analysis

*Divide these words into their parts. Some of them include Latin parts: **scio** = Latin for* know, ***con*** *= Latin for* with, ***inter*** *= Latin for* between, ***corp*** *= Latin for* body, ***mit*** *= Latin for* send, *and **trans*** *= Latin for* across. *What does the word as a whole mean? What does each part contribute?*

1. conscious (¶2) _____

2. unconscious (¶2) _____

3. interaction (¶2) _____

4. internalize (¶2) _____

5. incorporate (¶2) _____

6. transmitted (¶3) _____

7. background (¶4) _____

8. highlands (¶8) _____

C. Grammatical Function

Using a dictionary when necessary, fill the blanks with words related to the word that is given.

	VERB	NOUN	ADJECTIVE	ADVERB
1.	_____	belief	_____	_____
2.		culture	_____	_____
3.	_____	diversity	_____	
4.	modify	_____		
5.	prefer	_____	_____	_____
6.	socialize	_____	_____	_____
7.	tolerate	_____	_____	_____
		_____	_____	

Complete each of the following sentences with the word in parentheses or a related word from your chart, depending on which grammatical function the missing word should have. Change the forms of verbs and nouns as necessary.

1. There are many cultures in the world, and many countries today are also culturally _____. (diversity)

2. Even in our own country it is natural to feel most comfortable with people who are _____ similar to us. (culture)

3. Every cultural or ethnic group has a _____ for certain foods. (prefer)

4. Some people have a high _____ for different foods; others cannot _____ the idea of eating certain things. (tolerate)

5. Problems can arise in certain _____ situations when it would be impolite not to eat something new. (socialize)

6. It can be difficult to _____ our eating habits. (modify)

7. It is also hard to change our _____. (belief)

Text Analysis

A. The Grammar-Meaning Connection

Although speakers and writers generally use the **active voice**, they use the **passive voice** when they want to focus attention, not on the doer of the action, but on what is done or who it is done to.

EXAMPLES:
a. Children *learn* cultural patterns unconsciously for the most part. (*active voice*)
b. Cultural patterns *are learned* (by children) unconsciously for the most part. (*passive voice*)

Study the passive verb forms in the sentences below. The first one is done as an example. What is the auxiliary in a passive verb phrase? What is the form of the main verb? For each sentence, answer the following questions:
a. Who does the action?
b. Why do you think the author chose the passive voice?

1. Sometimes culture **is taught** directly.
   a. People like parents, grandparents, and teachers do the action of teaching culture directly.
   b. The focus is on the direct teaching of culture rather than on who does the teaching. Another reason for using the passive may be that it is not necessary to mention who does the teaching because it is well known.
2. Culture **is absorbed** unconsciously.
3. No swimming **was permitted** after five.
4. Meat cut by the knife **is** immediately **conveyed** to the mouth with the fork.
5. Human nature **is appropriated** by cultural systems and *molded* in hundreds of different directions.

Change each sentence above to the active voice. Which, if any, sound just as good in the active voice?

B. Text Organization

What basic ideas about culture should you remember after reading this passage? Reveal them by completing the chart with the main idea in each paragraph or paragraph set.

PARAGRAPHS	MAIN IDEA
¶1:	_____
¶2–3:	_____
¶4:	_____
¶5–8:	_____
¶9:	_____

Writing Task

1. Write a paragraph defining culture in your own words and providing examples from a culture you know.
2. Write a paragraph contrasting the idea of culture you had before reading this selection with the idea you have now. Begin with a general statement of what you learned or how your thinking changed. For example, *Before reading this selection, I used to think that… / I didn't know that… /* Be sure to make both your old idea and your new understanding clear with detailed explanation and examples.

SELECTION TWO

Before Reading

This selection is from the book, *Gestures: The Do's and Taboos of Body Language Around the World*. The author has written several books of use to international travelers and international business people.

Sit in a park or cafe for thirty minutes. Observe people (excluding couples in love) who pass by or who are sitting near you. Take notes on the following:

- How far apart are their heads as they talk?
- How close are they as they walk?
- How often do they touch each other?
- How often do they look each other in the eye?
- How loudly do they speak?
- How often do they gesture with their hands? Do they use any other part of the body to gesture?

Share your findings with your classmates.

Touching by Roger E. Axtell

1   On my first trip to the Middle East, my Arab business contact and I toured the city, walking along the street visiting customers. He wore his long robe, the air was hot and dusty, a priest chanted the call to prayers from a nearby minaret, and I felt as far away from my American home as one could possibly be. At that moment, my business friend reached over, took my hand in his, and we continued walking along, his hand holding mine.

2   It didn't take me long to realize that something untoward was happening here, that some form of communication was being issued…but I didn't have the faintest idea what that message was. Also, I suddenly felt even farther from home.

3   Probably because I was so stunned, the one thing I didn't do was pull my hand away. I later learned that if I had jerked my hand out of his, I could have committed a Sahara-sized[1] *faux pas*.[2] In his country, this act of taking my hand in his was a sign of great friendship and respect.

4   That was my first lesson about space relationships between different people. I quickly learned that it was a world of extremes—important extremes—with some cultures seeking bodily contact and others studiously avoiding it. Ken Cooper, in his book *Nonverbal Communication For Business Success* (AMACOM, NY 1979), writes that he once covertly observed conversations in outdoor cafes in several different countries and counted the

---

[1] **Sahara-sized** referring to the Sahara Desert in Africa, meaning very large

[2] *faux pas* social mistake (French)

number of casual touches (of self or of the other party) per hour. The results: San Juan, Puerto Rico, 180 per hour; Paris, 110 per hour; Florida, 2 per hour; London, 0 per hour.

5   I also learned that the Middle East was not the only region where it is quite acceptable for two men to walk cradling an elbow, arm-in-arm, or even holding hands. Korea, Indochina, Greece, and Italy are also regarded as "touch-oriented" countries. Such physical displays in those countries usually signal friendship. Touching between men—often seen as an indication of homosexuality in North America—is quite the opposite. In some of the most "touch-oriented" areas homosexuality is coldly rejected.

6   Here, on a scale of "touch" or "don't touch," is a geographic measuring stick:

Don't Touch	**Touch**	**Middle Ground**
Japan	Middle East countries	France
United States & Canada	Latin countries	China
England	Italy	Ireland
Scandinavia	Greece	India
Other Northern	Spain & Portugal	
European countries	Some Asian countries	
Australia	Russia	
Estonia		

7   Can the casual act of touching be all that important? The answer is "yes"— important enough to make bold headlines in at least one country's national newspapers:

When Queen Elizabeth paid one of her periodic visits to Canada, a Canadian provincial transport minister escorted her through a crowd by gently touching her elbow; he may have even touched the small of her back. Newspaper headlines in England screamed protests: "Hands off our Queen," said one; "Row Over Man Who Touched Queen," read another.

The reason behind that uproar was that it is an unwritten rule among the British that no one touches the Queen. Even when shaking hands, the rule is that she must make the first move.

8   In the United States, office workers and school teachers are warned and trained to avoid any casual touching of their employees or students. A university professor of communications explains that "an innocuous touch on someone's hand or arm can be misconstrued as a sexual move, especially if we let it linger." Unwanted touching in U.S. business offices can lead to law suits for sexual harassment[3] while teachers may be accused of molestation if they frequently hug, pat, or touch their students.

9   Yet there are strange contradictions, especially in the United States. Here are two examples:

I once asked an audience of U.S. businessmen what they would do if they boarded a crowded airplane, sat next to a large man and found themselves pressing elbows, maybe even shoulders and upper arms as

---

3 **sexual harassment** unwanted sexual advances

well, throughout the whole trip. "Nothing," was the consensus. "It happens all the time," they agreed. I countered, "Well, what would you do then if that same man then touched your knee with his hand?" The reaction was unanimous: "Move the knee." "And," one added, "if, God forbid, he *grabbed* my knee, I would punch him in the nose."

The second contradiction regarding rules for touching occurs on elevators and subways. On a crowded elevator or an underground train at commuting time, people will stand shoulder-to-shoulder, arm-to-arm, and accept such rubbing of shoulders without complaint. But, the rule is "Touch *only* from shoulder to elbow. No other parts of the body."

10   Cultures are colliding every day over this dilemma of "to touch or not to touch." In New York City, Korean immigrants in recent years have started new lives by opening retail shops of all kinds. But, when American customers make a purchase and receive their change, the Korean merchants place the money on the counter to avoid any physical contact. "They won't touch my hand," one customer noticed. "They won't even place coins in my hand. It's somewhat cold and insulting. And furthermore, they won't look me in the eyes."

11   One Korean merchant explained in a national television interview that in his homeland they are taught to avoid physical contact of any kind. The same with direct eye contact. "We are taught that either gesture could have sexual connotations," he added, "so we carefully avoid them."

12   And here's a surefire way for a North American to make a Japanese acquaintance feel uncomfortable. Just go up and place your arm around him, as you would a college buddy or big brother. Even though the Japanese permit themselves to be jammed into subways and trains, they are not regarded as a touching society. To explain this, anthropologist Edward T. Hall says the Japanese handle any unease about being packed into public places by averting eyes, avoiding eye contact, drawing within themselves and thus "touching without feeling."

13   Closely related to the societal customs of touching is that of spatial relationships. Anthropologists tell us that each of us walks around inside "bubbles of personal space." The size of the bubble represents our personal territory, territorial imperative,[4] or "personal buffer zones."[5] We neither like nor tolerate it when someone invades our bubble. We become distinctly uncomfortable.

14   But as we travel to different places around the world, we learn that some cultural bubbles are larger or smaller than others. Here is a ruler for measuring the bubbles between nationalities:

- The American "bubble" extends about 12 to 15 inches, and so we may stand a combined 24 to 30 inches apart. Scientists point out this just happens to be an arm's length away (which carries a certain symbolism, doesn't it?). Anthropologist George Renwick says "When two Americans stand facing one another in any normal social or business situation, one could stretch out his arm and put his thumb in the other person's ear."

---

[4] **territorial imperative**   the need to have a certain amount of space we must consider our own

[5] **buffer zones**   neutral spaces between two places, things, or people to keep them safely apart

- Orientals, and especially the Japanese, stand even farther apart, Renwick adds. When it comes to ordinary business or social situations, they have the largest bubbles of all. However, as we have learned, in their own public settings, where crowding is impossible to avoid, they accept body contact or just seem to ignore it by "retreating within themselves."

- Latins and Middle Easterners, on the other hand, stand much closer than Americans. They may stand, literally, toe-to-toe. They may even place a hand on the other's forearm or elbow, or finger the lapel of the other person.

Americans claim it takes years of experience, plus steely resolve, to stand that close and smell that many breaths. Some observers in Latin America even have a name for this charade. They call it "the conversational tango." That's the "dance" done by an American or European freshly arrived in Latin America who is confronted by this sudden and startling custom of closeness. The first reaction of the visitor is to step backward. But the Latin will follow. So, the visitor steps back again. The Latin follows. And so it goes, in a poorly choreographed tango. ...As one observer put it, "The dance stops only when the American is backed into a corner."

15   But even as these words are written, touch codes are changing all over the world. In the United States, politicians have learned the value of touch. They frequently give two-handed handshakes, casually touch the elbow of another, or lightly touch the back of the person standing next to them. "Pressing flesh" has become a byword on political campaigns. Also, Japanese managers posted in U.S. factories are steeling themselves and learning to accept finger-crunching handshakes, back patting, and maybe even a friendly arm around the shoulder for the softball team photo.

16   The "hugging professor," Leo Buscaglia,[6] tours cities and campuses presenting captivating lectures on the joy of hugging. His popular books and video and audio tapes make his audiences realize that separateness and aloofness can be a lonely, cold existence.

17   Finally, in Helen Colton's wonderful book, *The Gift of Touch,* she describes how Swedish actress Liv Ullman was once touring famine-stricken lands on behalf of UNICEF. In Bangladesh, after a warm visit with a woman there, Ullman gave the woman a hug. But she felt the woman suddenly draw away. Through her interpreter, Ullman asked why. The woman answered, "In my country, we kiss feet when we say goodbye." Ullman, the quintessential lady, unhesitatingly bent down and kissed the woman's feet. Then they hugged, each woman having exchanged the parting ritual of her own world.

---

[6] **Leo Buscaglia**   an American professor and writer

Comprehension Check

1. What did the author's Arab business contact do? How did the author, an American, react? Why?

2. How did the British press react to a Canadian government official guiding the Queen through a crowd? Why?

3. What are some of the subtleties of touching rules in the United States?

4. What was the problem between Korean storekeepers in New York City and their American customers? What are the rules in Korea that conflict with American rules?

5. How do the Japanese, who are generally nontouchers, handle crowded conditions?

6. What kind of rules do all cultures have regarding personal space? How do these vary from culture to culture?

7. What are some indications that the "buffer zone" in the United States is changing somewhat?

8. How did Liv Ullman handle the difference between parting rules in Sweden and Bangladesh?

Sharing Your Thoughts

1. If your country is included in paragraph 6, is it listed as a "Don't Touch," a "Middle Ground," or a "Touch" country? Do you agree with this label? If your country is not listed, where would you list it? In general, do you agree with the list in paragraph 6? Explain your answer.

2. How did your findings in the Before Reading task agree with the author's classification in paragraph 6 of the culture(s) you observed?

3. Do you think personal bubbles or buffer zones vary from person to person within the same culture? How much variation is permitted? Under what circumstances? Explain.

4. How do you react when confronted with touching or space behavior that conflicts with yours?

5. What does *direct eye contact* mean in your culture? How do you feel if someone violates the rule of your culture with regard to eye contact?

6. Do you think it is easier to adapt to another culture's eating rules, such as those discussed in the last selection, or personal space rules? Explain your answer.

7. In addition to rules regarding touching and distance, what other cultural differences might cause awkward situations like the example at the beginning of this selection? Describe such situations.

Vocabulary

A. Content Vocabulary

Complete the following statements about touching and space with the correct word from the list. Use each word only once. Change the form of verbs if the grammar of the sentence requires it.

avoid	**collide**	**faintest**
misconstrue	**realize**	**sign**
uproar	**warn**	

1. In some cultures people touch each other frequently; in others, they carefully _____ physical contact.

2. There can be difficult moments when conflicting cultural patterns _____. In these cases a person from one culture may _____ the action of someone from another culture. For example, what was intended as a(n) _____ of friendliness in one culture may be understood as an insult in another culture.

3. Sometimes it takes time to _____ that the other person has a different set of rules. This may cause some embarrassing moments, or even, if public figures are involved, an international _____.

4. The innocent offender often does not have the _____ idea of what he or she did wrong.

5. To avoid these problems, it is a good idea to _____ people about the rules of touching before they travel.

B. Grammatical Function

The words in the following sentences can function as nouns or verbs without a change in form. Are the italicized words functioning as nouns or verbs? Write N or V, as the case may be, next to each one.

1. Eye contact can **signal** _____ sexual interest.

2. In some countries men holding hands is a **display** _____ of friendship.

3. The only acceptable way to shake the hand of the Queen of England is to wait for her to make the first **move** _____.

4. Japanese people have to **crowd**_____ into trains during rush hour.

5. Japanese businessmen working in the United States have to **steel** _____ themselves in order to tolerate the friendly touching of their North American counterparts.

A suffix indicates a change of function in these cases. Complete the following sentences with one of the words in parentheses.

6. The British public was _____ (startle/startling/startled) when the Canadian official touched the Queen's elbow.

7. No one is likely to _____ (complaint/complain) if you touch from shoulder to elbow in _____ (crowd/crowding/crowded) places.

8. It takes _____ (steel, steely) resolve for a Japanese person to accept a pat on the back or an arm around the shoulder.

9. It may seem like a _____ (contradiction/contradict/contradictory) that it is okay to touch the elbow of the person next to you on an airplane, but not his or her knee.

Text Analysis

Supporting General Statements

General statements made about cultural differences require examples to make ideas clear; Axtell provides them in great number. Some of his examples are **anecdotes**, or specific incidents that really occurred.

*Answer questions **a**, **b**, and **c** about the examples listed below:*

a. Why does Axtell use the example?
b. Do you think it is well chosen for the intended purpose? Explain.
c. Which of the examples are anecdotes?

1. the hand-holding incident (¶1–¶3)
2. Cooper's report on touching in various cultures (¶4)
3. the incident involving the Queen of England and the examples of touching in the United States (¶7–¶8)
4. the examples of touching on planes and subways (¶9)
5. the Korean and Japanese examples (¶10–¶12)
6. the conversational tango (¶14)
7. U.S. politicians and Japanese managers (¶15)
8. Liv Ullman's experience in Bangladesh (¶17)

Writing Task

1. Write a one-paragraph summary of "Touching." Before writing, complete the chart with the main point Axtell makes in the paragraph groups to show you what ideas to include in the summary. Illustrate each idea with a carefully selected example if needed to make the idea clear.

Paragraphs Main Idea

¶4–12: _____

¶13–14: _____

¶15–16: _____

2. Write up your notes from the Before Reading task. Include place and time of observation, people observed (sex, approximate age, etc.), what you noted about their behavior in response to the Before Reading questions, and general conclusions, if any.

Before Reading

Judith Ortiz Cofer, an English professor at the University of Georgia, was born in Puerto Rico and raised in New Jersey. She has written autobiographical essays, a novel, and poems. The following selection is an excerpt from her book: *The Latin Deli*.

With a group of classmates, make a list of problems that people face when they leave their own culture and live in another. If you begin with general problems like differences in foods and rules of social interaction, try to include specific examples of each. Compare lists with another group or as a class.

DON'T MISREAD MY SIGNALS

by Judith Ortiz Cofer

1   On a bus to London from Oxford University, where I was earning some graduate credits one summer, a young man, obviously fresh from a pub,[1] approached my seat. With both hands over his heart, he went down on his knees in the aisle and broke into an Irish tenor's rendition of "Maria" from *West Side Story*.[2] I was not amused. "Maria"[3] had followed me to London, reminding me of a prime fact of my life: You can leave the island of Puerto Rico, master the English language, and travel as far as you can, but if you're a Latina, especially one who so clearly belongs to Rita Moreno's[4] gene pool, the island travels with you.

2   Growing up in New Jersey and wanting most of all to belong, I lived in two completely different worlds. My parents designed our life as a microcosm of their *casas*[5] on the island—we spoke Spanish, ate Puerto Rican food bought at the *bodega* and practiced strict Catholicism complete with Sunday mass in Spanish.

3   I was kept under tight surveillance by my parents, since my virtue and modesty were, by their cultural equation, the same as their honor. As teenagers, my friends and I were lectured constantly on how to behave as proper *señoritas*.[6] But it was a conflicting message we received, since our Puerto Rican mothers also encouraged us to look and act like women by dressing us in clothes our Anglo schoolmates and their mothers found too "mature" and flashy. I often felt humiliated when I appeared at an American friend's birthday party wearing a dress more suitable for a semiformal. At Puerto Rican festivities, neither the music nor the colors we wore could be too loud.

4   I remember Career Day in high school, when our teachers told us to come dressed as if for a job interview. That morning I agonized in front of my closet, trying to figure out what a "career girl" would wear, because the only model I had was Marlo Thomas on TV. To me and my Puerto Rican girlfriends, dressing up meant wearing our mother's ornate jewelry and clothing.

---

[1] **pub**   bar (British English)

[2] *West Side Story*   musical play about Puerto Ricans in New York

[3] "Maria"   song from *West Side Story* sung by an Anglo male who has fallen in love with a Puerto Rican girl named Maria

[4] **Rita Moreno**   Puerto Rican actress who has dark hair and eyes, and looks very Hispanic

[5] *casa*   house (Spanish)

[6] *señoritas*   unmarried young ladies (Spanish)

5   At school that day, the teachers assailed us for wearing "everything at once"—meaning too much jewelry and too many accessories. And it was painfully obvious that the other students in their tailored skirts and silk blouses thought we were hopeless and vulgar. The way they looked at us was a taste of the cultural clash that awaited us in the real world, where prospective employers and men on the street would often misinterpret our tight skirts and bright colors as a come-on.7

6   It is custom, not chromosomes, that leads us to choose scarlet over pale pink. Our mothers had grown up on a tropical island where the natural environment was a riot of primary colors, where showing your skin was one way to keep cool as well as to look sexy. On the island, women felt freer to dress and move provocatively since they were protected by the traditions and laws of a Spanish Catholic system of morality and machismo, the main rule of which was: *You may look at my sister, but if you touch her I will kill you.* The extended family and church structure provided them with a circle of safety on the island; if a man "wronged" a girl, everyone would close in to save her family honor.

7   Off-island, signals often get mixed. When a Puerto Rican girl who is dressed in her idea of what is attractive meets a man from the mainstream culture who has been trained to react to certain types of clothing as a sexual signal, a clash is likely to take place. She is seen as a Hot Tamale,8 a sexual firebrand. I learned this lesson at my first formal dance when my date leaned over and painfully planted a sloppy, overeager kiss on my mouth. When I didn't respond with sufficient passion, he said in a resentful tone: "I thought you Latin girls were supposed to mature early." It was the first time I would feel like a fruit or vegetable —I was supposed to *ripen*, not just grow into womanhood like other girls.

8   These stereotypes, though rarer, still surface in my life. I recently stayed at a classy metropolitan hotel. After having dinner with a friend, I was returning to my room when a middle-aged man in a tuxedo stepped directly into my path. With his champagne glass extended toward me, he exclaimed, "Evita!"9

9   Blocking my way, he bellowed the song "Don't Cry For Me, Argentina."10 Playing to the gathering crowd, he began to sing loudly a ditty to the tune of "La Bamba"11—except the lyrics were about a girl named Maria whose exploits all rhymed with her name and gonorrhea.

10   I knew that this same man—probably a corporate executive, even worldly by most standards—would never have regaled a white woman with a dirty song in public. But to him, I was just a character in his universe of "others," all cartoons.

11   Still, I am one of the lucky ones. There are thousands of Latinas without the privilege of the education that my parents gave me. For them every day is a struggle against the misconceptions perpetuated by the myth of the Latina as a whore, domestic worker or criminal.

12   Rather than fight these pervasive stereotypes, I try to replace them with a more interesting set of realities. I travel around the U.S. reading from my books of poetry and my novel. With the stories I tell, the dreams and fears I examine in my work, I try to get my audience past the particulars of my skin color, my accent or my clothes.

13   I once wrote a poem in which I called Latinas "God's brown daughters." It is really a prayer, of sorts, for communication and respect. In it, Latin women pray "in Spanish to an Anglo God/ with a Jewish heritage," and they are "fervently hoping/ that if not omnipotent,/ at least He be bilingual."

---

7 **come-on**   sexually exciting action inviting a person to respond

8 **Hot Tamale**   literally a spicy Mexican food

9 **Evita**   nickname given to Eva Perón—wife of the Argentinean dictator, Juan Perón—by her adoring fans

10 **"Don't Cry for Me, Argentina"**   song from the musical play *Evita* about the life of Eva Perón

11 **"La Bamba"**   lively Mexican song and dance

Comprehension Check

1. What was the author's life in New Jersey like? How did she feel growing up there?
2. What was the difference between the way American girls dressed and the way Puerto Rican girls dressed? What problem did this cause?
3. What was the conflicting message the Puerto Rican girls received in their upbringing?
4. What were some of the customs and morals on the island where their parents grew up? How were girls protected?
5. What was the stereotype of Latin women held by the men who sang songs to Ortiz Cofer? How did their behavior make her feel?
6. How does she try to disprove the stereotype?
7. What is the main idea of this article?

Sharing Your Thoughts

1. List the different ways the cultures of Puerto Rico and England or the United States clash, according to Ortiz. What explanation for the differences, if any, does she suggest?
2. List the different feelings that the author mentions or that can be inferred from her comments. Complete sentences such as:

   Ortiz felt humiliated when _____

   Ortiz probably felt angry when _____

   Would you have felt the same if you had been in her place? Why or why not?
3. Based on the selection, how do you think the author's parents felt about raising their Puerto Rican children in New Jersey?
4. What makes us feel like we do not belong if we are a member of a minority group or live in a foreign culture? What effect can the feeling of not belonging have? What can we do about it?
5. Do the types of things that happened to the author happen only to women? Explain.
6. Have you ever felt that you were stereotyped as a member of your ethnic group or as a male or a female? How did it make you feel? What can you do about being the object of stereotyping? What do you think of the way Ortiz Cofer handled incidents in which she was stereotyped?
7. Do you ever judge and stereotype people by the way they look or dress? If so, why do you think you do this? When we stereotype people, what are we doing to them? to ourselves?
8. Should people who leave their homes and live in another culture try to assimilate to the new culture as much as possible? What are some advantages of assimilation and what are some disadvantages?

Vocabulary

A. Content Vocabulary

Complete the following statements about growing up in another culture with the correct word from the list. Use each word only once. Change the form of verbs if the grammar of the sentence requires it.

amused	**flashy**	**lecture**
misconceptions	**misinterpret**	**replace**
signal	**suitable**	**surveillance**

1. Ortiz Cofer's parents brought their Puerto Rican values to New Jersey. They were strict with their daughter: They kept her under tight _____ and _____ her on how to be a proper young lady.

2. The Puerto Rican girls, like their mothers, wore loud-colored clothes and a lot of jewelry that North Americans considered too _____. The Puerto Rican girls sometimes felt uncomfortable because their clothes were not _____ according to North American taste.

3. As Ortiz grew into adulthood, she found out that Anglo men _____ sexy and provocative clothes as a come-on or sexual _____.

4. She was not _____ when men treated her like a character in a play like *West Side Story* or *Evita*.

5. Her way of dealing with _____ about her culture is to try to _____ the stereotypical ideas about Latin women with a more realistic picture.

B. Inferring Meaning from Context

Locate the following words in the selection. Can you infer their meaning from the context in which they appear? What words in the context help you figure out their meaning? Notice that in some cases, knowing what part of the word means can help you infer its meaning. Check your inferences with a dictionary if necessary.

1. fresh (¶1) _____

2. microcosm (¶2) _____

3. loud (¶3) _____

4. assailed (¶5) _____

5. mainstream (¶7) _____

6. firebrand (¶7) _____

7. overeager (¶7) _____

8. ditty (¶9) _____

9. worldly (¶10) _____

Text Analysis

A. Figurative Language

> Writers express comparisons imaginatively using similes and
> metaphors. A **simile** is an explicit comparison using *like* or *as*.
> A **metaphor** suggests a comparison without using *like* or *as*.
>
> SIMILE: She looks like an angel.
>
> METAPHOR: She is an angel.

*Locate two similes in paragraph 7 and a metaphor in paragraph 10. Explain in
your own words the ideas and feelings you think they are intended to
communicate. Do you think they are effective? Explain.*

B. Supporting General Statements

*Like the author of Selection Two, p. 129, Ortiz Cofer illustrates some of her
ideas with anecdotes. Find four anecdotes and evaluate each by answering the
following questions:*

- Why does Ortiz Cofer use this particular anecdote? [What idea is the
  anecdote or example intended to illustrate?]
- Do you think this anecdote is well chosen for the intended purpose? Explain.

Writing Task

1. Write sentences with similes to show how you would feel in certain situations. Ask yourself the questions below, and then answer them imaginatively, using sentences with similes.

   a. How would I feel if I were dressed differently from all the people at a party?

   b. How do I feel when a stranger stares at me?

   c. How would I feel if a stranger sang a dirty song to me?

   d. How do I feel when my parents keep me under tight surveillance?

2. Write a paragraph or two about yourself and a misunderstanding some people seem to have about you. You might want to begin or end it with, "Just because I _____, it doesn't mean that I am _____." Use an anecdote to illustrate what the misunderstanding was and how it made you feel. Exchange first drafts of your writing with a partner. Read each other's writing and determine if the anecdote illustrates the idea well and has enough details to be clear to the reader. If not, revise accordingly.

3. Write a conversation between Ortiz and the teacher who criticized the way she dressed for Career Day or between Ortiz and one of the men in her anecdotes. Each person should speak at least five times in the conversation.

SELECTION FOUR

Before Reading

B. Traven (1890–?) was born in Chicago but lived most of his life in Mexico. His many books and stories have been published in thirty languages, but he has been largely neglected as a writer in the United States, perhaps because at the time he was writing, his views were considered too radical. He wrote mainly about oppressed Indians in Mexico, a theme of universal relevance.

1. What is an assembly line? What is its role in manufacturing? What kind of products are usually produced on assembly lines?
2. In what types of cultures do people use and value assembly lines? Explain.

NOTE: This story is long. If desired, it can be read in two parts: paragraphs 1–44 and paragraphs 45–98. The Comprehension Check questions are divided into these two parts.

Assembly Line

by B. Traven

1   Mr. E. L. Winthrop of New York was on vacation in the Republic of Mexico. It wasn't long before he realized that this strange and really wild country had not yet been fully and satisfactorily explored by Rotarians and Lions,[1] who are forever conscious of their glorious mission on earth. Therefore, he considered it his duty as a good American citizen to do his part in correcting this oversight.

2   In search for opportunities to indulge in his new avocation, he left the beaten track and ventured into regions not especially mentioned, and hence not recommended, by travel agents to foreign tourists. So it happened that one day he found himself in a little, quaint Indian village somewhere in the State of Oaxaca.

3   Walking along the dusty main street of this pueblecito,[2] which knew nothing of pavements, drainage, plumbing, or of any means of artificial light save candles or pine splinters, he met with an Indian squatting on the earthen-floor front porch of a palm hut, a so-called jacalito.

4   The Indian was busy making little baskets from bast and from all kinds of fibers gathered by him in the immense tropical bush which surrounded the village on all sides. The material used had not only been well prepared for its purpose but was also richly colored with dyes that the basket-maker himself extracted from various native plants, barks, roots and from certain insects by a process known only to him and the members of his family.

5   His principal business, however, was not producing baskets. He was a peasant who lived on what the small property he possessed—less than fifteen acres of not too fertile soil—would yield, after much sweat and labor and after constantly worrying over the most wanted and best suited distribution of rain, sunshine, and wind and the changing balance of birds and insects beneficial or harmful to his crops. Baskets he made when there was nothing else for him to do in the fields, because he was

---

[1] **Rotarians and Lions** members of Rotary Clubs or Lions Clubs— international service organizations for men (the author thinks of them as promoters of capitalism)

[2] **pueblecito** little town (*pueblo* means town; *-ito* is a Spanish suffix meaning *small*)

unable to dawdle. After all, the sale of his baskets, though to a rather limited degree only, added to the small income he received from his little farm.

6 In spite of being by profession just a plain peasant, it was clearly seen from the small baskets he made that at heart he was an artist, a true and accomplished artist. Each basket looked as if covered all over with the most beautiful, sometimes fantastic ornaments, flowers, butterflies, birds, squirrels, antelope, tigers, and a score of other animals of the wilds. Yet, the most amazing thing was that these decorations, all of them symphonies of color, were not painted on the baskets but were instead actually part of the baskets themselves. Bast and fibers dyed in dozens of different colors were so cleverly—one must actually say intrinsically—interwoven that those attractive designs appeared on the inner part of the basket as well as on the outside. Not by painting but by weaving were those highly artistic effects achieved. This performance he accomplished without ever looking at any sketch or pattern. While working on a basket these designs came to light as if by magic, and as long as a basket was not entirely finished one could not perceive what in this case or that the decoration would be like.

7 People in the market town who bought these baskets would use them for sewing baskets or to decorate tables with or window sills, or to hold little things to keep them from lying around. Women put their jewelry in them or flowers or little dolls. There were in fact a hundred and two ways they might serve certain purposes in a household or in a lady's own room.

8 Whenever the Indian had finished about twenty of the baskets he took them to town on market day. Sometimes he would already be on his way shortly after midnight because he owned only a burro to ride on, and if the burro had gone astray the day before, as happened frequently, he would have to walk the whole way to town and back again.

9 At the market he had to pay twenty centavos[3] in taxes to sell his wares. Each basket cost him between twenty and thirty hours of constant work, not counting the time spent gathering bast and fibers, preparing them, making dyes and coloring the bast. All this meant extra time and work. The price he asked for each basket was fifty centavos, the equivalent of about four cents. It seldom happened, however, that a buyer paid outright the full fifty centavos asked—or four reales as the Indian called that money. The prospective buyer started bargaining, telling the Indian that he ought to be ashamed to ask such a sinful price. "Why, the whole dirty thing is nothing but ordinary petate straw which you find in heaps wherever you may look for it; the jungle is packed full of it," the buyer would argue. "Such a little basket, what's it good for anyhow? If I paid you, you thief, ten centavitos for it you should be grateful and kiss my hand. Well, it's your lucky day, I'll be generous this time, I'll pay you twenty, yet not one green centavo more. Take it or run along."

10 So he sold finally for twenty-five centavos, but then the buyer would say, "Now, what do you think of that? I've got only twenty centavos change on me. What can we do about that? If you can change me a twenty-peso bill, all right, you shall have your twenty-five fierros."[4] Of course, the Indian could not change a twenty-peso bill and so the basket went for twenty centavos.

11 He had little if any knowledge of the outside world or he would have known that what happened to him was happening every hour of every day to every artist all over the world. That knowledge would perhaps have made him very proud, because he would have realized that he belonged to the little army which is the salt of the earth and which keeps culture, urbanity and beauty for their own sake from passing away.

12 Often it was not possible for him to sell all the baskets he had brought to market, for people here as elsewhere in the world preferred things

---

[3] **centavo** one hundredth of a Mexican peso—the monetary unit of Mexico

[4] **fierro** 25 fierros = five centavos

made by the millions and each so much like the other that you were unable, even with the help of a magnifying glass, to tell which was which and where was the difference between two of the same kind.

13 Yet he, this craftsman, had in his life made several hundreds of those exquisite baskets, but so far no two of them had he ever turned out alike in design. Each was an individual piece of art and as different from the other as was a Murillo from a Velásquez.[5]

14 Naturally he did not want to take those baskets which he could not sell at the market place home with him again if he could help it. In such a case he went peddling his products from door to door where he was treated partly as a beggar and partly as a vagrant apparently looking for an opportunity to steal, and he frequently had to swallow all sorts of insults and nasty remarks.

15 Then, after a long run, perhaps a woman would finally stop him, take one of the baskets and offer him ten centavos, which price through talks and talks would perhaps go up to fifteen or even to twenty. Nevertheless, in many instances he would actually get no more than just ten centavos, and the buyer, usually a woman, would grasp that little marvel and right before his eyes throw it carelessly upon the nearest table as if to say, "Well, I take that piece of nonsense only for charity's sake. I know my money is wasted. But then, after all, I'm a Christian and I can't see a poor Indian die of hunger since he has come such a long way from his village." This would remind her of something better and she would hold him and say, "Where are you at home anyway, Indito?[6] What's your pueblo? So, from Huehuetonoc? Now, listen here, Indito, can't you bring me next Saturday two or three turkeys from Huehuetonoc? But they must be heavy and fat and very, very cheap or I won't even touch them. If I wish to pay the regular

price I don't need you to bring them. Understand? Hop along, now, Indito."

16 The Indian squatted on the earthen floor in the portico of his hut, attended to his work and showed no special interest in the curiosity of Mr. Winthrop watching him. He acted almost as if he ignored the presence of the American altogether.

17 "How much that little basket, friend?" Mr. Winthrop asked when he felt that he at least had to say something as not to appear idiotic.

18 "Fifty centavitos, patroncito,[7] my good little lordy, four reales," the Indian answered politely.

19 "All right, sold," Mr. Winthrop blurted out in a tone and with a wide gesture as if he had bought a whole railroad. And examining his buy he added, "I know already who I'll give that pretty little thing to. She'll kiss me for it, sure. Wonder what she'll use it for?"

20 He had expected to hear a price of three or even four pesos. The moment he realized that

---

[5] **Murillo** and **Velásquez** Spanish painters of the 1600s; both were from Seville and both became very famous; each one had a very distinctive style

[6] **Indito** the Spanish suffix -ito can suggest that a person is of lower rank (lowly Indian)

[7] **patroncito** the Spanish suffix -ito can also suggest respect (my good boss)

he had judged the value six times too high, he saw right away what great business possibilities this miserable Indian village might offer to a dynamic promoter like himself. Without further delay he started exploring those possibilities. "Suppose, my good friend, I buy ten of these little baskets of yours which, as I might as well admit right here and now, have practically no real use whatsoever. Well, as I was saying, if I buy ten, how much would you then charge me apiece?"

21 The Indian hesitated for a few seconds as if making calculations. Finally he said, "If you buy ten I can let you have them for forty-five centavos each, señorito gentleman."

22 "All right, amigo. And now, let's suppose I buy from you straight away one hundred of these absolutely useless baskets, how much will cost me each?"

23 The Indian, never fully looking up to the American standing before him and hardly taking his eyes off his work, said politely and without the slightest trace of enthusiasm in his voice, "In such a case I might not be quite unwilling to sell each for forty centavitos."

24 Mr. Winthrop bought sixteen baskets, which was all the Indian had in stock.

25 After three weeks' stay in the Republic, Mr. Winthrop was convinced that he knew this country perfectly, that he had seen everything and knew all about the inhabitants, their character and their way of life, and that there was nothing left for him to explore. So he returned to good old Nooyorg and and felt happy to be once more in a civilized country, as he expressed it to himself.

26 One day going out for lunch he passed a confectioner's and, looking at the display in the window, he suddenly remembered the little baskets he had bought in that faraway Indian village.

27 He hurried home and took all the baskets he still had left to one of the best-known candy-makers in the city.

28 "I can offer you here," Mr. Winthrop said to the confectioner, "one of the most artistic and at the same time the most original of boxes, if you wish to call them that. These little baskets would be just right for the most expensive chocolates meant for elegant and high-priced gifts. Just have a good look at them, sir, and let me listen."

29 The confectioner examined the baskets and found them extraordinarily well suited for a certain line in his business. Never before had there been anything like them for originality, prettiness and good taste. He, however, avoided most carefully showing any sign of enthusiasm, for which there would be time enough once he knew the price and whether he could get a whole load exclusively.

30 He shrugged his shoulders and said, "Well, I don't know. If you asked me I'd say it isn't quite what I'm after. However, we might give it a try. It depends, of course, on the price. In our business the package mustn't cost more than what's in it."

31 "Do I hear an offer?" Mr. Winthrop asked.

32 "Why don't you tell me in round figures how much you want for them? I'm not good in guessing."

33 "Well, I'll tell you, Mr. Kemple: since I'm the smart guy who discovered these baskets and since I'm the only Jack who knows where to lay his hands on more, I'm selling to the highest bidder, on an exclusive basis, of course. I'm positive you can see it my way, Mr. Kemple."

34 "Quite so, and may the best man win," the confectioner said. "I'll talk the matter over with my partners. See me tomorrow same time, please, and I'll let you know how far we might be willing to go."

35 Next day when both gentlemen met again Mr. Kemple said: "Now, to be frank with you, I know art on seeing it, no getting around that. And these baskets are little works of art, they surely are. However, we are no art dealers, you realize that of course. We've no other use for these pretty little things except as fancy packing for our French pralines made by us. We can't pay for them what we might pay considering them pieces of art. After all to us they're only wrappings. Fine wrappings, perhaps, but nevertheless wrappings. You'll see it our way I hope, Mr.——— oh yes, Mr. Winthrop. So, here is our offer, take it or leave it: a dollar and a quarter apiece and not one cent more."

36   Mr. Winthrop made a gesture as if he had been struck over the head.

37   The confectioner, misunderstanding this involuntary gesture of Mr. Winthrop, added quickly, "All right, all right, no reason to get excited, no reason at all. Perhaps we can do a trifle better. Let's say one-fifty."

38   "Make it one-seventy-five," Mr. Winthrop snapped, swallowing his breath while wiping his forehead.

39   "Sold. One-seventy-five apiece free at port of New York. We pay the customs and you pay the shipping. Right?"

40   "Sold," Mr. Winthrop said also and the deal was closed.

41   "There is, of course, one condition," the confectioner explained just when Mr. Winthrop was to leave. "One or two hundred won't do for us. It wouldn't pay the trouble and the advertising. I won't consider less than ten thousand, or one thousand dozens if that sounds better in your ears. And they must come in no less than twelve different patterns well assorted. How about that?"

42   "I can make it sixty different patterns or designs."

43   "So much the better. And you're sure you can deliver ten thousand let's say early October?"

44   "Absolutely," Mr. Winthrop avowed and signed the contract.

45   Practically all the way back to Mexico, Mr. Winthrop had a notebook in his left hand and a pencil in his right and he was writing figures, long rows of them, to find out exactly how much richer he would be when this business had been put through.

46   "Now, let's sum up the whole goddamn thing," he muttered to himself. "Damn it, where is that cursed pencil again? I had it right between my fingers. Ah, there it is. Ten thousand he ordered. Well, well, there we got a clean-cut profit of fifteen thousand four hundred and forty genuine dollars. Sweet smackers.[8] Fifteen grand[9] right into papa's pocket. Come to think of it, that Republic isn't so backward after all."

---

[8] smackers   dollars (old-fashioned slang term)

[9] grand $1,000 (slang)

47   "Buenas tardes, mi amigo, how are you?" he greeted the Indian whom he found squatting in the porch of his jacalito as if he had never moved from his place since Mr. Winthrop had left for New York.

48   The Indian rose, took off his hat, bowed politely and said in his soft voice, "Be welcome, patroncito. Thank you, I feel fine, thank you. Muy buenas tardes. This house and all I have is at your kind disposal." He bowed once more, moved his right hand in a gesture of greeting and sat down again. But he excused himself for doing so by saying, "Perdoneme, patroncito, I have to take advantage of the daylight, soon it will be night."

49   "I've got big business for you, my friend," Mr. Winthrop began.

50   "Good to hear that, señor."

51   Mr. Winthrop said to himself, "Now, he'll jump up and go wild when he learns what I've got for him." And aloud he said: "Do you think you can make one thousand of these little baskets?"

52   "Why not, patroncito? If I can make sixteen, I can make one thousand also."

53   "That's right, my good man. Can you also make five thousand?"

54   "Of course, señor. I can make five thousand if I can make one thousand."

55   "Good. Now, if I should ask you to make me ten thousand, what would you say? And what would be the price of each? You can make ten thousand, can't you?"

56   "Of course, I can, señor. I can make as many as you wish. You see, I am an expert in this sort of work. No one else in the whole state can make them the way I do."

57   "That's what I thought and that's exactly why I came to you."

58   "Thank you for the honor, patroncito."

59   "Suppose I order you to make me ten thousand of these baskets, how much time do you think you would need to deliver them?"

60   The Indian, without interrupting his work, cocked his head to one side and then to the other as if he were counting the days or weeks it would cost him to make all these baskets.

61   After a few minutes he said in a slow voice, "It will take a good long time to make so many baskets, patroncito. You see, the bast and the fibers must be very dry before they can be used properly. Then all during the time they are slowly drying, they must be worked and handled in a very special way so that while drying they won't lose their softness and their flexibility and their natural brilliance. Even when dry they must look fresh. They must never lose their natural properties or they will look just as lifeless and dull as straw. Then while they are drying up I got to get the plants and roots and barks and insects from which I brew the dyes. That takes much time also, believe me. The plants must be gathered when the moon is just right or they won't give the right color. The insects I pick from the plants must also be gathered at the right time and under the right conditions or else they produce no rich colors and are just like dust. But, of course, jefecito, I can make as many of these canastitas as you wish, even as many as three dozens if you want them. Only give me time."

62   "Three dozens? Three dozens?" Mr. Winthrop yelled, and threw up both arms in desperation. "Three dozens!" he repeated as if he had to say it many times in his own voice so as to understand the real meaning of it, because for a while he thought that he was dreaming. He had expected the Indian to go crazy on hearing that he was to sell ten thousand of his baskets without having to peddle them from door to door and be treated like a dog with a skin disease.

63   So the American took up the question of price again, by which he hoped to activate the Indian's ambition. "You told me that if I take one hundred baskets you will let me have them for forty centavos apiece. Is that right, my friend?"

64   "Quite right, jefecito."

65   "Now," Mr. Winthrop took a deep breath, "now, then, if I ask you to make me one thousand, that is, ten times one hundred baskets, how much will they cost me, each basket?"

66   That figure was too high for the Indian to grasp. He became slightly confused and for the first time since Mr. Winthrop had arrived he interrupted his work and tried to think it out. Several times he shook his head and looked vaguely around as if for help. Finally, he said, "Excuse me, jefecito, little chief, that is by far too much for me to count. Tomorrow, if you will do me the honor, come and see me again and I think I shall have my answer ready for you, patroncito."

67   When on the next morning Mr. Winthrop came to the hut he found the Indian as usual squatting on the floor under the overhanging palm roof working at his baskets.

68   "Have you got the price for ten thousand?" he asked the Indian the very moment he saw him, without taking the trouble to say "Good Morning!"

69   "Si, patroncito, I have the price ready. You may believe me when I say it has cost me much labor and worry to find out the exact price, because, you see, I do not wish to cheat you out of your honest money."

70   "Skip that, amigo. Come out with the salad. What's the price?" Mr. Winthrop asked nervously.

71   "The price is well calculated now without any mistake on my side. If I got to make one thousand canastitas each will be three pesos. If I must make five thousand, each will cost nine pesos. And if I have to make ten thousand, in such a case I can't make them for less than fifteen pesos each." Immediately he returned to his work as if he were afraid of losing too much with such idle talk.

72   Mr. Winthrop thought that perhaps it was his faulty knowledge of this foreign language that had played a trick on him.

73   "Did I hear you say fifteen pesos each if I eventually would buy ten thousand?"

74   "That's exactly and without any mistake what I've said, patroncito," the Indian answered in his soft courteous voice.

75   "But now, see here, my good man, you can't do this to me. I'm your friend and I want to help you get on your feet."

76   "Yes, patroncito, I know this and I don't doubt any of your words."

77   "Now, let's be patient and talk this over quietly as man to man. Didn't you tell me that if I would buy one hundred you would sell each for forty centavos?"

78 "Si, jefecito, that's what I said. If you buy one hundred you can have them for forty centavos apiece, provided that I have one hundred, which I don't."

79 "Yes, yes, I see that." Mr. Winthrop felt as if he would go insane any minute now. "Yes, so you said. Only what I can't comprehend is why you cannot sell at the same price if you make me ten thousand. I certainly don't wish to chisel on the price. I am not that kind. Only, well, let's see now, if you can sell for forty centavos at all, be it for twenty or fifty or a hundred, I can't quite get the idea why the price has to jump that high if I buy more than a hundred."

80 "Bueno, patroncito, what is there so difficult to understand? It's all very simple. One thousand canastitas cost me a hundred times more work than a dozen. Ten thousand cost me so much time and labor that I could never finish them, not even in a hundred years. For a thousand canastitas I need more bast than for a hundred, and I need more little red beetles and more plants and roots and bark for the dyes. It isn't that you just can walk into the bush and pick all the things you need at your heart's desire. One root with the true violet blue may cost me four or five days until I can find one in the jungle. And have you thought how much time it costs and how much hard work to prepare the bast and fibers? What is more, if I must make so many baskets, who then will look after my corn and my beans and my goats and chase for me occasionally a rabbit for meat on Sunday? If I have no corn, then I have no tortillas to eat, and if I grow no beans, where do I get my frijoles from?"

81 "But since you'll get so much money from me for your baskets you can buy all the corn and beans in the world and more than you need."

82 "That's what you think, señorito, little lordy. But you see, it is only the corn I grow myself that I am sure of. Of the corn which others may or may not grow, I cannot be sure to feast upon."

83 "Haven't you got some relatives here in this village who might help you to make baskets for me?" Mr. Winthrop asked hopefully.

84 "Practically the whole village is related to me somehow or other. Fact is, I got lots of close relatives in this here place."

85 "Why then can't they cultivate your fields and look after your goats while you make baskets for me? Not only this, they might gather for you the fibers and the colors in the bush and lend you a hand here and there in preparing the material you need for the baskets."

86 "They might, patroncito, yes, they might. Possible. But then you see who would take care of their fields and cattle if they work for me? And if they help me with the baskets it turns out the same. No one would any longer work his fields properly. In such a case corn and beans would get up so high in price that none of us could buy any and we all would starve to death. Besides, as the price of everything would rise and rise higher still how could I make baskets at forty centavos apiece? A pinch of salt or one green chili would set me back more than I'd collect for one single basket. Now you'll understand, highly estimated caballero and jefecito, why I can't make the baskets any cheaper than fifteen pesos each if I got to make that many."

87 Mr. Winthrop was hard-boiled, no wonder considering the city he came from. He refused to give up the more than fifteen thousand dollars which at that moment seemed to slip through his fingers like nothing. Being really desperate now, he talked and bargained with the Indian for almost two full hours, trying to make him understand how rich he, the Indian, would become if he would take this greatest opportunity of his life.

88 The Indian never ceased working on his baskets while he explained his points of view.

89 "You know, my good man," Mr. Winthrop said, "such a wonderful chance might never again knock on your door, do you realize that? Let me explain to you in ice-cold figures what fortune you might miss if you leave me flat on this deal."

90 He tore out leaf after leaf from his notebook, covered each with figures and still more figures, and while doing so told the peasant he would be the richest man in the whole district.

91 The Indian without answering watched with a genuine expression of awe as Mr. Winthrop wrote down these long figures, executing

complicated multiplications and divisions and subtractions so rapidly that it seemed to him the greatest miracle he had ever seen.

92 The American, noting this growing interest in the Indian, misjudged the real significance of it. "There you are, my friend," he said. "That's exactly how rich you're going to be. You'll have a bankroll of exactly four thousand pesos. And to show you that I'm a real friend of yours, I'll throw in a bonus. I'll make it a round five thousand pesos, and all in silver."

93 The Indian, however, had not for one moment thought of four thousand pesos. Such an amount of money had no meaning to him. He had been interested solely in Mr. Winthrop's ability to write figures so rapidly.

94 "So, what do you say now? Is it a deal or is it? Say yes and you'll get your advance this very minute."

95 "As I have explained before, patroncito, the price is fifteen pesos each."

96 "But, my good man," Mr. Winthrop shouted at the poor Indian in utter despair, "where have you been all this time? On the moon or where? You are still at the same price as before."

97 "Yes, I know that, jefecito, my little chief," the Indian answered, entirely unconcerned. "It must be the same price because I cannot make any other one. Besides, señor, there's still another thing which perhaps you don't know. You see, my good lordy and caballero, I've to make these canastitas my own way and with my song in them and with bits of my soul woven into them. If I were to make them in great numbers there would no longer be my soul in each, or my songs. Each would look like the other with no difference whatever and such a thing would slowly eat up my heart. Each has to be another song which I hear in the morning when the sun rises and when the birds begin to chirp and the butterflies come and sit down on my baskets so that I may see a new beauty, because, you see, the butterflies like my baskets and the pretty colors on them, that's why they come and sit down, and I can make my canastitas after them. And now, señor jefecito, if you will kindly excuse me, I have wasted much time already, although it was a pleasure and a great honor to hear the talk of such a distinguished caballero like you. But I'm afraid I've to attend to my work now, for day after tomorrow is market day in town and I got to take my baskets there. Thank you, señor, for your visit. Adiós."

98 And in this way it happened that American garbage cans escaped the fate of being turned into receptacles for empty, torn, and crumpled little multicolored canastitas into which an Indian of Mexico had woven dreams of his soul, throbs of his heart: his unsung poems.

Comprehension Check

Part 1, Paragraphs 1–44

1. Mr. Winthrop was on vacation in Mexico. What other purpose or mission did he discover while he was there?

2. How does the Indian make a living?

3. What was exceptional about the baskets? How did people use them? Are these uses worthy of the baskets? Explain.

4. How did Mexican townspeople treat the Indian? How were prices for the baskets established when the Indian sold them in town? What does this suggest about the attitude of some Mexican townspeople toward rural Indians? What does it suggest about the economic system?

5. How does Mr. Winthrop view the Indian?

6. Who will benefit most from the business deal Mr. Winthrop wants to make with the Indian?

7. What argument does Mr. Winthrop use in negotiating prices with the Indian?

8. What business strategies do Mr. Winthrop and Mr. Kemple, the confectioner, use on each other in making their deal?

Part 2, Paragraphs 45–98

9. When Mr. Winthrop returns to Mexico, what does he propose to the Indian? How will Mr. Winthrop benefit from the deal?

10. How does the Indian respond to Mr. Winthrop's proposal? Can he make the number of baskets Mr. Winthrop wants? Why can't they come to an agreement?

11. Mr. Winthrop cannot understand the Indian's point of view on two levels, economic and artistic. What exactly does he have trouble understanding?

12. What does the Indian have trouble understanding and how does this relate to the title?

Sharing Your Thoughts

1. This story involves contact among three cultures: Mexican Indian, Mexican non-Indian, and North American. The cultures are shown to differ in how people relate to each other and what they value or consider important. What do you learn about each of these cultures in these two areas? How do they differ?

2. Mr. Winthrop and the Indian represent two economic systems, another area in which cultures differ. Why is it so difficult for members of the two systems to come to an agreement?

3. As suggested in paragraph 11, a person who is an artist and a person who is not an artist—in a sense—live in different worlds. What are some of the differences? What do you think each one thinks of the other?

4. There are only two principal characters in this story. Which one do you like better and why? Do you think the characters are portrayed fairly? Why or why not? What, if any, evidence of stereotyping is there?

5. Why do you think the Indian doesn't have a name in the story?

6. Have you ever tried to negotiate or discuss something with a person who thinks differently from you? Were you able to communicate? How did you feel during the interaction?

Vocabulary

Content Vocabulary

Complete the following statements about the story with words from the list. Use each word only once. Change the form of verbs if the grammar of the sentence requires it.

accomplished	bargain	cheat
deal	dyes	exquisite
gather	get on his feet	grasp
profits	stock	tax
weave	willing	

1. The Indian farmer in this story is also a(n) _____ artist who makes baskets from fibers he _____ near his village. He makes the _____ to color these fibers from native plants as well. Into each basket he _____ a beautiful and unique design.

2. In spite of their beauty, selling his _____ creations is not easy. He has to travel a long distance to the market and pay a(n) _____ to sell there. In addition, he rarely receives his asking price of fifty centavos because customers _____ with him to get the lowest price possible. They sometimes _____ him out of a little more by pretending they do not have the correct change.

3. Mr. Winthrop, who sees the value of the baskets, buys all sixteen baskets that the Indian had in _____.

4. Back in New York, Winthrop finds a candy maker who is _____ to pay a high price for the baskets. After making an exclusive _____ with the man for 10,000 baskets, Winthrop returns to Mexico.

5. With visions of great _____ in mind, Winthrop tries to convince the poor Indian that making 10,000 baskets will help him _____ and become an economic success.

6. Winthrop goes home empty-handed because he does not understand the Indian's way of life or appreciate the artistic value of the Indian's work; he cannot _____ that the Indian can never make 10,000 baskets by hand.

Text Analysis

Elements of Fiction

In some stories **characters** come alive as individuals. In others, such as this one, they seem to be important to the writer for what they represent.

1. To reveal ideas that Traven may have had in mind in creating these characters, fill in the chart below showing how they differ, or make your own chart. Some ways they differ are suggested in the guide below; you will probably find more. Then find evidence in the story that illustrates these differences. Types of evidence might include words and actions of the characters or observations of the narrator.

AREA OF DIFFERENCE	MR. WINTHORP	INDIAN
a. occupation	_____	_____
b. personality	_____	_____
c. communication style	_____	_____
d. aim in life	_____	_____
e. _____	_____	_____
f. _____	_____	_____

2. What do you infer about Traven's views of North American and Mexican-Indian cultures through these characters?

Writing Task

1. Based on the chart you prepared in Text Analysis 1, write three to five paragraphs contrasting North American and Mexican-Indian cultures (in Traven's view) as represented by Mr. Winthrop and the Indian. Use one of the two types of organization presented in Text Analysis, p 89. That is, either discuss first one culture and then the other, or discuss the differences in your chart one by one, giving examples from both cultures.

2. Imagine you are the Indian telling a friend about your encounter with Mr. Winthrop. Write the story from your point of view. Be sure to include what Mr. Winthrop proposed, your reaction to him and to the proposal, and his reaction to your response.

SELECTION FIVE

Before Reading

Chitra Banerjee Divakaruni, a young Indian poet, teaches creative writing at Foothill College in California. Yuba City is in northern California.

Talk with a group of your classmates about problems that children have when they go to school in a new country. What kinds of help can parents give their children in this situation?

Yuba City School

by Chitra Banerjee Divakaruni

From the black trunk I shake out
my one American skirt, blue serge
that smells of mothballs. Again today
Neeraj came crying from school. All week
5 the teacher has made him sit
in the last row, next to the fat boy
who drools and mumbles,
picks at the spotted milk-blue
skin of his face, but knows
10 to pinch, sudden-sharp,
when she is not looking.

The books are full of black curves,
dots like the eggs the boll-weevil lays
each monsoon in furniture-cracks
15 in Ludhiana.[1] Far up in front
the teacher makes word-sounds
Neeraj does not know. They float
from her mouth-cave, he says,
in discs, each a different color.

---

[1]Ludhiana city in the Punjab region of northern India

20   Candy-pink for the girls
       in their lace dresses, marching
       shiny shoes. Silk-yellow
       for the boys beside them,
       crisp blond hair, hands raised
25   in all the right answers. Behind them
       the Mexicans, whose older brothers,
       he tells me, carry knives,
       whose catcalls[2] and whizzing rubber bands
       clash, mid-air, with the teacher's
30   voice, its sharp purple edge.
       For him, the words are
       a muddy red, flying low and heavy,
       and always the one he has learned to understand:
       idiot, idiot, idiot.

35   I heat the iron over the stove. Outside
       evening blurs the shivering
       in the eucalyptus.[3] Neeraj's shadow
       disappears into the hole
       he is hollowing all afternoon.
40   The earth, he knows, is round, and if
       one can tunnel all the way through,
       he will end up in Punjab,
       in his grandfather's mango orchard,
       his grandmother's songs lighting
45   on his head, the old words
       glowing like summer fireflies.

       In the playground, Neeraj says,
       invisible hands snatch at his uncut hair,[4]
       unseen feet trip him from behind,
50   and when he turns, ghost laughter
       all around his bleeding knees.

---

2 catcalls loud whistles or cries expressing disapproval, as at a sporting event

3 eucalyptus tall tree that produces oil used for treating colds

4 Neeraj's uncut hair Neeraj and his family are Sikh immigrants. Their religion prohibits cutting the hair.

He bites down on his lip
to keep in the crying. They are
waiting for him to open his mouth,
55 so they can steal his voice.

I test the iron with little drops of water
that sizzle and die. Press down
on the wrinkled cloth. The room fills
with a smell like singed flesh.
60 Tomorrow in my blue skirt I will go
to see the teacher, my tongue
stiff and swollen
in my unwilling mouth, my few
English phrases. She will pluck them
65 from me, nail shut my lips. My son
will keep sitting in the last row
among the red words that drink his voice.

Comprehension Check

1. Who is the speaker in this poem?
2. What problems is the son having in school? Are they real or imaginary?
3. What is his usual school day like?
4. What is the mother planning to do?
5. Why will she wear her blue skirt?
6. Does she think she will be successful in the task ahead of her? Explain.

Sharing Your Thoughts

1. How do you think the mother feels in this situation? How would you feel if you were in her position?
2. How do you think Neeraj feels in this situation? How would you feel in his position?
3. Living in an alien culture causes stress for Neeraj and his mother. What kinds of stress does it cause for them? Compare their problems with those of any minority group in its own country. What similarities and differences do you find? Share anecdotes with your classmates that illustrate your points.

Text Analysis

A. Figurative Language

The **similes** and **metaphors** Divakaruni uses in this poem contribute in important ways to the reader's understanding of the feelings of people living in a new culture.

1. Reread the poem and mark all references to spoken or written language. Referring to what you have just marked, answer these questions.
   a. How does the teacher's language sound to Neeraj?
   b. How does Neeraj feel about the way his teacher speaks to him? to the other children?
   c. What is Neeraj's impression of the words in the books?
   d. What meaning, if any, comes from the colors associated with the language images?
   e. How does the mother feel about using English?
   f. How do other people treat Neeraj and his mother because of their language problems?
   g. How does Neeraj feel about his native language?
   h. Why are there so many references to language in this poem?

2. Find other images in the poem that appeal to your sense of smell, hearing, touch or feeling, and sight. Do the images tend to be happy or sad images? What do they contribute to the meaning of the poem?

B. Text Organization

What is the mother doing at the beginning of the first stanza of this poem? What is she doing in the beginning of the last stanza? Why do you think the poet structured the poem in this way? What does this tell us about the passage of time in the poem?

Writing Task

1. Imagine you are Neeraj or his mother. Write a letter to a friend or relative in India explaining how things are going for you in California and how you feel about your new life.

2. Did you (or a child of yours) ever have a problem at school where parental intervention was necessary? Write two or three paragraphs in which you explain the problem and describe the meeting at school and its results. Comment on how you and the other participants in the situation felt.

A FINAL LOOK

Discussion

1. Work with a partner, in a small group, or as a whole class. Drawing on all five selections in this unit and the quote on the introductory page, discuss the focus questions.

2. In Unit Four we saw some stereotypes of males and females. How are stereotypes of ethnic groups similar to gender stereotypes? What is your stereotypical idea of North Americans? Do you know how your ethnic group is stereotyped by others? Where do these stereotypes come from? How do you feel about them?

3. How does living in a foreign culture affect the parent-child relationship? If you read Unit Two, have you learned anything in this unit that can help you understand the problem between Hank López and his father in Unit Two, Selection Two, p. 39?

4. What does the proverb "When in Rome, do as the Romans do" say about visiting or living in another culture? Do you think people should always follow this advice? Explain.

Writing

1. Choose one of the following topics, and write several paragraphs narrating a personal experience. Write the question words *who, what, where, when, why, how,* and *how long* on a piece of paper. Make notes after each question word to be sure you include the necessary details and background information in your writing. Be sure to include details about how you and the other people in your anecdote felt in the situation.

    a. a personal intercultural experience similar to the ones you have read about in this unit

    b. an experience with stereotyping

    c. a situation in which you felt out of place or different from others

2. Referring specifically to ideas and examples in selections in this unit, as well as to your general knowledge of cultural differences and problems of living or working in a different culture, do one of the following:

    a. Write to Mr. Winthrop explaining why his business deal failed.

    b. Write to one of the men who sang to Ortiz Cofer and explain why he is offensive and should change his way of dealing with people.

    c. Write a letter giving advice to a friend who is going to visit another country for two or three weeks, stay in another country for several years, or move permanently to another culture.

3. Which of these selections can you relate to best? In two or three paragraphs, describe your reaction to it, and explain why you reacted as you did.

UNIT SIX

Humans and Other Animals

> The difference in mind between man and the higher animals, great as it is, certainly is one of degree and not of kind.
>
> – Charles Darwin

FOCUS

➤ What do other animals provide for humans?

➤ What are possible relationships between humans and other animals?

➤ How do these relationships affect the lives of people and the lives of animals?

➤ How should humans treat other animals?

SELECTION ONE

Before Reading

After graduating from college in 1956, Gloria Steinem went to India on a Chester Bowles Asian Fellowship. She then began a career as a journalist, feminist, and political activist. In 1972, she founded *Ms.* magazine.

This selection is an excerpt from her book, *Revolution from Within*, which is about improved self-esteem for both men and women.

1. For a variety of reasons, humans have always formed relationships with other animals. What are some of these relationships? What are the reasons for them? How do you think people feel about the animals in these relationships? How do you think the animals feel?

2. In a group, discuss the direct contact you have or have had with animals. Survey your group to find out

   a. how many students have a pet

   b. the pets that students most commonly have

   c. the benefits of having pets

   d. the reasons some students do not have a pet

   e. how many students have had other contact with animals, such as raising animals for food, working with laboratory animals, or studying animals in the wild

   Tabulate the results and discuss them with the class.

3. Preview the selection. What do you think animals could have to do with the self-esteem of humans?

People and Other Animals by Gloria Steinem

1 *B*onding with animals—or rather, admitting the bond we work so hard to ignore—is one way of increasing health and strengthening a sense of self. A wide variety of studies have shown that on the average, people who have pets or live close to animals have lower blood pressure, heart rates, stress levels, and incidence of depression, while enjoying longer life expectancies. Anecdotal evidence[1] shows they also have higher levels of responsibility, independence, self-confidence, and optimism. If you haven't experienced the power of this bonding with pets, start a conversation with any group of friends who have them, and watch the faces light up as they tell stories of creatures with whom they share their homes. Even people institutionalized for catatonic withdrawal[2] have responded for the first time when given an affectionate animal to hold, as have the institutionalized elderly so depressed or overmedicated that they would respond to nothing else. In eighteenth-century Germany and England, hospitals and retreats for the insane discovered that cats, dogs, horses, and birds were healing catalysts, as if the animals' freely given energy could pierce a human wall of isolation.

---

[1] anecdotal evidence   evidence from personal experience, not based on scientific studies

[2] catatonic withdrawal   a psychiatric condition in which a patient is detached and lacks interest in his surroundings, characterized by unfocused eyes and lack of action

2   In this country, programs that teach handicapped people to ride horseback have increased their confidence and independence, and others that allow autistic[3] children to swim with dolphins have resulted in unprecedented levels of response and speech. Some observers have insisted that the dolphins seemed to sense the kids' vulnerability and protect them. Among a group of women prisoners in Washington State, recidivism[4] was eliminated when they were given dogs to train and care for. In Ohio, suicide and depression among the criminally insane were reduced by allowing prisoners to care for fish and small animals in their cells (Beth W. McLeod, "Someone to Care For," *Christian Science Monitor*, Feb. 13, 1989).

3   For skeptics who say this is the power of expectation—that like a placebo,[5] any intervention works if those participating believe it will—there are also plenty of accidental discoveries. In a California hospital, for instance, nurses were asked to care for a patient's Seeing Eye dog by keeping it at their station. To the surprise of everyone, nurses began to report less job stress, and patients became more active and ambulatory. Among people who have animals but become too ill to keep them at home, there is often an unexpected and rapid decline. In major cities hit hard by the AIDS epidemic, pets have had such a clear impact on the self-esteem of homebound patients that volunteer groups now help to maintain them when their owners can no longer cope. Thanks to one such program in New York City called POWARS (Pet Owners With AIDS/ARC Resource Service), volunteers pay daily visits to feed and walk the pets of bedridden patients. "People with AIDS and ARC often feel like pariahs and outcasts," explains Steve Kohn, a cofounder of POWARS, but animals provide the greatest gift: "a feeling that they are unconditionally loved" ("Loving Paws, Helping Hands," *New York Times*, May 16, 1991).

4   In Northern California, the Animal Assisted Therapy Program, a project of the Society for the Prevention of Cruelty to Animals, has selected kittens and roosters, dogs, guinea pigs, and sometimes even a boa constrictor for their sociability and taken them into children's wards and prisons, abuse shelters, and retirement homes—anyplace where people are feeling robbed of affection and identity. "Animals don't care if a person is losing sight or can't walk," as one of the program leaders explained. "All they want is to love you, and that quality brings out therapeutic things in us." There is also another goal: "What we're primarily doing is helping animals by promoting the idea that they are a very valuable part of our lives" (McLeod, "Someone to Care For").

5   In fact, animals have been found to boost human morale, communication, and self-esteem more reliably and quickly than almost any other kind of therapy. The animals themselves seem to sense their impact and to thrive—unlike their isolated fate in many zoos and other institutions. As a result of the success of such programs, forty-eight states now permit pets in hospitals, all fifty states allow them in nursing homes, and the National Institutes of Health has officially noted "the crucial role pets may play" in physical and mental health—a big change from a decade ago when the presence of any animal was forbidden in health-care facilities.

6   Perhaps the least expected testimony to our potential for radical empathy is its crossing not just of species lines, but of elements. In addition to dolphins,

---

[3] autistic   suffering from a mental illness in which the person does not communicate

[4] recidivism   returning to a life of crime

[5] placebo   a substance that does not do anything, given instead of real medicine

other underwater creatures respond to human beings—and vice versa—as scuba divers or aquarium lovers can testify. Diana James, a colleague whose pet for twenty-seven years was a medium-sized turtle, found she and he developed a bond. When she had a cold or a migraine, he became sympathetically ill, and when he was wedged under rocks in his aquarium and in danger of drowning, she awoke in another room to rescue him. In an expedition organized by marine explorers Jacques Cousteau and his son Philippe, scuba divers descended into one of the few ocean areas where spear fishermen, ships' motors, and dragnets had never been, and found an underwater life that was curious, friendly, and unafraid. Fish swam close to their human visitors and allowed themselves to be touched and petted. Only because Philippe Cousteau filmed these remarkable scenes were they believed. On the other hand, in ocean areas where humans have brought great danger, sea life seems to learn caution and fear in just one generation.

7   Clearly, human beings fare better when we feel an empathetic bond with the other passengers on this Spaceship Earth. When we are not being the terrorists on this spaceship, they seem to thrive around us, too.

8   I often wonder: What would life with animals be like if, as Chief Seattle[6] said, we shared "the same breath"? I've felt that possibility only once, while living in India.

9   In our student hostel in Delhi, small gray monkeys often left their perch in trees outside our windows and came in to visit. They sat on our desks and watched while we studied. They hid our pencils and jewelry when we were out, watched with amusement as we searched for things they finally "found" for us. They were delightful companions—graceful, funny, mysterious, and never boring. By being so alive in the moment, they made us feel more alive and aware, too.

10   Later, in a South Indian village where I stayed with a family for a few days, I remember elephants gliding past each morning with their keeper, or *mahout,* on the way to the fields. Often the little boy of the household would give them a treat of plantains,[7] but one morning, he mischievously poked one elephant's trunk with a sharp pin instead. She squealed, but did nothing—until, on the way back from that evening's drink at the river, she raised her trunk over the garden wall and drenched the boy with a trunkful of water she had saved up for the purpose. Then she calmly lumbered on.

11   As his mother and the *mahout* explained to the little boy, this was *shabash*—very clever—but it was also serious elephant wisdom. Without hurting him, but also without sacrificing one whit of her dignity, the elephant had taught him a lesson in fairness he would never forget.

12   In a way, animals are professors of self-esteem: unself-conscious, confident, and utterly themselves. I thought again of what humans could learn while reading about Koko, a female gorilla who was taught sign language by Dr. Francine Patterson, a primatologist. Thanks to Koko's ability to understand some spoken language and respond in a vocabulary of 500 signed[8] words, we

---

[6] **Chief Seattle**   Indian of the Suquamish tribe in Washington State who is credited with stating that the white man uses the earth and its creatures for his own purposes, not appreciating that "all things share the same breath—the beasts, the tree, the man"

[7] **plantain**   a type of large banana that must be cooked before eaten

[8] **signed**   hand motions (sign language) to communicate as deaf/mute people do

know some of her thoughts on everything from her favorite foods to using a camera. We know about her dislike for someone she called an "obnoxious nut" and her gentleness and love for a kitten that was given to her as a pet— as well as her sadness and mourning when that kitten was killed by a car.

13   Here is one of the exchanges Dr. Patterson recorded:

14   "I turn to Koko: 'Are you an animal or a person?' Koko's instant response: 'Fine animal gorilla'" (Francine Patterson, "Conversations with a Gorilla," *National Geographic*, October 1978; 154)

15   Self-esteem is natural, and only humans create inequality by simply believing in it. By unhardening our hearts to animals, perhaps we open them to ourselves.

Comprehension Check

1. What is bonding?

2. Read through the selection again and notice each mention of people who benefit from contact with animals. Who benefitted? Where did the contact take place? What was the beneficial effect? Make and complete a chart with the following headings:

PEOPLE   SETTING   EFFECT

3. The use of animals as part of the therapy for the mentally and physically ill is called *pet therapy*. What do those most in need of pet therapy often have in common? What do the animals provide people in these situations?

4. What does the incident with the nurses show?

5. What is the purpose of POWARS?

6. What effect does bonding with people have on the animals?

7. What species of animals can humans relate to and benefit from?

8. What did the author's experiences with animals in India teach her?

9. What do we learn from Koko, the gorilla?

10. What is the main idea of this selection?

Sharing Your Thoughts

1. Think about the urban environment in which many people live and the stress they suffer. How can they improve their lives by means of bonds with an animal?

2. Do you know of any cases where people benefit from bonds with animals other than the typical pet? Share examples with your classmates.

3. How does Steinem believe bonds with animals are related to human self-esteem? What specific examples from your own experience or knowledge can you think of, if any, that demonstrate the effect of animals on human self-esteem?

4. Steinem says that we humans work hard to ignore our bond to animals. What do you think she means? In what specific ways do we ignore the bond?

5. Why do you think we humans ignore our bond with animals? Do we do it intentionally? What, if any, effect does this have on humans? on animals?

Vocabulary

A. Content Vocabulary

Complete the following statements about people and animals with words from the list. Use each word only once. Change the form of verbs if the grammar of the sentence requires it.

boost	catalyst	empathy
expectancy	handicapped	impact
isolated	reduce	thrive

1. Animals can have a positive _____ on the self-esteem and health of humans. The presence of animals can _____ stress, lower blood pressure, lead to more social contacts, and _____ morale.

2. Their presence is like a(n) _____ that triggers improvement in patients with mental and emotional problems and can also help the physically _____. Living close to animals can even increase a person's life _____.

3. The benefits are mutual. When people and animals feel _____ for each other, the animals also _____, knowing that they play a useful role. Clearly animals who have strong bonds with humans are happier than animals who are _____ in zoos or laboratories.

B. Word Analysis

Locate the following words in the selection. Check the context in which they each appear. Divide them into their meaningful parts. What is the meaning of the whole? What does each part contribute? Notice that in some cases, knowing what part of the word means can help you infer its meaning. Use a dictionary if necessary.

1. overmedicated (¶1) _____

2. unprecedented (¶2) _____

3. homebound (¶3) _____

4. bedridden (¶3) _____

5. outcasts (¶3) _____

6. unconditionally (¶3) _____

7. unself-conscious (¶12) _____

8. primatologist (¶12) _____

Text Analysis

Supporting General Statements

Recall the main idea of this selection as decided upon by your class (Comprehension Check 10). The author uses factual examples as well as personal anecdotes to support her main idea.

1. What are some of her factual examples? What personal anecdotes does she use?
2. What does each kind of example add?
3. Why do you think Steinem uses both types?

Writing Task

Write at least one paragraph in which you relate an incident or anecdote that illustrates one of the following:
- an animal helping someone
- the intelligence of an animal
- the sense of humor or personality of an animal

Begin with a general statement of the animal behavior you will illustrate. Then give enough details so the reader can picture the behavior and will be convinced that the animal was helpful, smart, or funny. Exchange first drafts with a partner; read each other's writing and determine if there is enough detail for the reader to understand and picture what you are describing. If not, revise accordingly.

SELECTION TWO

Before Reading

This selection is an adapted excerpt from a brochure published by the Humane Farming Association, an organization that campaigns against factory farming.

1. Steinem emphasized the positive aspects of human-animal relationships. However, there are many ways that humans use animals for their own benefit without giving much thought to the effects on the animals or on people. Some of these uses are obvious while others are less well known. As a class, brainstorm a list of ways animals serve human needs.

2. One of the ways animals serve human needs you probably listed in Before Reading is supplying humans with food. Write down the foods you ate yesterday that included animal products. What do you think the farms these products come from are like?

3. If anyone in the class lives or has lived on a farm, share your experiences and feelings about living on a farm and having farm animals.

FOOD FOR THOUGHT

from The Humane Farming Association

1 Consider these facts about food production in the United States:

• Eighty percent of the hogs born in the U.S. are placed in bare wire mesh cages or tiny cement pens until they weigh 50 pounds. Then they are crowded into "finishing pens" with no straw or bedding to be fattened up for the trip to the slaughterhouse when they reach 210–220 pounds.

• Ninety-eight percent of our eggs come from factory farms where four or five laying hens are crowded into 12″ by 18″ cages with no room to stretch their wings, move about or engage in any of the natural activities of chickens such as nest building. Those who are low on the pecking order[1] have no escape, and cannibalism is widespread.

• In the name of "gourmet food" veal factories take newborn male calves and chain them alone in crates 22″ by 58″ for their whole lives. To obtain the light colored meat sold as "premium" or "milk-fed" veal, they are kept anemic on a liquid diet of growth stimulators, antibiotics, powdered skim milk, and mold inhibitors, and they are allowed absolutely no exercise.

2 Does this sound like the traditional family farm? Unfortunately, family farms in the U.S. are being replaced by factory farms where these practices are commonplace. Yet most people are not aware of the way the animals they consume as food are raised. Not only are these conditions bad for the animals, but the results are dangerous for humans as well.

---

[1] **pecking order**   the hierarchical social order in a group of chickens in which chickens lower in the hierarchy allow themselves to be pecked (hit with the beak) by those higher up

FACTORY FARM DISEASE—
A HUMAN DILEMMA

3   Factory farm conditions result in severe physiological as well as behavioral animal afflictions. Anemia, influenza, intestinal diseases, mastitis, metritis, orthostasis, pneumonia, and scours are only the beginning of a long list of ailments plaguing factory farm animals.

4   By ignoring traditional animal husbandry methods such as exercise, fresh air, wholesome food, and proper veterinary care, factory farms are a breeding ground for countless infectious diseases. Factory farms attempt to counter the effects of grossly deficient husbandry, overcrowding, and intensive confinement by administering continuous doses of antibiotics and other drugs to the animals. This "cost effective" practice has a significant negative impact on the health of the consumer, as well as the animal.

5   The deprivation to which animals are subjected on factory farms has provoked concern among knowledgeable veterinarians, family farmers, and humanitarians for several years. Today, criticism of factory farm practices is widespread among human health care professionals as well.

6   Medical doctors now warn that the tragedy of factory farming reaches well beyond the farm animals themselves. According to a broad spectrum of scientists, the high level of contaminants in factory farm products now poses a serious danger to human health. Studies in the *New England Journal of Medicine* and research by the U.S. Centers for Disease Control, National Resources Defense Council, and the U.S. Food and Drug Administration all warn that the levels of antibiotics and other contaminants in commercially raised meat constitute a serious threat to the health of the consumer.

ANTIBIOTICS—SQUANDERING A
MEDICAL MIRACLE

7   Almost 50% of all antibiotics manufactured in the United States are poured directly into animal feeds. This accounts for over $435 million each year for the pharmaceutical companies.

8   The most commonly used antibiotics are penicillin and tetracycline. The squandering of these important drugs in livestock production is wreaking havoc for physicians in the treatment of human illness. Widespread overuse of antibiotics is resulting in the evolution of new strains of virulent bacteria whose resistance to antibiotics poses a great threat to human health. Doctors are now reporting that, due to their uncontrolled use of factory farms, these formerly lifesaving drugs are often rendered useless in combating human disease.

9   Dr. Jere Goyan, Dean of the School of Pharmacy at the University of California, San Francisco, tells us that the indiscriminate use of antibiotics in animal feed is leading to "a major national crisis in public health. Unless we take action now to curb the use of these drugs in the livestock industry, we will not be able to use them to treat human disease." Dr. Karim Ahmed, head scientist of the National Resources Defense Council, has long urged Congress to impose immediate controls on the use of antibiotics in animal feed. According to Dr. Ahmed, unless swift action is taken, "we are going to have an epidemic of untreatable stomach ailments, many of which will end in death."

10   *Unfortunately, the crisis has already begun.* Scientists now calculate that the misuse of penicillin and tetracycline in animal feed is implicated in more than 2,000,000 cases of *Salmonella* poisoning each year, resulting in as many as 2,000 human deaths.

11   These illnesses and deaths need not occur. The routine use of antibiotics and other chemicals in animal feed is a dangerously irresponsible attempt to counter the harsh, disease-ridden conditions to which animals are subjected on factory farms.

ANIMAL FACTORIES VS. FAMILY FARMS

12   Factory farm equipment and drug companies tell us that farmers need intensive animal confinement facilities in order to make a large profit. In reality, it is the equipment companies and giant pharmaceutical corporations such as Lilly, Upjohn, American Cyanamid, and Pfizer (which collectively sell farmers over 15 million pounds of antibiotics each year) that profit most from factory farming.

13   Family farms are being squeezed out of business by their inability to raise the necessary capital to compete with huge factory farms. Traditional farming is labor intensive, but factory farming is capital intensive. Farmers who do manage to raise the money for confinement systems quickly discover that the small savings in labor costs are not enough to cover the increasingly expensive facilities, energy, caging, and drug costs.

THE STRESS CONNECTION

14   Agribusiness companies will tell us that factory farm animals are "happy" and "as well cared for as your own pet dog or cat." Nothing could be further from the truth.

15   The life of a factory farm animal is characterized by acute deprivation, stress, and disease. Hundreds of millions of animals are forced to live in cages or crates just barely larger than their own bodies. While one species may be caged alone without any social contact, another species may be crowded so tightly together that they fall prey to stress-induced cannibalism. Cannibalism is particularly prevalent in the cramped confinement of hogs and laying hens. Unable to groom, stretch their legs, or even turn around, the victims of factory farms exist in a relentless state of distress.

16   "When animals are intensively confined and under stress, as they are on factory farms, their autoimmune systems are affected and they are prone to infectious diseases," reports veterinarian Dr. Bruce Feldmann. "When animals are raised with care and responsibility there is no need for continuous low-level antibiotic feed additives. It is as simple as that."

17   The public relations firms[2] retained by agribusiness companies will pubicly deny the existence of farm animal stress. Ironically, these PR campaigns are paid for out of the millions of dollars made selling drugs to treat stress and stress-induced diseases on factory farms.

NO LAWS PROTECT FARM ANIMALS

18   If a kennel, stable, zoo, or other establishment treated animals in a manner common on factory farms, they could be fined or lose their license to operate. If a private citizen was discovered confining a dog or cat in a manner common on factory farms, he/she could be charged with cruelty to animals. There is an area, however, that society's laws protecting animals do no touch.

19   The powerful agribusiness and pharmaceutical lobbies[3] have seen to it that *farm animals are explicitly excluded from the federal Animal Welfare Act.* There are virtually no laws which protect farm animals from even the most harsh and brutal treatment as long as it takes place in the name of production and profit. It is left *entirely* to the preference of the individual company how many egg-laying hens are stuffed into each little wire cage, or whether an artificially inseminated sow must spend her entire pregnancy chained to the floor of a cement-bottomed cage.

---

[2] **public relations (PR) firms**   businesses dedicated to maintaining friendly relations between an organization and the general public

[3] **lobbies**   groups whose purpose is to influence legislators to pass laws that are in their interest

Comprehension Check

1. What are the effects of factory farming on animals? on people? on family farms?
2. How does agribusiness justify the conditions of factory farming?
3. Who benefits from factory farming?
4. Why aren't farm animals protected by the federal Animal Welfare Act?

Sharing Your Thoughts

1. How do the conditions described in this selection contrast with conditions on traditional farms? What value do people give to animals under traditional farming conditions? How is that changed by factory farming?
2. How does stress affect people and animals? Why would farmers deliberately put animals in stressful conditions?
3. What, if anything, did you take for granted about your diet before you read the selection that you might think about now?
4. How can the way our food is produced be changed so that it is more humane for the animals involved and healthier for the human consumers? Do you think such changes will come about? Why or why not?

Vocabulary

A. Content Vocabulary

Complete the following statements about factory farming with words from the list. Use each word only once. Change the form of verbs if the grammar of the sentence requires it.

ailments	anemic	beyond
cages	calves	feed
pens	prone	threat
warn	wreak havoc	

1. Many people in the United States may still imagine that farm animals are happy and well cared for. Unfortunately, this is no longer the usual case. Hens are crowded into small wire _____; pigs are kept in small cement _____; baby _____ are deprived of exercise and proper nutrition to ensure that they will be _____ so that their meat will be pale and tender.

2. These animals suffer from many _____; therefore, antibiotics are routinely put into animal _____ in order to keep disease under control.

3. Scientists _____ that the overuse of antibiotics has an impact that extends _____ the animals themselves because people also consume the antibiotics when they eat the meat, dairy products, and eggs of these overmedicated animals.

4. The result is the evolution of resistant strains of bacteria, which poses a serious _____ to human health. In fact, resistant strains of bacteria are already beginning to _____ in the treatment of human illness as the usual antibiotics are no longer effective in fighting these bacteria.

5. If animals were treated more humanely, they would be less _____ to illness and wouldn't need this constant dose of antibiotics. They would be healthier, and so would we.

B. Word Analysis

Locate the following words in the selection. Check the context in which they each appear. Divide them into their meaningful parts. What is the meaning of the whole? What does each part contribute? Notice that in some cases, knowing what part of the word means can help you infer its meaning. Use a dictionary if necessary.

1. fattened (¶1) _____

2. slaughterhouse (¶1) _____

3. newborn (¶1) _____

4. widespread (¶1, ¶5, ¶8) _____

5. commonplace (¶2) _____

6. countless (¶4) _____

7. overcrowding (¶4) _____

8. livestock (¶8) _____

9. overuse (¶8) _____

10. lifesaving (¶8) _____

11. indiscriminate (¶9) _____

12. untreatable (¶9) _____

13. misuse (¶10) _____

14. inability (¶13) _____

15. agribusiness (¶14, ¶17 ¶19) _____

Text Analysis

A. Cause and Effect

> Many phenomena in the world can be understood in terms of cause and effect. A **cause** is the source or origin of a condition or situation; an **effect** is the result of the condition or situation. The relationships among causes and effects can be complex. *A* can be the direct cause of *B*, or it can be one factor contributing to *B*, the effect. Also, an effect may in turn become a cause of something else. For example, factory farming conditions cause stress (stress is the effect or result of the farming conditions), but stress then becomes a cause of numerous diseases.

1. Reread this selection. Find cause and effect expressed in paragraphs 3, 4, 5, 6, 8, 9, 10, 12, and 16. Mark the statements or groups of statements that are causes with a *C* and those that are effects with an *E*. Look also for words that express cause and effect. Some are quite obvious like *result*, and others are more subtle like *wreaking havoc.*

2. Compare your answers for question 1 with those of your classmates. Even if you do not agree completely, your discussion will help you understand the causes and effects that this issue involves.

3. The statement of the main idea of this selection involves a cause and an effect. Locate it in paragraph 2.

B. Persuasion

The overall purpose of the brochure from which this excerpt comes is to persuade readers to work for the improvement of the inhumane conditions on factory farms and the inclusion of farm animals under the federal Animal Welfare Act. Although you do not have this final conclusion in hand, this excerpt illustrates the first step of persuasion, which is to make readers aware of facts or situations of which they might not otherwise be aware.

1. In presenting the facts, writers with a persuasive purpose usually use words with emotional impact. The writer of this selection uses words that have strong negative connotations and thus show that the purpose of the brochure is not strictly informative but also persuasive. Find words with emotional impact in paragraphs 3, 4, 5, 6, 8, 9, 11, 15, and 19. Try to rewrite these sentences using vocabulary that is less emotional.

2. Another characteristic of persuasive writing is the use of arguments, in this case, the reasons why we should work for improving inhumane conditions on factory farms. There are two principal reasons we should do something about factory farming. One is directly related to animals; the other is directly related to people. What are they?

3. Paragraphs 12, 14, and 17 present the arguments of the opposition. What are they? What does the writer of the brochure say in response?

Writing Task

1. Imagine your family owns a small farm in the United States that depends heavily on human labor rather than machinery. Write a letter to the editor of a newspaper explaining what is happening to your farm as large factory farms take over agriculture, and how this change is affecting the public. Letters to an editor are more effective if brief and direct. Exchange letters with a partner; read each other's letters and determine if they are clear enough for the reader to understand the points. If not, revise accordingly.

2. Write a letter to your representative in Congress (if you do not live in the United States, imagine you do) protesting the fact that farm animals are not protected by the federal Animal Welfare Act. In order to persuade your representative to work to have the law amended, you will have to use convincing arguments or reasons supported by facts. Before beginning to write, list the reasons for your position, and put them in a logical order (most to least important or vice versa). Select the facts to support your reasons. Exchange letters with a partner; read each other's letters and determine if the arguments are clear, convincing, and well supported. If not, revise accordingly.

3. Write at least one paragraph describing your reaction to this selection. How do you feel about the information presented in the selection? Did the selection open your mind to any new ideas? Do you think the writer is exaggerating? Explain.

SELECTION THREE

Before Reading

Jane Goodall began observing and writing about chimpanzees in Tanzania, Africa, in the early 1960s. Her work was not readily accepted by animal behaviorists who considered it nonscientific to do qualitative rather than quantitative research. Nevertheless, an enormous amount has been learned about chimps as a result of her work. This article appeared in the *New York Times Magazine*.

1. As a class, brainstorm a list of things that you know about chimpanzees or that come to mind when you think of chimpanzees.
2. What type of plea do you think Jane Goodall makes?

NOTE: This article is long. If desired, it can be read in two parts: paragraphs 1 to 23 and paragraphs 24 to 46.

A PLEA FOR THE CHIMPS

by Jane Goodall

1 The chimpanzee is more like us, genetically, than any other animal. It is because of similarities in physiology, in biochemistry, in the immune system, that medical science makes use of the living bodies of chimpanzees in its search for cures and vaccines for a variety of human diseases.

2 There are also behavioral, psychological and emotional similarities between chimpanzees and humans, resemblances so striking that they raise a serious ethical question: are we justified in using an animal so close to us—an animal, moreover, that is highly endangered in its African forest home—as a human substitute in medical experimentation?

3 In the long run, we can hope that scientists will find ways of exploring human physiology and disease, and of testing cures and vaccines, that do not depend on the use of living animals of any sort. A number of steps in this direction already have been taken, prompted in large part by a growing public awareness of the suffering that is being inflicted on millions of animals. More and more people are beginning to realize that nonhuman animals—even rats and guinea pigs—are not just unfeeling machines but are capable of enjoying their lives, and of feeling fear, pain and despair.

4 But until alternatives have been found, medical science will continue to use animals in the battle against human disease and suffering. And some of those animals will continue to be chimpanzees.

5 Because they share with us 99 percent of their genetic material, chimpanzees can be infected with some human diseases that do not infect other animals. They are currently being used in research on the nature of hepatitis non-A non-B, for example, and they continue to play a major role in the development of vaccines against hepatitis B.

6 Many biomedical laboratories are looking to the chimpanzee to help them in the race to find a

vaccine against acquired immune deficiency syndrome. Chimpanzees are not good models for AIDS research; although the AIDS virus stays alive and replicates within the chimpanzee's bloodstream, no chimp has yet come down with the disease itself. Nevertheless, many of the scientists involved argue that only by using chimpanzees can potential vaccines be safely tested.

7   Given the scientists' professed need for animals in research, let us turn aside from the sensitive ethical issue of whether chimpanzees should be used in medical research, and consider a more important issue: how are we treating the chimpanzees that are actually being used?

8   Just after Christmas I watched, with shock, anger and anguish, a videotape—made by an animal rights group during a raid—revealing the conditions in a large biomedical research laboratory, under contract to the National Institutes of Health, in which various primates, including chimpanzees, are maintained. In late March, I was given permission to visit the facility.

9   It was a visit I shall never forget. Room after room was lined with small, bare cages, stacked one above the other, in which monkeys circled round and round and chimpanzees sat huddled, far gone in depression and despair.

10   Young chimpanzees, 3 or 4 years old, were crammed, two together, into tiny cages measuring 22 inches by 22 inches and only 24 inches high. They could hardly turn around. Not yet part of any experiment, they had been confined in these cages for more than three months.

11   The chimps had each other for comfort, but they would not remain together for long. Once they are infected, probably with hepatitis, they will be separated and placed in another cage. And there they will remain, living in conditions of severe sensory deprivation, for the next several years. During that time, they will become insane.

12   A juvenile female rocked from side to side, sealed off from the outside world behind the glass doors of her metal isolation chamber. She was in semidarkness. All she could hear was the incessant roar of air rushing through vents into her prison.

13   In order to demonstrate the "good" relationship the lab's caretaker had with this chimpanzee, one of the scientists told him to lift her from the cage. The caretaker opened the door. She sat, unmoving. He reached in. She did not greet him—nor did he greet her. As if drugged, she allowed him to take her out. She sat motionless in his arms. He did not speak to her, she did not look at him. He touched her lips briefly. She did not respond. He returned her to her cage. She sat again on the bars of the floor. The door closed.

14   I shall be haunted forever by her eyes, and by the eyes of the other infant chimpanzees I saw that day. Have you ever looked into the eyes of a person who, stressed beyond endurance, has given up, succumbed utterly to the crippling helplessness of despair? I once saw a little African boy, whose whole family had been killed during the fighting in Burundi. He too looked out at the world, unseeing, from dull, blank eyes.

15   Though this particular laboratory may be one of the worst, from what I have learned, most of the other biomedical animal-research facilities are not much better. Yet only when one has some understanding of the true nature of the chimpanzee can the cruelty of these captive conditions be fully understood.

16   Chimpanzees are very social by nature. Bonds between individuals, particularly between family members and close friends, can be affectionate, supportive, and can endure throughout their lives. The accidental separation of two friendly individuals may cause them intense distress. Indeed, the death of a mother may be such a psychological blow to her child that even if the child is 5 years old and no longer dependent on its mother's milk, it may pine away and die.

17   It is impossible to overemphasize the importance of friendly physical contact for the well-being of the chimpanzee. Again and again one can watch a frightened or tense individual relax if she is patted, kissed or embraced reassuringly by a companion. Social grooming, which provides hours of close contact, is undoubtedly the single most important social activity.

18   Chimpanzees in their natural habitat[1] are active for much of the day. They travel extensively

---

1 habitat   the environment in which an animal or plant usually lives

within their territory, which can be as large as 50 square kilometers for a community of about 50 individuals. If they hear other chimpanzees calling as they move through the forest, or anticipate arriving at a good food source, they typically break into excited charging displays, racing along the ground, hurling sticks and rocks and shaking the vegetation. Youngsters, particularly, are full of energy, and spend long hours playing with one another or by themselves, leaping through the branches and gamboling along the ground. Adults sometimes join these games. Bunches of fruit, twigs and rocks may be used as toys.

19   Chimpanzees enjoy comfort. They construct sleeping platforms each night, using a multitude of leafy twigs to make their beds soft. Often, too, they make little "pillows" on which to rest during a midday siesta.

20   Chimps are highly intelligent. They display cognitive abilities that were, until recently, thought to be unique to humans. They are capable of cross-model transfer of information—that is, they can identify by touch an object they previously have only seen, and vice versa. They are capable of reasoned thought, generalization, abstraction and symbolic representation. They have some concept of self. They have excellent memories and can, to some extent, plan for the future. They show a capacity for intentional communication that depends, in part, on their ability to understand the motives of the individuals with whom they are communicating.

21   Chimpanzees are capable of empathy and altruistic behavior. They show emotions that are undoubtedly similar, if not identical, to human emotions—joy, pleasure, contentment, anxiety, fear and rage. They even have a sense of humor.

22   The chimpanzee child and the human child are alike in many ways: in their capacity for endless romping and fun; their curiosity; their ability to learn by observation, imitation and practice; and, above all, in their need for reassurance and love. When young chimpanzees are brought up in a human home and treated like human children, they learn to eat at table, to help themselves to snacks from the refrigerator, to sort and put away cutlery, to brush their teeth, to play with dolls, to

switch on the television and select a program that interests them and watch it.

23   Young chimpanzees can easily learn over 200 signs of the American language of the deaf and use these signs to communicate meaningfully with humans and with one another. One youngster, in the laboratory of Dr. Roger S. Fouts, a psychologist at Central Washington University, has picked up 68 signs from four older signing chimpanzee companions, with no human teaching. The chimp uses the signs in communication with other chimpanzees and with humans.

24   The chimpanzee facilities in most biomedical research laboratories allow for the expression of almost none of these activities and behaviors. They provide little—if anything—more than the warmth, food and water, and veterinary care required to sustain life. The psychological and emotional needs of these creatures are rarely catered to, and often not even acknowledged.

25   In most labs the chimpanzees are housed individually, one chimp to a cage, unless they are part of a breeding program. The standard size of each cage is about 25 feet square and about 6 feet high. In one facility, a cage described in the catalogue as "large," designed for a chimpanzee of up to 25 kilograms (55 pounds), measures 2 feet 6 inches by 3 feet 8 inches, with a height of 5 feet 4 inches. Federal requirements for cage size are dependent on body size; infant chimpanzees, who are the most active, are often imprisoned in the smallest cages.

26   In most labs, the chimpanzees cannot even lie with their arms and legs outstretched. They are not let out to exercise. There is seldom anything for them to do other than eat, and then only when food is brought. The caretakers are usually too busy to pay much attention to individual chimpanzees. The cages are bleak and sterile, with bars above, bars below, bars on every side. There is no comfort in them, no bedding. The chimps, infected with human diseases, will often feel sick and miserable.

27   What of the human beings who administer these facilities—the caretakers, veterinarians and scientists who work at them? If they are decent, compassionate people, how can they condone, or

even tolerate, the kind of conditions I have described?

28 They are, I believe, victims of a system that was set up long before the cognitive abilities and emotional needs of chimpanzees were understood. Newly employed staff members, equipped with a normal measure of compassion, may well be sickened by what they see. And, in fact, many of them do quit their jobs, unable to endure the suffering they see inflicted on the animals yet feeling powerless to help.

29 But others stay on and gradually come to accept the cruelty, believing (or forcing themselves to believe) that it is an inevitable part of the struggle to reduce human suffering. Some become hard and callous in the process, in Shakespeare's words, "all pity choked with custom of fell deeds."

30 A handful of compassionate and dedicated caretakers and veterinarians are fighting to improve the lot of the animals in their care. Vets are often in a particularly difficult position, for if they stand firm and try to uphold high standards of humane care, they will not always be welcome in the lab.

31 Many of the scientists believe that a bleak, sterile and restricting environment is necessary for their research. The cages must be small, the scientists maintain, because otherwise it is too difficult to treat the chimpanzees—to inject them, to draw their blood or to anesthetize them. Moreover, they are less likely to hurt themselves in small cages.

32 The cages must also be barren, with no bedding or toys, say the scientists. This way, the chimpanzees are less likely to pick up diseases or parasites. Also, if things are lying about, the cages are harder to clean.

33 And the chimpanzees must be kept in isolation, the scientists believe, to avoid the risk of cross-infection, particularly in hepatitis research.

34 Finally, of course, bigger cages, social groups and elaborate furnishings require more space, more caretakers—and more money. Perhaps, then, if we are to believe these researchers, it is not possible to improve conditions for chimpanzees imprisoned in biomedical research laboratories.

35 I believe not only that it is possible, but that improvements are absolutely necessary. If we do not do something to help these creatures, we make a mockery of the whole concept of justice.

36 Perhaps the most important way we can improve the quality of life for the laboratory chimps is to increase the number of carefully trained caretakers. These people should be selected for their understanding of animal behavior and their compassion and respect for, and dedication to their charges. Each caretaker, having established a relationship of trust with the chimpanzees in his care, should be allowed to spend time with the animals over and above that required for cleaning the cages and providing the animals with food and water.

37 It has been shown that a chimpanzee who has a good relationship with his caretaker will cooperate calmly during experimental procedures, rather than react with fear or anger. At the Dutch Primate Research Center at Rijswijk, for example, some chimpanzees have been trained to leave their group cage on command and move into small, single cages for treatment. At the Stanford Primate Center in California, a number of chimpanzees were taught to extend their arms for the drawing of blood. In return they were given a food reward.

38 Much can be done to alleviate the pain and stress felt by younger chimpanzees during experimental procedures. A youngster, for example, can be treated when in the presence of a trusted human friend. Experiments have shown that young chimps react with high levels of distress if subjected to mild electric shocks when alone, but show almost no fear or pain when held by a sympathetic caretaker.

39 What about cage size? Here we should emulate the animal-protection regulations that already exist in Switzerland. These laws stipulate that a cage must be, at minimum, about 20 meters square and 3 meters high for pairs of chimpanzees.

40 The chimpanzees should never be housed alone unless this is an essential part of the experimental procedure. For chimps in solitary confinement, particularly youngsters, three to four hours of friendly interaction with a caretaker should be mandatory. A chimp taking part in hepatitis research, in which the risk of cross-infection is, I am told, great, can be provided with a companion of a compatible species if it doesn't infringe on existing regulations—a rhesus monkey, for example, which cannot catch or pass on the disease.

41   For healthy chimpanzees there should be little risk of infection from bedding and toys. Stress and depression, however, can have deleterious effects on their health. It is known that clinically depressed humans are more prone to a variety of physiological disorders, and heightened stress can interfere with immune function. Given the chimpanzee's similarities to humans, it is not surprising that the chimp in a typical laboratory, alone in his bleak cage, is an easy prey to infections and parasites.

42   Thus, the chimpanzee also should be provided with a rich and stimulating environment. Climbing apparatus should be obligatory. There should be many objects for them to play with or otherwise manipulate. A variety of simple devices designed to alleviate boredom could be produced quite cheaply. Unexpected food items will elicit great pleasure. If a few simple buttons in each cage were connected to a computer terminal, it would be possible for the chimpanzees to feel they at least have some control over their world— if one button produced a grape when pressed, another a drink, or another a video picture. (The Canadian Council on Animal Care recommends the provision of television for primates in solitary confinement, or other means of enriching their environment.)

43   Without doubt, it will be considerably more costly to maintain chimpanzees in the manner I have outlined. Should we begrudge them the extra dollars? We take from them their freedom, their health and often their lives. Surely, the least we can do is try to provide them with some of the things that could make their imprisonment more bearable.

44   There are hopeful signs. I was immensely grateful to officials of the National Institutes of Health for allowing me to visit the primate facility, enabling me to see the conditions there and judge them for myself. And I was even more grateful for the fact that they gave me a great deal of time for serious discussions of the problem. Doors were opened and a dialogue begun. All who were present at the meetings agreed that, in light of present knowledge, it is indeed necessary to give chimpanzees a better deal in the labs.

45   Plans are now under way for a major conference to discuss ways and means of bringing about such change. Sponsored by the N.I.H. and organized by Roger Fouts (who toured the lab with me) and myself, this conference—which will be held in mid-December at the Jane Goodall Institute in Tucson, Ariz.—will bring together for the first time administrators, scientists and animal technicians from various primate facilities around the country and from overseas. The conference will, we hope, lead to the formulation of new, humane standards for the maintenance of chimpanzees in the laboratory.

46   I have had the privilege of working among wild, free chimpanzees for more than 26 years. I have gained a deep understanding of chimpanzee nature. Chimpanzees have given me so much in my life. The least I can do is to speak out for the hundreds of chimpanzees who, right now, sit hunched, miserable and without hope, staring out with dead eyes from their metal prisons. They cannot speak for themselves.

Comprehension Check

Part 1, Paragraphs 1–23

1. Why are chimpanzees used in medical research?
2. What is Goodall's position regarding the use of animals, particularly chimpanzees, in research?
3. What is the immediate question the author explores in this article?
4. What did the author see at the primate facility that was under contract to the National Institutes of Health?
5. How are young chimpanzees similar to young humans?

Part 2, Paragraphs 24–46

6. What happens to chimpanzees when they have to live in the sterile laboratory environment that Goodall describes?
7. Why don't the people who work at primate research labs see the conditions as inadequate, unnatural, and cruel?
8. What dilemma do humane veterinarians, those who want appropriate and good conditions for animals, find themselves in?
9. What suggestions does Goodall make for improving the conditions of chimps in labs?
10. What was the author's purpose for writing this article?

Sharing Your Thoughts

1. List the characteristics of chimpanzees in a natural setting. How does a laboratory setting affect each of these natural characteristics?
2. What evidence do you find in this article to support the quote by Charles Darwin on the introductory page?
3. How do you think you would react if you worked in the type of primate lab that Goodall describes?
4. What is your opinion of using animals in medical research? List the pros and cons. Why is this a controversial issue?

Vocabulary

A. Content Vocabulary

Complete the following statements about chimps with words from the list. Use each word only once. Change the form of verbs if the grammar of the sentence requires it.

alleviate	**bleak**	**bonds**
brought up	**callous**	**condone**
confined	**insane**	**justified**
resemblance		

1. Jane Goodall raises the question of whether we are _____ in using chimpanzees in research. When chimps are _____ like human children, their behavioral _____ to humans is remarkable.

2. Like people, chimps are sociable and affectionate, and in their natural habitat they establish strong _____ with other chimps.

3. Unfortunately, in laboratory settings they are _____ to small cages with inadequate space and nothing to play with. This _____ environment provides no more than is needed to keep them alive.

4. Some people who work in labs become hard and _____ about these conditions and are not concerned about the chimps' welfare. Other employees cannot _____ these conditions and, unable to change them, quit their jobs.

5. Chimps cannot endure such deprivation; some go _____.

6. Goodall argues that it would not take much effort to improve conditions and _____ the suffering of the chimps.

B. Word Analysis

Locate the following words in the selection. Check the context in which they appear. Divide them into their meaningful parts. What is the meaning of the whole? What does each part contribute? Use a dictionary if necessary.

1. caretaker (¶13, ¶36, ¶37, ¶38, ¶40) _____

2. motionless (¶13) _____

3. overemphasize (¶17) _____

4. outstretched (¶26) _____

5. powerless (¶28) _____

6. handful (¶30) _____

7. bearable (¶43) _____

Text Analysis

A. Text Organization

Complete the information for the introductory paragraphs.

Paragraphs 1–7: Introduction

1. States the topic, which is _____

2. Raises the question of whether _____

3. States the purpose of the whole article, which is to _____

_____

4. Gets the reader interested by _____

To reveal how well-organized this article is, describe the contribution each set of paragraphs listed below makes to the whole piece of writing. If possible, locate one sentence that states the main idea of that set of paragraphs.

Paragraphs

¶8–14: _____

¶15–23: _____

¶24–26: _____

¶27–30: _____

¶31–34: _____

¶35–43: _____

¶44–45: _____

¶46: _____

B. The Grammar-Meaning Connection

The **passive voice** (Text Analysis, p. 127) is often used in scientific writing. In paragraph 3, for example, we find:

> A number of steps in this direction already *have been taken*, prompted in large part by a growing public awareness of the suffering that *is being inflicted* on millions of animals.

Locate other examples of the passive voice in paragraphs 4, 5, 6, 7, 10, 22, 36, 37, 38, 40, 42. What are the reasons for using this grammatical structure in scientific writing?

Writing Task

1. Write a letter to the director of the primate lab Goodall visited, making recommendations to improve conditions for the animals and explaining why improving the conditions is important. Before beginning to write, list your recommendations as they come to mind, and put them in a logical order (most to least important or vice versa). For each recommendation, list your reasons. In thinking of your reasons, keep in mind cause and effect: Bad conditions lead to bad effects. Remember, you want to convince this person to take some action. After drafting your letter, exchange letters with a partner; read each other's writing and determine if the reasons are clear, convincing, and where possible, supported by facts. If not, revise accordingly.

2. Write a letter to the editor of a newspaper in which you are either for or against the use of animals in research. Before beginning to write, list the reasons for your position, and put them in a logical order (most to least important or vice versa). Remember, you want to convince the public to agree with your position. After drafting your letter, exchange letters with a partner; read each other's writing and determine if the reasons are clear, convincing, and where possible, supported by facts. If not, revise accordingly.

3. Write a one- or two-paragraph summary of this article using your work in Text Analysis A as a guide. Refer to Writing Task, p. 72 to refresh your memory about writing summaries.

SELECTION FOUR

Before Reading

This is a true story that appeared in *Reader's Digest*. In addition to many magazine articles, Jo Coudert has written novels and plays. Animals are one of her particular interests.

1. As a class, brainstorm a list of things that come to mind when you think of pigs.
2. You read something about pet therapy in Selection One, p. 160, and learned that bonds with animals can benefit people. Preview this story. How do you think the pig in the story can benefit his owner?

The Pig Who Loved People

by Jo Coudert

He wasn't what you'd expect in a pet—or even in a pig

1 THE PHONE RANG at Bette and Don Atty's house in Johnstown, N.Y. It was a friend calling to ask if they'd like a pig.

2 "His name is Lord Bacon. He's four months old, and he's smarter than any dog," the friend said to Don. "He adores people, and with Bette working at home, I thought she might like the company."

3 For a year Don had stood by helplessly as his wife suffered from agoraphobia, a fear of open spaces and crowds, apparently triggered by stress at work. Even after she had quit her job, just going to the local mall could bring on an anxiety attack. She couldn't leave the house unless Don was with her.

4 Now Bette was standing nearby, overhearing the conversation, and she shook her head no. "Think about it," Don urged. "It'll be good for you to have a special pet."

5 Bette recalled reading in one of the many psychology books she had consulted about her condition that caring for another creature strengthens a person's inner being. *But could a pig help my nerves?*

6 "All right," she said reluctantly. "I suppose some farmer'll take him if we have to get rid of him."

7 Two hours later the owner delivered Lord Bacon in a wire cage. He was a miniature variety who stood 14 inches high and 24 inches long. Shaped like a root-beer keg on stilts, he weighed 45 pounds.

8 Don laughed when he saw him. "That snout looks like he ran into a wall doing 90!" Even Bette joined in: "I've got an old hairbrush with better-looking bristles than these."

9   When the cage was opened, Lord Bacon trotted out wagging his straight tail, looked around and headed for Bette. She knelt to greet him. He heaved himself up on his hind legs, laid his head on her shoulder and kissed her on the cheek with his leathery snout. She looked at the pig and, for the first time in a long time, smiled.

10   The rest of the day, Bette and Don watched as the pig bustled about, exploring the house. He sat up on his bottom and begged for a treat. He gently chewed on Don's beard when Don put him on his lap. When they whistled, he came to them.

11   That night the pig tried to follow Bette and Don upstairs, but with his potbelly he couldn't negotiate the steps. Bette made up a bed for him in the kitchen, then sat on the floor and stroked him. "It's all right. We'll be here in the morning," she told him.

12   The next morning, instead of dreading having to face another day, Bette was actually eager to see her new pet. Lord Bacon scrambled to greet her and rubbed against her leg. It was like being massaged with a Brillo[1] pad. From then on, Bette was destined always to have this red rash of affection on her leg.

13   After breakfast the pig followed Bette into the small home office where she prepared tax returns, and settled down beside her desk. Bette found that when she grew edgy, if she reached down and petted him and said a few words, it made her feel calmer.

14   Very soon the pig was a member of the household. When Don brought home a doggy bed to put next to Bette's desk, the animal looked it over and decided that, with some alterations, it would do nicely. He planted his hoofs, ripped open the tartan pillow, pulled out the stuffing and then crawled inside the cover, content.

15   One evening when Bette and Don drew up their armchairs to watch television, the pig pushed a chair over with his snout and sat up in front of it, as if to say, "Hey, I want to be part of this too." As he watched figures on the screen, his head bobbed from side to side.

16   Lord Bacon disliked loud noises. Bette's phone hung on a post beside her desk, and the pig figured out that it stopped ringing when Bette picked it up. If Bette wasn't there to answer immediately, he yanked the receiver off the hook, stood over it and grunted into the mouthpiece.

17   *I wonder what my clients must think*, Bette thought, only half amused.

18   One day a client came to see her about his tax return and was so charmed by her pet that he returned later with his children. Soon other neighbors were stopping by to see Lord Bacon. Finding this to be too formidable a name for such a friendly, small pig, the kids took to calling him Pigger, and Pigger he became from then on.

19   Once when a small group had gathered, Bette felt herself growing tense. Realizing they were all too fascinated by the pig to look at her, however, she began to enjoy the company.

20   "It's fun coming home from work now," Don told Bette. "The first thing you say is, 'Guess what Pigger did today. He pulled the blankets off the bed,' or whatever, and we get to laughing and it feels like when we were first married."

21   "You laugh," Bette said, "but it wasn't so funny when he locked me out this morning." Pigger had followed Bette in and out of the house and had watched her close the door behind her. That morning as he went inside, he took the initiative

---

1 **Brillo**   a brand of steel wool used for scrubbing pots

himself—except that the door was on the latch and his mistress was still outside. Luckily, she had a spare key.

22 More and more Bette realized that Pigger was a superb mimic and would imitate whatever she and Don did. If she shook her head, Pigger would too. If she twirled, Pigger would twirl. Soon Bette was teaching tricks to her pig that few dogs would learn. His reward was dog biscuits.

23 In Pigger's company Bette was beginning to be more like her old self—so much so that her father tried to persuade her to bring Pigger to a senior-citizens meeting. Bette demurred. "Pigger can run like the wind and feint like a soccer player," she said, "but he hates a leash. He plants his feet and won't walk. I'd look pretty silly, wouldn't I, a grown lady dragging a pig?"

24 The next night Don came home with a baby stroller. "What's that?" Bette demanded.

25 "It's a pigmobile, so you can take Pigger to the seniors' meeting." Pigger loved the stroller. He sat up in it, blanket around his shoulders, green visor on his head, as Don pushed him about.

26 Bette finally agreed to take Pigger to the meeting. Her nerves tightened as she drove up. She turned off the motor and sat in the car, trembling. She stroked Pigger, seat-belted beside her, and felt calmer. *I've got to conquer my fears,* she told herself. *I can't spend the rest of my life being afraid.* She struggled out, settled Pigger in the pigmobile and wheeled him into the building.

27 The seniors were intrigued. "What is *that* ?" they asked. Bette lifted Pigger to the floor. He immediately singled out the oldest woman and trotted over to nuzzle her cheek. The other seniors broke into laughter and crowded around to pet him.

28 Bette found herself answering questions, at first haltingly, then with enthusiasm. She told the seniors that pigs are smarter than dogs and twice as clean. "Pigger loves it when I put him into the bathtub once a week for a good scrub," she said.

29 To show off how smart he was, she called to Pigger and told him he was a handsome hog. Pigger strutted about proudly. Then she scolded him for being piggy. Pigger lowered his head in shame and, for good measure, let his tongue hang out. His audience cheered.

30 Word got around, and soon Bette and Pigger set out on what Don referred to as pig gigs. At a nearby nursing home, she wheeled Pigger from room to room to visit with the patients. In one, an old woman sat staring at her hands in her lap. Suddenly her head came up, and her face cracked in the beginning of a smile. She held out her hands, then wrapped her arms around herself. "What is it?" Bette asked. "Do you want to hug him?" An aide whispered to Bette that the woman had not smiled, spoken or taken an interest in anything since her husband died years before.

31 Bette picked up Pigger and let the old woman pet him. Pigger stayed as quiet as could be, with his ears cocked and his mouth drawn up in a grin.

32 On later visits, when Pigger came through the front door in his pigmobile, the call would go out: "Pigger's here!" A commotion would start in the halls—the squeak of wheelchairs, the tap-tap of walkers, the shuffle of slippered feet—as residents hurried to see him.

33 The more Bette saw of sick and helpless people, the more thoughts of her own illness faded away. "I used to hate myself," she told Don, "but now I'm beginning to thank God every day for being me. Pigger is my therapy."

34   One day it occurred to Bette that Pigger might carry a message to schoolchildren. Soon she faced an audience of youngsters and invited them to ask Pigger if he would ever take drugs. Pigger shook his head emphatically while grunting and snorting disgust at the idea. Asked if he'd stay in school and study hard, Pigger bowed low and nodded his head.

35   The children were curious about what Pigger liked to eat. "Dog biscuits, of course. Also beans, corn, carrots, apples and Cheerios.[2] But the two things Pigger loves best are popcorn and ice cream. At the Dairy Queen, he gets his own dish of ice cream, which he eats neatly from a spoon," Bette explained.

36   The kids' comments about Pigger ranged from: "He feels like a pot scrubber," to "He has cute ears," to "He looks like my uncle." One little boy, hugging Pigger, said wistfully, "I wish you could come home with me. I know you'd love me." Bette had to hold firmly on the leash to keep Pigger from following the boy.

37   Sometimes Bette and Don would be shopping in the supermarket, and from the next aisle a child's voice would ring out: "There's the pig's mother and father!" An embarrassed parent would be dragged over to be introduced to "the pig's family."

38   When strangers stopped, stared, and asked what Pigger was, Don explained, "To us, he's a pig, but to him, he's people." Sometimes Don quoted Winston Churchill:

39   "Dogs look up to us. Cats look down on us. Pigs treat us as equals." And Pigger would confirm this by grunting.

    In one year Bette and Pigger made 95 public appearances together, mostly before old people and children. Bette handled each occasion with poise and flair.

40   In July, Pigger was invited to attend the 1990 Fulton County, New York, Senior Citizens Annual Picnic. The day before, Bette opened the back door. "Why don't you go out and cool off in your pool, Pigger?" she suggested.

41   Pigger trotted into the yard, and Bette went back to work. Half an hour later, something made her check on him. He was lying in his favorite napping spot in the shade of a barberry bush. He wasn't breathing.

42   Bette felt panic coming on. She began to wail. *No, I mustn't carry on. Pigger never liked loud noises.* She phoned the police to come take his body. She called two friends to keep her company until Don got home. Then she knew she was going to make it.

43   Pigger had succumbed to a pulmonary aneurysm. But Bette has her own theory on why he died. "I think Pigger had a heart so big, it just burst with all that love. He helped me become my old self, and he brightened so many other lives. There'll never be another Pigger."

---

2 **Cheerios**   a brand of dry breakfast cereal

Comprehension Check

1. Why did Bette and Don Atty adopt a pig?
2. Describe how Lord Bacon/Pigger reacted to Bette and Don. How did he integrate himself into their household and their lives? What kind of personality did he have?
3. What was the pigmobile? Why did they use it?
4. How did other people, especially elderly people and children, react to Pigger?
5. How did Bette change as a result of Pigger's presence?

Sharing Your Thoughts

1. Why is Pigger more successful at helping Bette than Don is?
2. What is your opinion of the relationship between Pigger and Don and Bette Atty? Would your reaction be different if Pigger were some other animal? Explain.
3. How do you think Pigger felt about helping people?
4. What purpose do you think the writer might have had in telling the story of Pigger?
5. What are other types of true stories that we find in newspapers and magazines? Why do you think they are told?
6. How would Pigger's life on a factory farm differ from his life as a pet therapist? Consider living conditions, health, food, the bond with people, and so forth.

Vocabulary

Content Vocabulary

Complete the following statements about the story with words from the list. Use each word only once. Change the form of verbs if the grammar of the sentence requires it.

creature	dread	edgy
face	get rid of	handle
mimic	reluctantly	reward
triggered		

1. Bette Atty had a condition called agoraphobia, which is a fear of open spaces and crowds. Her condition was apparently _____ by stress at work, and Bette had to quit her job and work at home.

2. The Attys adopted Pigger because Bette had read that taking care of another _____ could be therapeutic.

3. But a pig? Bette wasn't so sure, but she _____ agreed to give it a try. If it didn't work out and they had to _____ the pig, they figured a farmer would take him.

4. Before adopting this pet, Bette used to _____ each day, but after Pigger's arrival she looked forward to seeing him every morning.

5. Pigger was an entertaining companion; he was a superb _____ and imitated whatever Bette and Don did; he performed tricks and got dog biscuits as a(n) _____.

6. Pigger's presence also calmed Bette when she felt nervous or _____. With her pet at her side, Bette was confident enough to _____ groups of school children and the elderly.

7. Pigger really knew how to _____ people and did most of the work. As a result, Bette felt more relaxed and gradually overcame her condition.

Text Analysis

A. Figurative Language

Find **similes** that describe Pigger in paragraphs 7, 8, 12, and 35. Explain these comparisons in your own words. Why are they effective descriptions of Pigger?

B. Nonfiction Stories

"The Pig Who Loved People" is about something that really happened, written in story form. Like any well-told story, it has the elements of fiction: a **setting, characters**, and a **plot** (Elements of Fiction, p. 81).

1. What is the setting? Is it important to the story?
2. Who are the characters? What important details does the writer give you about them? What role does each play?
3. What is the plot of this story? What is the problem? Where do you think the plot reaches its highest point of interest, or climax? What happens in the resolution?

Writing Task

1. Write a true story, one to two pages long, about how a person you know faced a problem or challenge in life and dealt with it, whether successfully or unsuccessfully.

   To get ideas for the story, think of a person who has faced a problem. Freewrite about the problem, looking for a conflict in the person's life that can be the basis of your story. What are the opposing forces? If this idea does not work, repeat your freewriting for another person.

   When you have decided on the person whose story you will tell, list details about his or her personality and feelings about what happened to him or her. Note details you might want to give about the setting of the story.

   Exchange first drafts of your story with a classmate. Read each other's writing and try to visualize the setting, characters, and the events in the story. Write questions on your partner's paper where something is not clear. Try to improve your story, taking your partner's questions into consideration.

2. Write a three- to five-paragraph composition in which you use what you learned about pet therapy in Selection One, p. 160, to explain how Pigger helped Bette Atty.

   - In one or two introductory paragraphs, explain what pet therapy is and how pet therapy works.

   - In the body paragraphs, describe Bette's condition and how Pigger helped her and others.

   - In a concluding paragraph, provide a final comment about Pigger and how he functioned as a pet therapist.

SELECTION FIVE

Before Reading

D. H. Lawrence (1885–1930) was a prolific British writer, best known for his novels *Sons and Lovers* (1913) and *Lady Chatterley's Lover* (1928). Literary critic Diana Trilling noted in the introduction to *The Portable D. H. Lawrence* (Penguin Books) that he "challenge(d) our accepted ways of thinking and feeling" (p. 5) and that he had an "acute awareness of non-human life" (p. 18).

1. As a class, brainstorm a list of things that come to mind when you think of snakes.

2. How do you think a poem about a snake might relate to the human-animal bond?

3. This is a narrative poem; it tells a story. What are the basic elements of fiction that you might find in a narrative poem?

Snake

by D. H. Lawrence

1   A snake came to my water-trough
On a hot, hot day, and I in pyjamas for the heat,
To drink there.

2   In the deep, strange-scented shade of the great dark
      carob tree
I came down the steps with my pitcher
And must wait, must stand and wait, for there he was at
      the trough before me.

3   He reached down from a fissure in the earth-wall in the
      gloom
And trailed his yellow-brown slackness soft-bellied
      down, over the edge of the stone trough
And rested his throat upon the stone bottom,
And where the water had dripped from the tap, in a
      small clearness,
He sipped with his straight mouth,
Softly drank through his straight gums, into his slack
      long body,
Silently.

4   Someone was before me at my water-trough,
    And I, like a second-comer, waiting.

5   He lifted his head from his drinking, as cattle do,
    And looked at me vaguely, as drinking cattle do,
    And flickered his two-forked tongue from his lips, and
        mused a moment,
    And stooped and drank a little more,
    Being earth-brown, earth-golden from the burning
        bowels of the earth
    On the day of Sicilian[1] July, with Etna[2] smoking.

6   The voice of my education said to me
    He must be killed,
    For in Sicily the black black snakes are innocent, the
        gold are venomous.

7   And voices in me said, If you were a man,
    You would take a stick and break him now, and finish
        him off.

8   But must I confess how I liked him,
    How glad I was he had come like a guest in quiet, to
        drink at my water-trough
    And depart peaceful, pacified, and thankless
    Into the burning bowels of this earth?

9   Was it cowardice, that I dared not kill him?
    Was it perversity, that I longed to talk to him?
    Was it humility, to feel so honoured?
    I felt so honoured.

10 And yet those voices:
    If you were not afraid, you would kill him!

11 And truly I was afraid, I was most afraid,
    But even so, honoured still more
    That he should seek my hospitality
    From out the dark door of the secret earth.

12 He drank enough
    And lifted his head, dreamily, as one who has drunken,
    And flickered his tongue like a forked night on the air,
        so black,

---

[1] **Sicilian**   referring to Sicily, a large island that is part of Italy

[2] **Etna**   a volcano on the island of Sicily

Seeming to lick his lips,
And looked around like a god, unseeing, into the air,
And slowly turned his head,
And slowly, very slowly, as if thrice adream³
Proceeded to draw his slow length curving round
And climb again the broken bank of my wall-face.

13 And as he put his head into that dreadful hole,
And as he slowly drew up, snake-easing his shoulders,
and entered further,
A sort of horror, a sort of protest against his withdrawing
into that horrid black hole.
Deliberately going into the blackness, and slowly drawing
himself after,
Overcame me now his back was turned.

14 I looked round, I put down my pitcher,
I picked up a clumsy log
And threw it at the water-trough with a clatter.

15 I think it did not hit him;
But suddenly that part of him that was left behind convulsed
in undignified haste,
Writhed like lightning, and was gone
Into the black hole,the earth-lipped fissure in the wall-front
At which, in the intense still noon, I stared with fascination.

16 And immediately I regretted it.
I thought how paltry, how vulgar, what a mean act!
I despised myself and the voices of my accursed human
education.

17 And I thought of the albatross,⁴
And I wished he would come back, my snake.

18 For he seemed to me again like a king,
Like a king in exile, uncrowned in the underworld,
Now due to be crowned again.
And so, I missed my chance with one of the lords
Of life.
And I have something to expiate:
A pettiness.

---

³ thrice adream   three times asleep; perhaps in a very deep dreamlike state

⁴ albatross   refers to the poem "The Rime of the Ancient Mariner" by Samuel Taylor Coleridge in which the mariner, for
no reason, shoots an albatross, a large sea bird that is supposed to bring good luck. As a consequence he suffers a
terrible curse.

Comprehension Check

1. What is the setting of this poem?
2. What happens in the poem?
3. Why did the speaker think he should kill the snake?
4. Why didn't the speaker kill the snake?
5. What did the speaker do instead of killing the snake?
6. How did the speaker feel about his action?

Sharing Your Thoughts

1. What is the physical setting and mood in stanzas 1 to 5? What change takes place beginning with stanza 6? What is the reason for the change?
2. Why was the speaker afraid? Why was he honored?
3. Reread the last four lines of the poem. What chance did the speaker miss? How do you think he expiated his action?
4. For you, what is the message or meaning of this poem?
5. What are some of the things you do because the "voice of your education" tells you to (i.e., out of habit without giving it much thought)?
6. Have you ever had the experience of realizing that something you were taught to do might not be correct? Do you think that this happens often? Why or why not? What problems or benefits can result from not following the "voice of (one's) education"?
7. What does this poem suggest about Lawrence's views of nonhuman life?

Text Analysis

A. Stanzas

Lawrence goes back and forth between describing what happens and his thoughts about it. Which does he do in each group of stanzas?

STANZAS

1–5: _____

6–11: _____

12–15: _____

16–18: _____

B. Figurative Language

Poets sometimes give human qualities to animals, objects, or abstract ideas. This figurative use of language is called **personification**. For example, if you read the poem in Unit Two, "Those Winter Sundays," the speaker personified the house when he referred to its "chronic angers" because people, not houses, get angry.

1. Find the words and phrases the poet uses to show that he views the snake as human*like*, king*like*, and god*like*.

2. Why did he personify the snake?

Writing Task

1. Write a paragraph about something you did and regretted or felt guilty about. Why did you do it? If at all, how did you expiate, or make up for, your action?

2. Write a paragraph about something questionable that people in your culture might do without thinking because they are ruled by the "voice of their education." Describe the action or behavior. How are people educated to behave that way? What is your opinion of this type of action or behavior?

A FINAL LOOK

Discussion

1. Work with a partner, in a small group, or as a whole class. Drawing on all five selections in this unit, and the photo and quote on the introductory page, discuss the focus questions.

2. How does your culture influence the way you think of animals? Consider, for example, your relationship to them and your use of animals for food.

3. Three quite different topics dealing with the human-animal bond were presented in this unit: therapy, farming, and research. Which of the three seems to you to be especially important? Why?

4. Referring to all the selections in this unit, discuss the consequences of ignoring and of nurturing the human-animal bond. What action might be taken by individuals and countries to increase the nurturing of animals and to make people more aware of the need to treat them humanely?

5. Some people like to keep exotic animals such as lions, tigers, wolves, snakes, and alligators. Do you think this is a good idea? Why or why not?

Writing

1. Have you changed any of your attitudes related to animals (e.g., about food that comes from animals, about a particular species of animal) as a result of what you have read? If so, write two or three paragraphs explaining what you learned, how it affected your attitude, and, if anything, what you plan to do about it. When you use other people's ideas, remember to give proper credit.

2. Read the quote below. Think about the selections in this unit and your own experience. Write one page in reaction to the quote.

    > Throughout history, humans have been forming relationships with other animals. Some of these relationships have been mutually beneficial, but many have served human needs or wants at the expense of the animals involved. It is important that we as humans recognize these relationships and how they affect both animals and us. If we understand that we, as humans, are also animals and share many common characteristics with other members of the animal kingdom, we will be more sensitive to the rights of animals and will consequently be capable of making more responsible decisions concerning our personal relationships with animals. (Adapted from *People and Animals, A Humane Education Curriculum Guide*, National Association for Humane and Environmental Education.)

UNIT SEVEN

Humans and Their Environment

Human beings have built dams, drained wetlands, diverted rivers, cleared brush and scrublands, and permitted overgrazing of grasslands since ancient times. But the environmental crisis we now confront is quantitatively and qualitatively different from anything before, simply because so many people have been inflicting damage on the world's ecosystem during the present century that the system as a whole—not simply its various parts—may be in danger.

– Paul Kennedy
Preparing for the Twenty-first Century

FOCUS

➤ What kinds of damage are humans doing to their environment?

➤ What are the sources of this damage? Why are people treating the environment this way?

➤ Why is economic growth needed? What are some of the dangers of totally free and unrestricted economic growth?

➤ What should the relationship between humans and the Earth be?

195

SELECTION ONE

Before Reading

The following selection was written by Jeremy Iggers for the *Minneapolis-St. Paul Star Tribune*.

1. Scan the title and headings of Selection One. What does the word *threat* mean? What do you already know about the ten major threats and their causes? Which of these threats have you been aware of in places where you have lived?

2. Scan several of the sections. What three aspects of the topic does each section cover?

---

10 Major Threats to the Environment

How people can help to reduce potential danger

By JEREMY IGGERS
Minneapolis-St. Paul Star Tribune

All the talk about global warming, the hole in the ozone layer and loss of genetic diversity can be confusing and overwhelming. Here are brief explanations of 10 major threats to the environment, including the potential danger if the trend isn't remedied and how people can respond.

Global warming

1 **The situation:** There is growing evidence that the Earth is warming because of carbon dioxide (and to a lesser extent methane) in the atmosphere. Carbon dioxide is released when fossil fuels[1] are burned. Rice paddies and livestock are significant sources of methane.

The danger: Rising temperatures could melt polar ice caps, raise sea levels and submerge coastal areas. They also could disrupt agriculture and ecosystems, resulting in desertification[2] and famine.

What we can do: Reduce carbon dioxide emissions by developing alternative energy sources such as solar power and wind energy to replace fossil fuels. Cut automotive emissions of carbon dioxide by developing more efficient engines and encouraging other means of transportation, including mass transit.

The ozone hole

2 **The situation:** The ozone layer that shields the planet from harmful ultraviolet radiation[3] is deteriorating as industrial chemicals, including chlorinated fluorocarbons (CFCs),[4] are released into the atmosphere. Jet exhaust is another significant cause of ozone depletion.

The danger: The Environmental Protection Agency announced this month that the ozone layer is being destroyed faster than previously believed. The EPA said this destruction could result in 11 million additional cases of skin cancer and 200,000 additional deaths in the United States in the next 50 years.

What we can do: Reduce CFC emissions by proper maintenance and disposal of sources such as refrigerators, air conditioners, insulating foam, chemical solvents and fire extinguishers. Support stricter controls on industrial use of CFCs.

Air pollution

3 **The situation:** Burning fossil fuels, notably gasoline, fuel oil and coal, releases particulates,[5] heavy metals (lead and cadmium), acid gases and organic contaminants into the atmosphere. These emissions can travel long distances in the upper atmosphere. Fossil-fuel combustion also creates nitrous oxide, which falls back to Earth as nitrous acid, a major component of acid rain.[6]

The danger: Organic and acid contaminants can increase rates of lung cancer and respiratory diseases, and destroy plant and animal life. In Mexico City, one of the worst-polluted cities in the world, seven out of 10 children are born with higher lead levels in their blood than the

---

[1] fossil fuels   fuels from once-living substances; for example, petroleum and coal

[2] desertification   the transformation of good land to desert

[3] ultraviolet radiation   invisible light from the sun that can cause skin cancer

[4] chlorinated fluorocarbons (CFCs)   chemical compound used in air conditioners, spray cans, and foam

[5] particulates   small, separate particles in the air

[6] acid rain   rain polluted by harmful emissions

World Health Organization's standards, and it is estimated that one out of every 100 children is born with some form of mental retardation as a result. Air pollution also is taking a devastating toll on other animal and plant life. It is estimated that by early next century, Germany will have lost 90 percent of its trees.

What we can do: Minimize reliance on fossil fuels by using mass transit, car pools or other transportation. Use natural gas, which emits fewer contaminants than coal or oil. Use unleaded gasoline. Because burning garbage produces air pollution, reduce waste by recycling, reusing and not buying things you don't need. Insist on stricter pollution standards.

4 Water pollution

The situation: Toxic chemicals are sometimes dumped directly into lakes and rivers or into municipal sewage systems. Runoff of agricultural chemicals is also a major source of water pollution. Lakes, rivers and oceans can also be contaminated by raw sewage, which can spread disease-causing bacteria. Runoff of animal waste from feedlots and nitrate fertilizers from farm fields is a significant source of nitrate contamination.

Other forms of water pollution are acid rain and toxic rain, which result when smokestack emissions from factories mix with rain. The deaths of thousands of lakes in the northeastern United States and Canada have been linked to emissions from Midwest smokestacks.

The danger: Drinking water drawn from polluted lakes and rivers can cause mental retardation, cancer and kidney and liver disease. Hazardous concentrations of chemicals have been found in fish taken from polluted lakes and rivers. Where sewage treatment is inadequate, water can transmit cholera, typhus and dysentery. Acid rain also can lower agricultural productivity by making the soil more acidic.

What we can do: Reduce air pollution—see the recommendations above. Properly dispose of engine oil, paint, solvents and other liquid wastes to keep them out of the water system. Lobby[7] governments to require industries and municipal sewage systems to establish "zero discharge" goals.

5 Garbage

The situation: Landfills are filling up. Many cities use incinerators, but burning garbage releases toxic chemicals into the atmosphere and concentrates toxic chemicals in the ash, which in many cases must be handled as hazardous material.

The danger: Burning and dumping trash lead to increased emissions of toxic chemicals into the air and water, and the need for more land as a burial ground for garbage. Improperly maintained landfills leach[8] toxic chemicals into rivers and other waters.

What we can do: Environmental advocates recommend source reduction—cutting the amount of garbage we produce by using less packaging and fewer disposable products, reusing disposable packaging and recycling. Nearly every product eventually enters the waste stream,[9] so simply stop buying things you don't need.

6 Rain forests

The situation: Tropical forests are being cut down at a rate of 35.2 million acres—and area the size of New York state—every year. In Central America rain forests are cleared for cattle ranching. Elsewhere forests are being cut to supply tropical hardwoods to developed countries. Expanding populations and growing needs for farmland also are causing forest loss. Half of the world's tropical forests are gone, and if the destruction continues at the current rate, most of the world's rain forests will be gone by the end of the century.

The danger: Rain forests have been described as the lungs of the planet because they take in carbon dioxide and release oxygen. The diversity of plant and animal life in the rain forests is far richer than in other areas of the world. Plants and genetic material[10] from rain forests have been extremely valuable in agriculture and pharmacology—they are the original sources of many of today's most important drugs. The destruction of rain forests can also disrupt climatic patterns.

What we can do: Don't buy tropical lumber products unless you can be sure they are not endangered species and were logged using sustainable methods. Avoid "rain forest beef"—meat produced in countries where rain forests are cleared for pasture. It is most often used in food processing, pet food and fast-food products. Write Congress demanding trade sanctions against countries that permit the destruction of rain forests.

7 Topsoil loss

The situation: Soil scientists estimate that between a third and half of the topsoil in the United States has been lost within the past 200 years. Much of the loss is caused by wind and water erosion. Plowing leaves the soil without protective covering, allowing wind to blow it away. In hillier areas, rain can wash away topsoil.

The danger: Loss of topsoil means loss of soil nutrients and a resulting loss of agricultural productivity. Soil erosion is also America's largest nonpoint source[11] of water pollution—as soil runs off into rivers, silting[12] hampers river navigation and kills aquatic life. Loss of topsoil results in greater use of agricultural chemicals to make up for poor topsoil, which in turn results in increased chemical runoff and water pollution.

---

[7] **lobby**   to influence legislators to pass laws that protect a group's interests

[8] **leach**   to filter through soil and rock on the way from land to water

[9] **waste stream**   the total of what we throw away

[10] **genetic material**   deoxyribonucleic acid (DNA); the material that genes, which determine the characteristics of living organisms, are made of

[11] **nonpoint source**   a general source, not from one specific point

[12] **silting**   filling up with fine particles of dirt

What we can do: Buy organic produce.[13] Certified organic farmers must use proper conservation practices, including minimum tillage,[14] contour planting,[15] crop rotation[16] and planting cover crops,[17] all of which keep soil from being blown or washed away. Eat less meat. Much of the most vulnerable land is used to grow feed grains for cattle. Support economic incentives for farmers to use sustainable agricultural practices.

8 Aquifer depletion

The situation: We are draining our aquifers—underground reservoirs—faster than they can be replenished. It has been estimated that at current consumption rates, the Ogallala aquifer—the nation's largest stretching from Texas to the Dakotas—will be depleted within 30 years. Rural America depends on groundwater for virtually all its water needs. Nearly half of all Americans depend on groundwater for domestic use, but almost 70 percent of the water pumped from aquifers is used for irrigation. According to 1986 statistics, California uses 2.7 million more acre-feet[18] of groundwater per year than is naturally replenished.

The danger: As the water table[19] drops, wells go dry and must be dug deeper or replaced with new wells at high cost, with higher pumping costs to draw the water from a greater depth. Otherwise, farmers must shift to dry land agriculture[20] or abandon production. Depletion of the aquifer also weakens geologic structures.

What we can do: Consumers can use water-saving shower heads and toilets, and recycle "gray water"[21] for gardening and other uses. Support enforcement of legislation that protects water supplies.

9 Endangered species

The situation: Human activity wipes out more than a thousand plant and animal species every year, and many more species are pushed to the edge of extinction. The causes vary: overhunting, habitat[22] destruction, degradation of the environment through pollution, the disappearance of "primitive" plant and animal varieties as farmers and animal breeders concentrate on a handful of high-yielding varieties.

The danger: The loss of species can be seen as tragic in itself, but there are further consequences. The loss of a species disrupts the ecosystem in which it lives. As plant and animal varieties disappear, we lose potentially valuable sources of new crops, medicines and genetic material that could be used to breed disease resistance or other desirable characteristics into modern plant and animal varieties.

What we can do: Support laws that restrict trade in endangered species.

10 Overpopulation

The situation: It is estimated that the world's population sometime in the next century will be between 11 billion and 14 billion people. More than 90 percent of the anticipated growth will take place in the developing world.[23] In 1989, for the third straight year, the world ate more than it produced. World food reserves are currently estimated at 30 days.

The danger: The potential consequences of current population growth rates include famine, widespread environmental destruction, epidemics and political unrest.

What we can do: Limit family size. It is estimated that people in industrialized countries consume resources at 60 times the rate of people in developing countries. Experts disagree on strategies for limiting population growth in developing countries. Some advocate direct support for family planning programs; others argue those programs are effective only if the underlying problem of poverty is addressed.

Sources: *The Rainforest Book* (Living Planet), by Scott Lewis with the Natural Resources Defense Council, and *It's a Matter of Survival* (Harvard University), by Anita Gordon and David Suzuki. Other recommended readings include the annual State of the World reports issued by the Worldwatch Institute and *The End of Nature* (Doubleday), by Bill McKibben.

---

[13]**organic produce** fruits and vegetables grown without chemical fertilizers or pesticides

[14]**tillage** plowing, turning of the soil

[15]**contour planting** planting in rows that follow the curve of the hill, to avoid soil erosion

[16]**crop rotation** over time, growing different crops on an area of land, to preserve the land's productivity

[17]**cover crops** any crops planted between commercial crops to hold the soil

[18]**acre-feet** a measure of volume; in this case the volume of water that would cover one acre of land (4,840 square yards) with one foot of water

[19]**water table** a level underground at which water collects

[20]**dry land agriculture** a system in which land is unplanted in a rainy season and collects water, then planted with a long-rooted crop in the dry season

[21]**gray water** water after it is used for bathing and washing dishes and clothes

[22]**habitat** the environment where an organism usually lives

[23]**developing world** poorer countries with less-developed economies

Comprehension Check

Decide which student or students will be responsible for explaining each threat to the class. Reread your section of the article carefully. Answer these questions about your section:

1. What is the threat and what are some of its causes?
2. What are the dangers if nothing changes?
3. What changes are recommended? How will each of these changes help?

The sections in the selection are summaries of large, complicated problems. You can expect that they will not give you enough material to understand the problem completely. Write some questions that still remain after you have read the section carefully.

Prepare a short oral presentation in which you explain the threat, the potential dangers, and the actions that people can take. Use the simplest words possible so your classmates can understand. Use numbering to simplify problems and solutions.

EXAMPLE:
There are three reasons why_____. First...Second...Third...

If necessary, teach your classmates difficult vocabulary that is not glossed.

Sharing Your Thoughts

1. Listen to the presentations of each of the ten threats to the environment. At the end of each, nonpresenters should be able to summarize the threat, the potential dangers, and the actions that people can take. If you cannot do this, ask the presenters to explain again what you did not understand.
2. Share your unanswered questions about each threat to the environment. Where would you look to find information to answer them?
3. As specifically as possible, discuss how the lifestyle in wealthy nations like the United States is harmful to the environment. Are you familiar with a lifestyle that might be better for the environment? If so, in what ways might this lifestyle be better?
4. Talk about ways in which one threat to the environment is connected to another or others.

   EXAMPLE:
   Garbage and air pollution are connected. If we burn garbage, we release toxic chemicals into the air. We have to stop burning garbage in open areas.

5. Which threats would be easiest to get people to take action on? Which would be hardest? Explain.

Vocabulary

A. Providing Definitions

Each group did the vocabulary work for part of this article. Combine your knowledge and, as a class, provide simple definitions of the following important vocabulary which will be useful in reading the selections that follow. Refer to a dictionary if you need to.

1. disrupt (Sections 1, 6, 9) _____

2. ecosystem (Sections 1, 9) _____

3. famine (Sections 1, 10) _____

4. emit, emissions (Sections 1, 3, 4, 5) _____

5. ozone layer (Section 2) _____

6. deteriorating (Section 2) _____

7. release (Sections 2, 3, 5, 6) _____

8. deplete, depletion (Sections 2, 8) _____

9. source (Sections 2, 4, 5, 9) _____

10. contaminate, contaminants (Section 3) _____

11 . rely on, reliance on (Section 3) _____

12. dump (Section 4) _____

13. sewage (Section 4) _____

14. runoff (Sections 4, 7) _____

15. waste (Sections 4, 5) _____

16. pollution, polluted (Sections 3, 4, 7, 9) _____

17. toxic (Sections 4, 5) _____

18. hazardous (Sections 4, 5) _____

19. dispose of, disposable (Sections 4, 5) _____

20. landfill (Section 5) _____

21. burial (Section 5) _____

22. trash (Section 5) _____

23. recycling (Section 5) _____

24. diversity (Section 6) _____

25. sustainable (Section 6) _____

26. species (Sections 6, 9) _____

27. endangered (Sections 6, 9) _____

28. topsoil (Section 7) _____

29. erosion (Section 7) _____

30. replenish (Section 8) _____

31. habitat destruction (Section 9) _____

32. degradation (Section 9) _____

33. food reserves (Section 10) _____

34. resources (Section 10) _____

B. Content Vocabulary

Complete the following statements about threats to the environment with words from the list. Use each word only once. Change the form of verbs if the grammar of the sentence requires it.

deteriorate	**emissions**	**endangered**
erosion	**habitats**	**hazardous**
landfills	**pollution**	**resources**
sewage		

1. Many human activities threaten life on our planet. For example, destruction of forests contributes to air _____ and the _____ of topsoil because trees are nature's air filters and their root systems hold soil in place.

2. We pollute our air with _____ from automobiles and factories. We pollute our water when we bury _____ waste in _____ or dispose of raw _____ in lakes and rivers.

3. Animals have become extinct or are _____ because we kill them for quick profit, or we destroy their _____.

4. Despite these problems, the quality of our life does not need to _____ if we are careful of how we use our limited _____ and take the environment into consideration when we make decisions.

Text Analysis

Text Organization

Before reading "Ten Major Threats to the Environment," you noted that each section was organized by the same three boldfaced headings: **The situation**, **The danger**, and **What we can do**. Why do you think the writer chose to use such uniform headings? What advantages are there for readers? for the writer?

Writing Task

1. Freewrite about the environmental problem that concerns you most. One of these questions may help you get started.
   - What is your experience with the problem?
   - What worries you?
   - Is there anything you can do to help the situation?

   Reread your writing. Look for and mark ideas you might want to write about in more detail on some other occasion. Keep your freewriting for possible use for the writing exercise in A Final Look.

2. Writing about a topic that is new to you or that you do not understand well can make you think about the topic and help you understand it. Write about one of the threats to the environment that you were not aware of or knew little about. Use these questions as a guide to help you get started.
   - What are you able to understand easily about the problem, its causes, and what can be done?
   - What don't you understand well? What more would you like to learn about the threat?

   Reread your writing. Is anything clearer to you now than before you did this writing? Summarize what you learned from this experience in a sentence or two.

Before Reading

This selection is an excerpt from the book *Diet for a Gentle World*. The purpose of the book is to make readers more aware of what they choose to eat by showing the far-reaching and close-to-home effects of these choices.

1. As a class, list the ways you can think of that trees are important to humans and the ecology of the planet. Compare your list with the Puerto Rican Conservation Trust advertisement on p. 207.

2. What is a rain forest? Where are they found? What do you already know about the value of rain forests and what is happening to them?

The Destruction of the Rain Forests   by Les Inglis

1 *S*tatistics abound in discussions of the environment. We are bombarded with *millions* and *billions* and *trillions* as we try to understand the problems facing us. Sometimes the numbers make sense to us, but too often we have no frame of reference when regional or global statistics are offered, and the numbers dazzle without educating. In this age of huge resources of information, we encounter more numbers than we can remember, and we are occasionally suspicious, too, knowing that some people will try to prove anything with statistics. As writers try harder to convey the impact of environmental problems, they rattle off still more numbers, and our sense of hopelessness grows. But the environment is not a quantitative aspect of our lives—it is qualitative. We don't have to reckon with parts per million of pollutants and billions of cubic feet to sense smog[1] in the Los Angeles basin or in many other cities. We know when a well runs dry or our gardens don't get enough rain. We can remember that as children we saw more butterflies and dragonflies and frogs, and we know that something has happened—all without statistics. We can set aside the numbers and know what we see, and it does not require a giant leap of consciousness to accept that our world—nature as we know it— is truly threatened. One of the threats we've heard so much about is the loss of the world's rain forests.

2 Perhaps the rain forests of Central America may not seem like our backyard, but they are closer to Houston than New York is. In Costa Rica, outside the capital city of San José, is a small biological reserve, operated by the Association for the Conservation and Reforestation of San Rafel. It is called El Chompipe, which means "the turkey" in Spanish. A large hill or small mountain among many larger mountains, the group looking like a turkey if you have lots of imagination, El Chompipe is a cloud forest, a very special kind of rain forest. Nearly every day of the year, thick clouds form and cover the hill, wetting the trees and brush and ground plants almost constantly. A walk along the few

---

[1] **smog**   a blend of two words, smoke + fog; dense, dirty air, with pollutants like carbon monoxide, nitrogen oxides, and sulfur oxides

trails on El Chompipe requires tall rubber boots because one's feet sink several inches into the mud, even on some of the established paths. Biologists have counted over 6,000 species of plants and animals on this reserve of less than 300 acres—more species than can be found in all of North America.

3   A Costa Rican rain forest is unlike any area in the United States. And although the lion's share of Costa Rica's rain forests has already been cleared, what remains almost vibrates with life wherever one looks. High up in the tops of mahogany trees, birds, animals, and a staggering variety of plants compete for sunlight with the leaves of the big trees themselves. What sunlight is not caught in the upper canopy filters down into the middle levels, where it nurtures skinny palm trees, themselves up to 100 feet high. At eye level, still other trees and vines make a home for countless insects, air plants, and orchids. Even fallen trees are not idle, as bromeliads hang and prosper on every foot of the rotting branches. On the ground are tiny, leafy plants, some sporting exotic flowers, and the occasional anthill teems with tiny life. Bird calls are the only sound, and the trained eye can still catch glimpses of toucans and macaws. This is the rain forest we are losing, and this is the source of about 30 percent of the oxygen in our air.

4   Rain forests are found in tropical areas around the world—in Central America and Brazil, in Africa, and in Southeast Asia. They are shrinking everywhere. Why? Because they are being cleared for agriculture, especially for grazing land and plantations, and for timber and charcoal.

5   A quarter-pound hamburger requires the destruction of fifty-five square feet of rain forest. That number has been tossed about and argued over for a few years now, but let's look at how such a statistic could even exist. Normally we think of an acre of farmland as producing a certain amount of crop every year. The land is going to be there forever, so relating a unit of crop production to an area of farmland makes sense only on a per-year basis. For example, if you clear an acre of forest and plant potatoes and produce 20,000 pounds of them in a season, the rate of production is 20,000 pounds per acre per year. You wouldn't say that the farmer destroyed an acre of forest for 20,000 pounds of potatoes because the land would presumably go on producing 20,000 pounds of potatoes, or some other crop, year after year. Without referring to the time period involved, comparing the acre of forest with 20,000 pounds of potatoes is meaningless.

6   How, then, can we compare fifty-five square feet of rain forest with a quarter pound of hamburger? Should we really be saying that that area of forest produces a quarter pound of beef *per year*? No, because—in the case of rain forests cleared for grazing—the land has only a few productive years before it will not support cattle grazing or other farming. Some areas will be abandoned after as few as three years, and others might support grazing for up to ten years, but the common experience is that the land quickly wears out and is not used perpetually for grazing. And so the fifty-five-square-foot-per-quarter-pound-hamburger statistic does make sense after all. It comes from merely dividing the area of rain forest cleared for grazing by all of the pounds of beef it produces *in its entire productive life*. Every rain forest hamburger does indeed represent an area of tropical splendor destroyed forever—the antithesis of sustainable agriculture.

7   Why does the land have such short-lived usefulness for grazing? The answer involves the delicate soil and the indelicate cattle. Rain forest soils are well adapted for the forests they support, cycling nutrients efficiently between the dense vegetation and the soil, but these soils cannot support grass because they

they lack a suitable quantity or quality of nutrients. In a newly cleared forest area, grass initially takes hold easily, and the cattle move onto the land to feed. The thin layer of soil can withstand only very low cattle density, so the number of cattle per acre almost always exceeds the sustainable level and the new forage plants are overgrazed as the ranchers seek a quick return from their land.

8   Overgrazing, unfortunately, doesn't simply mean that the grass has been eaten down too close to the earth. As excessive numbers of cattle range over the land, their hooves trample it, compacting the soil. The compacting action of animal feet is well known to farmers. In the Midwest, a farmer with a leaking hillside pond may pen up the pigs around the pond for a year or two to seal it. Eventually, the pigs' narrow hooves pressing down into the soft earth around the pond will compact the ground and stop the leaks. On overgrazed cleared forest land, the compacting action is the same, and soon rainwater tends to run off the packed soil rather than soak in.

9   Now several undesirable processes begin. As water runs off the land, it carries away some of the topsoil, exposing more rock at the surface. With less topsoil, more compacted earth, and less retained moisture in the ground, the grasses and forage plants thin out. Less moisture returns to the air from the ground because fewer plants grow, more water has run off, and the soil itself is drier. Now the air becomes drier as well and begins to warm. Warmer, drier air contributes to the reduction of plant life as the cycle of degradation feeds on itself in several ways. Rainfall decreases, and as dry spells occur, the dry wind begins to pick up dust and carry it away, further depleting the soil and now polluting the air. As streams dry up and become clogged with topsoil, water supplies dwindle. In only a few years, less water and less grass mean that the cleared grazing land will no longer support a practical or economical number of cattle. The farmer abandons the land and moves to newly cleared areas, expanding and perpetuating the destruction of the forests.

10   This process has earned a new name, a new word in our language: *desertification.* Not limited to tropical areas, it also applies to rangelands in the temperate parts of the world. If somewhat slower, desertification proceeds in much of the western part of the United States, where perhaps half the grazing productivity of the land has already been lost.

11   Here again an inappropriate economic system subsidizes a segment of agriculture—meat production—by failing to force producers to bear the cost of the natural destruction they cause. If grazing densities were forced by law to the low levels needed to make the grazing land sustainable (in this case, merely being able to hold its own and not dry up), the cost of rangeland beef would rise dramatically to perhaps five or ten times its present cost. Demand for beef would drop because of the high price, and the incentive to clear forests for grazing would largely disappear. An appropriate economic system would limit environmental damage in the rain forests and in our own backyard, the western rangeland.

12   But advancing theories about these matters is far easier than putting them into practice. Clearing rain forests has become a livelihood for many people and a source of quick profits for opportunists. Some Third World[2] governments—struggling to bring a better life to their people and, in some cases, to begin to approach the "good life" of the meat-eating, industrialized Western nations—have encouraged exploitation of their undeveloped areas

---

[2] Third World   a term often used to refer to poorer countries with less well developed economies

(too often *undeveloped* translates into *rain forest*). Even if the people and the governments in these developing countries make the connection between forest loss and eventual climatic disaster, they seem to be trying to "get ours now, before it's too late."

13   And who denounces this rape of nature—this cycle of slash, burn, graze, destroy, and abandon? Of course, it is we enlightened children of Western industrial privilege. We are the ones who cleared nearly all of our own forests generations ago and who now consume energy, meat, water, minerals, lumber, and capital at rates far out of proportion to our small share of the world's population and land area. We are the ones who even today clear our few remaining old-growth forests to ship logs to Japan, even if it means the end of the spotted owl and who knows how many other less-celebrated but equally doomed animals. We are the ones who live a lifestyle so rich and abundant that it cannot possibly be spread to the developing nations because the world hasn't enough resources to support it. To the hungry people of the Third World, we seem to be saying, "We've got ours; we deserve this lifestyle; and you must not destroy your own forests as we did so long ago. *You* must protect *our* (meaning *all people's)* environment." No wonder we aren't convincing them!

14   A newspaper column on rain forest and beef sparked a letter to the editor from a beef producers' association proudly stating that the United States now imports no beef from Central America. The message was that if you eat beef in the United States, you aren't causing rain forest destruction. But the world population is growing, and its beef consumption is growing per capita. With such an expanding demand on a world commodity, it doesn't matter where the hamburger we eat is grazed. If we buy less from the rain forest clearers, we will eat more of our own domestic beef and export less, and the rest of the world will buy more from the rain forest clearers. So even indirectly our consumption of domestic beef hurts the rain forests, despite what our beef producers will tell you. Also, we in the Western world cannot escape the responsibility for creating this unsustainable, nature-destroying idea of the good life—our earth-killing addiction to beef.

Comprehension Check

1. Why do writers often use statistics when writing about environmental problems? What is the potential danger of using statistics?

2. Why aren't statistics necessary to understand that our environment is threatened?

3. Using El Chompipe as an example, describe a rain forest.

4. Why are tropical rain forests important?

5. Why are tropical rain forests shrinking?

6. What is the difference between clearing forest for potatoes and for grazing cattle?

7. Why doesn't rain forest land last long when animals graze on it?

8. What could be done to be sure cattle don't destroy the land they graze on? What will the economic effect of this action be?

9. According to Inglis, what will happen if Americans stop importing beef produced on land that was once rain forest?

10. Why aren't wealthier nations able to convince less-developed nations to protect their rain forests?

11. Which of the ten major threats to the environment covered in Selection One are discussed in more detail in this article?

Ilustración: Jack Delano

HOW DO TREES BENEFIT THE URBAN ENVIRONMENT?

1. TREES PROVIDE OXYGEN
2. CLEAN AIR BY ABSORBING ODORS, POLLUTION, DUST AND HEAT
3. CONTRIBUTE TO ENERGY CONSERVATION BY SHADING HOMES, BUILDINGS AND CONCRETE ISLANDS
4. INCREASE ATMOSPHERIC MOISTURE
5. REDUCE WATER RUNOFF AND SOIL EROSION BY HOLDING WATER, INCREASING THE AMOUNT OF TIME WATER TAKES TO REACH THE GROUND
6. PRODUCE ORGANIC MATTER USED AS MULCH
7. PROVIDE COVER, FOOD AND HABITAT FOR SUBURBAN WILDLIFE
8. INCREASE PROPERTY VALUE AND PRIDE IN THE COMMUNITY
9. ABSORB UNWANTED SOUNDS
10. PROVIDE VISUAL BARRIERS TO UNPLEASANT URBAN LANDSCAPES
11. TRANSFORM BARREN AREAS INTO COMMUNITY RECREATION AREAS
12. PROVIDE PROTECTION FROM DAMAGING ULTRAVIOLET RAYS
13. PRODUCE A SENSE OF ROOTEDNESS, CONNECTEDNESS AND COMMUNITY

 Fideicomiso de Conservación de Puerto Rico

Sharing Your Thoughts

1. What is Inglis advocating regarding the:
   a. protection of rain forest land?
   b. production and cost of beef?
   c. eating habits of some nations?

   Does he make a convincing case? Why or why not? Why do you agree or disagree with him?

2. What other ideas, if any, do you have for protecting rain forest land?

3. What is your definition of a good life? Do you think it is possible for humans to live a good life without damaging the environment? Explain. What changes in the way we do things might be necessary for most people to have a good life without destroying the environment?

4. How good are human beings at making changes in the way they think and act? What problems in bringing about change do you see?

5. With a partner, make a drawing or poster to illustrate the steps in one of the following:
   a. What happens when a rain forest undergoes desertification? (¶7–¶9)
   b. What would happen if nations passed laws to limit grazing? (¶11)

Vocabulary

A. Content Vocabulary

Complete the following statements about the destruction of rain forests with words from the list. Use each word only once. Change the form of verbs if the grammar of the sentence requires it.

clear	climate	compact
delicate	demand	desert
destruction	profit	run off
shrink	support	sustainable

1. In many areas of the world, rain forests are _____ because people are _____ them for agriculture and grazing cattle. Unfortunately, rain forest soil is _____; it is good for rain forest plants, but does not _____ grazing or normal agriculture for long. Whoever clears the land gets only a short-term benefit.

2. To meet the _____ for beef and make a quick _____, ranchers put too many cattle on the land The weight of the cattle _____ the soil. When it rains, the water _____ and takes good topsoil with it.

3. Without topsoil, trees and plants that hold moisture in the air cannot grow. The _____ becomes drier and eventually the land turns to _____. The _____ of nature that occurs is the opposite of _____ agriculture.

B. Inferring Meaning from Context

Locate the following words in the selection. Can you infer their meaning from the context in which they appear? What words in the context help you figure out their meaning? Check your inferences with a dictionary if necessary.

1. dazzle (¶1) _____

2. convey (¶1) _____

3. rattle off (¶1) _____

4. reckon with (¶1) _____

5. trails (¶2) _____

6. sink (¶2) _____

7. the lion's share (¶3) _____

8. staggering (¶3) _____

9. nurtures (¶3) _____

10. sporting (¶3) _____

11. teems with (¶3) _____

12. glimpses (¶3) _____

Text Analysis

A. Text Organization

Suppose this excerpt from Inglis's book were going to be reprinted in a magazine. An editor has requested that you and a partner divide it into sections and give each section an appropriate heading that reflects its content. How many headings would you need? What would you suggest they be? Where would you put them?

B. Persuasion

One of the principal purposes for writing is to convince an audience, or readers, to believe or do something (Persuasion, p. 171); this is clearly Inglis's purpose. When writers or speakers try to persuade people, they analyze their audience carefully and plan the communication to convince that specific audience. Answering these questions will reveal how Inglis is directing his writing to a specific audience.

1. Who is Inglis's audience? Why does he use the pronoun *we*?
2. Why does he describe the rain forest in detail for this audience?
3. What questions does Inglis use to organize his writing? Why do you think he chose these questions and this technique?
4. Why does he discuss the comparison of rain forest land to a quarter-pound hamburger?
5. Why does he ask and answer the last question (¶13)? How does it fit with his persuasive purpose? Does he go easy or hit his audience rather hard here? Explain. Do you think his approach is correct? Why or why not?

Writing Task

1. Write a paragraph in which you describe some natural feature of your country like Inglis describes Costa Rica's El Chompipe rain forest. Before you begin writing, plan what aspects you will write about and what details you will use. Have a partner read your paragraph and point out places where your description is not clear; revise accordingly.

2. In paragraphs 7 to 9, Inglis describes the steps in the process of desertification. Write as many paragraphs as necessary to describe the steps in a process you know about, for example:
    * how something is built, made, or put together (e.g., a radio, a favorite meal, a dress)
    * how something old or in bad condition can be restored or fixed (e.g., a piece of furniture)
    * how something should be done for the best results (e.g., seeds planted)

3. Imagine you are a cattle rancher. Write a letter to the author of this selection arguing in favor of cattle ranching and against a law which would limit the number of cattle you can graze on your land. Before writing the letter, make notes to answer these questions:
    * How will the law affect you, your business, and the public?
    * Is there something unfair about the law?
    * What better solution is there?
    * What do you know about your audience (Les Inglis) that you should take into consideration when writing the letter?

Exchange letters with a partner; read each other's letters and determine if the arguments are clear, convincing, and well supported. If not, revise accordingly.

SELECTION THREE

Before Reading

Edward O. Wilson, an entomologist or specialist in insects, is Professor of Science at Harvard University and Curator in Entomology at Harvard's Museum of Comparative Zoology. This selection is taken from his 1992 Pulitzer Prize winning book, *The Diversity of Life*, in which he illustrates how human activity has caused the extinction of many forms of life and how we must become good protectors of the variety of life that still remains if we are to survive.

1. All people want and need a decent standard of living. Economies must grow to meet the needs of their populations, but they must grow in ways that do not use up or destroy the only renewable source of wealth—the natural world. This type of economic growth, called *sustainable growth*, is the opposite of the use of land seen in Selection Two, where a natural resource is destroyed, principally for short-term economic gain. What similar examples of the misuse of natural resources for short-term profit do you know of?

2. In this selection Edward O. Wilson demonstrates how ecosystems, especially forests, can provide sustainable economic growth for countries, making it more profitable to conserve resources than to destroy them. What do you think the title of this selection means?

UNMINED RICHES   by Edward O. Wilson

1   A revolution in conservation thinking during the past twenty years, a New Environmentalism, has led to the perception of the practical value of wild species. Except in pockets of ignorance and malice, there is no longer an ideological war between conservationists and developers. Both share the perception that health and prosperity decline in a deteriorating environment. They also understand that useful products cannot be harvested from extinct species. If dwindling wildlands are mined for genetic material rather than destroyed for a few more boardfeet of lumber and acreage of farmland, their economic yield will be vastly greater over time. Salvaged species can help to revitalize timbering, agriculture, medicine, and other industries located elsewhere. The wildlands are like a magic well: the more that is drawn from them in knowledge and benefits, the more there will be to draw.

2   The old approach to the conservation of biodiversity was that of the bunker.[1] Close off the richest wildlands as parks and reserves, post guards. Let the people work out their problems in the unreserved land, and they will come to appreciate the great heritage preserved inside, much as they value their cathedrals and national shrines. Parks and guards are necessary, without doubt. The approach has worked to some extent in the United States and Europe, but it cannot succeed to the desired degree in the developing countries. The reason is that the poorest people with the fastest-growing populations live next to the richest deposits of biological diversity. One Peruvian farmer clearing rain forest to feed his family, progressing from patch to patch as the soil is drained of nutrients, will cut more kinds of trees than are native to all of Europe. If there is no other way for him to make a living, the trees will fall.

3   Proponents of the New Environmentalism act on this reality. They recognize that only new ways of drawing income from land already cleared, or from intact wildlands themselves, will save biodiversity from the mill of human poverty. The race is on to develop methods, to

---

1 bunker   a protected place; originally a military fortification

draw more income from the wildlands without killing them, and so to give the invisible hand of free-market economics a green thumb.[2]

4   This revolution has been accompanied by another, closely related change in thinking about biodiversity: the primary focus has moved from species to the ecosystems in which they live. Star species such as pandas and redwoods are no less esteemed than before, but they are also viewed as protective umbrellas over their ecosystems. The ecosystems for their part, containing thousands of less-conspicuous species, are assigned equivalent value, enough to justify a powerful effort to conserve them, with or without the star species. When the last tiger on Bali was shot in 1937, the rest of the island's diversity lost none of its importance.

5   The humble and ignored are in fact often the real star species. An example of a species lifted from obscurity to fame by its biochemistry is the rosy periwinkle (*Catharanthus roseus*) of Madagascar. An inconspicuous plant with a pink five-petaled flower, it produces two alkaloids, vinblastine and vincristine, that cure most victims of two of the deadliest of cancers, Hodgkin's disease, mostly afflicting young adults, and acute lymphocytic leukemia, which used to be a virtual death sentence for children. The income from the manufacture and sale of these two substances exceeds $180 million a year. And that brings us back to the dilemma of the stewardship[3] of the world's biological riches by the economically poor. Five other species of periwinkles occur on Madagascar. One, *Catharanthus coriaceus*, is approaching extinction as the last of its natural habitat, in the Betsileo region of the central highlands, is cleared for agriculture.

6   Few are aware of how much we already depend on wild organisms for medicine. Aspirin, the most widely used pharmaceutical in the world, was derived from salicylic acid discovered in meadowsweet (*Filipendula ulmaria*) and later combined with acetic acid to create acetylsalicylic acid, the more effective painkiller. In the United States a quarter of all prescriptions dispensed by pharmacies are substances extracted from plants. Another 13 percent come from microorganisms and 3 percent more from animals, for a total of over 40 percent that are organism-derived. Yet these materials are only a tiny fraction of the multitude available. Fewer than 3 percent of the flowering plants of the world, about 5,000 of the 220,000 species, have been examined for alkaloids, and then in limited and haphazard fashion. The anticancer potency of the rosy periwinkle was discovered by the merest chance, because the species happened to be widely planted and under investigation for its reputed effectiveness as an antidiuretic.

7   The scientific and folkloric record is strewn with additional examples of plants and animals valued in folk medicine but still unaddressed in biomedical research. The neem tree (*Azadirachta indica*), a relative of mahogany, is a native of tropical Asia virtually unknown in the developed world. The people of India, according to a recent report of the U.S. National Research Council, treasure the species. "For centuries, millions have cleaned their teeth with neem twigs, smeared skin disorders with neem-leaf juice, taken neem tea as a tonic, and placed neem leaves in their beds, books, grain bins, cupboards, and closets to keep away troublesome bugs. The tree has relieved so many different pains, fevers, infections, and other complaints that it has been called the 'village pharmacy.' To those millions in India neem has miraculous powers, and now scientists around the world are beginning to think they may have been right."

8   One should never dismiss the reports of such powers as superstition or legend. Organisms are superb chemists. In a sense they are collectively better than all the world's chemists at synthesizing organic molecules of practical use. Through millions of generations each kind of plant, animal, and microorganism has experimented with chemical substances to meet its special needs. Each species has experienced astronomical numbers of mutations and genetic recombinations affecting its biochemical machinery. The experimental products thus produced have been tested by the unyielding forces of natural

---

2 **green thumb**   a person who is successful growing plants has a green thumb (here, the term refers to an interest in protecting the environment)

3 **stewardship**   caring for something; stewards take care of passengers on a ship

selection, one generation at a time. The special class of chemicals in which the species became a wizard is precisely determined by the niche it occupies. The leech, which is a vampire annelid worm, must keep the blood of its victims flowing once it has bitten through the skin. From its saliva comes the anticoagulant called hirudin, which medical researchers have isolated and used to treat hemorrhoids, rheumatism, thrombosis, and contusions, conditions where clotting blood is sometimes painful or dangerous. Hirudin readily dissolves blood clots that threaten skin transplants. A second substance obtained from the saliva of the vampire bat of Central and South America is being developed to prevent heart attacks. It opens clogged arteries twice as fast as standard pharmaceutical remedies, while restricting its activity to the area of the clot. A third substance called kistrin has been isolated from the venom of the Malayan pit viper.

9   The discovery of such materials in wild species is but a fraction of the opportunities waiting. Once the active component is identified chemically, it can be synthesized in the laboratory, often at lower costs than by extraction from raw harvested tissue. In the next step, the natural chemical compound provides the prototype from which an entire class of new chemicals can be synthesized and tested. Some of these less-than-natural substances may prove even more efficient on human subjects than the prototype, or cure diseases never confronted with chemicals of their structural class in nature. Cocaine, for example, is used as a local anesthetic, but it has also served as a blueprint[4] for the laboratory synthesis of a large number of specialized anesthetics that are more stable and less toxic and addictive than the natural product.

10   The same bright prospect exists with wild plants that can serve as food. Very few of the species with potential economic importance actually reach world markets. Perhaps 30,000 species of plants have edible parts, and throughout history a total of 7,000 kinds have been grown or collected as food but, of the latter, 20 species provide 90 percent of the world's food and just three—wheat, maize, and rice—supply more

than half. This thin cushion of diversity is biased toward cooler climates, and in most parts of the world it is sown in monocultures sensitive to disease and attacks from insects and nematode worms.

11   Fruits illustrate the pattern of underutilization. A dozen temperate-zone species—apples, peaches, pears, strawberries, and so on down the familiar roster—dominate the northern markets and are also used heavily in the tropics. In contrast, at least 3,000 other species are available in the tropics, and of these 200 are in actual use. Some, like cherimoyas, papayas, and mangos, have recently joined bananas as important export products, while carambolas, tamarindos, and coquitos are making a promising entry. But most consumers in the north have yet to savor lulos (the "golden fruit of the Andes"), mamones, rambutans, and the near-legendary durians and mangosteens, esteemed by aficionados[5] as the premier fruits of the world.

12   Our narrow diets are not so much the result of choice as of accident. We still depend on the plant species discovered and cultivated by our neolithic[6] ancestors in the several regions where agriculture began. These cradles of agriculture include the Mediterranean and Near East, Central Asia, the horn of Africa, the rice belt of tropical Asia, the uplands of Mexico and Central

---

[4] **blueprint**   an architectural drawing of a building used here to mean model

[5] **aficionados**   fans, people who like something very much (Spanish)

[6] **neolithic**   period at the end of the Stone Age when agriculture began

America, and middle to high elevations in the Andes. A few favored crops were spread around the world, woven into almost all existing cultures. Had the European settlers of North America not followed the practice, had they stayed resolutely with the cultivated crops native to the new land, citizens of the United States and Canada today would be living on sunflower seeds, Jerusalem artichokes, pecans, blueberries, cranberries, and muscadine grapes. Only these relatively minor foods originated on the continent north of Mexico.

13   Yet even when stretched to the limit of the neolithic crops, modern agriculture is only a sliver of what it could be. Waiting in the wings are tens of thousands of unused plant species, many demonstrably superior to those in favor. One potential star species that has emerged from among the thousands is the winged bean (*Psophocarpus tetragonolobus*) of New Guinea. It can be called the one-species supermarket. The entire plant is palatable, from spinach-like leaves to young pods usable as green beans, plus young seeds like peas and tubers[7] that, boiled, fried, baked or roasted, are richer in protein than potatoes. The mature seeds resemble soybeans. They can be cooked as they are or ground into flour or liquified into a caffeine-free beverage that tastes like coffee. Moreover, the plant grows at a phenomenal pace, reaching a length of 4 meters in a few weeks. Finally, the winged bean is a legume:[8] it harbors nitrogen-fixing nodules in its roots and has little need for fertilizer. Apart from its potential as a crop, it can be used to raise soil fertility for other crops. With a small amount of genetic improvement through selective breeding, the winged bean could raise the standard of living of millions of people in the poorest tropical countries.

14   [In the concluding chapter of *The Diversity of Life*, "The Environmental Ethic," Wilson writes,] We do not understand ourselves yet and descend farther from heaven's air if we forget how much the natural world means to us. Signals abound that the loss of life's diversity endangers not just the body but the spirit. If that much is true, the changes occurring now will visit harm on all generations to come.

15   The ethical imperative should therefore be, first of all, prudence. We should judge every scrap of biodiversity as priceless while we learn to use it and come to understand what it means to humanity. We should not knowingly allow any species or race to go extinct. And let us go beyond mere salvage to begin the restoration of natural environments in order to enlarge wild populations and stanch the hemorrhaging of biological wealth. There can be no purpose more enspiriting than to begin the age of re storation, reweaving the wondrous diversity of life that still surrounds us.

---

[7] tuber   an underground stem; potato and yuca, for example

[8] legume   a type of plant in which seeds grow in pods; peas, beans, lentils, for example

Comprehension Check

1. Why has there been a war between conservationists and developers in the past? According to Wilson, why has that war ended?

2. What is biodiversity, and why is it important to save it?

3. What are the old and new approaches to saving biodiversity?

4. Why is a new approach to saving biodiversity needed in developing countries where poor people live next to great natural wealth?

5. How can the lives of poor people be improved while still protecting forests?

6. What are some examples of medicines that come from nature? Where do they come from? What do they do?

7. What does Wilson mean when he says, "Organisms are superb chemists"? How is the leech a good example of this ability of living organisms?

8. What can scientists do after they learn about the medicinal power of certain plants?

9. What are the three plant species that provide more than 50 percent of the world's food? When were they discovered and cultivated? What plants are edible but not commonly consumed? What should modern agriculture do?

10. What does the last paragraph suggest will be the benefit to those who begin the age of restoration of natural environments?

Sharing Your Thoughts

1. What kind of activities is Wilson referring to when he says there has been a "war between conservationists and developers"? Do you agree that the war is over or is it still going on? What specific evidence can you give to support your opinion?

2. How will Wilson's proposal help poor people? Can it work alone or must it work in combination with other changes? If so, what other changes will also be needed?

3. Why are "star species" as well as others worth saving? What do you know about specific endangered species and efforts to protect them? What problems do people who are interested in saving them have to face?

4. Wilson also suggests there are many animal as well as plant foods that go unused. Why do these potential foods go unused? What problems will businesses face if they try to market them?

5. Do you think that business and industry will or will not see the value of protecting the natural world while trying to increase productivity and profits? Explain. What kinds of international agreements will be necessary to protect our planet?

6. Imagine that a foundation has asked you to create a program to raise the standard of living of poor people who live near a rain forest without destroying the forest.

   a. What kind of education would you provide the people?

   b. What kinds of economic activities would you consider?

   c. What problems would you face?

Vocabulary

A. Content Vocabulary

Complete the following statements about biodiversity with words from the list. Use each word only once. Change the form of verbs if the grammar of the sentence requires it.

available	biodiversity	derived
income	make a living	poverty
preserve	priceless	restoration
wilderness		

1. According to Edward O. Wilson, _____ areas, like rain forests, are _____; they are of great value.

2. We must _____ them not only as sources of food and medicines, but for what they do for man's spirit as well.

3. People near the rain forests, who live in _____, cut down trees to plant crops to survive. If we help them to _____ from the forest in other ways, they will protect it.

4. One way to produce _____ from the forests is to harvest food and medicinal plants from them.

5. Many of the medicines and foods we presently use are _____ from plants; there are even more to be discovered because we have studied only a few of the species that are _____.

6. The cooperation of business, government, conservationists, and citizens' groups can lead to the _____ of natural environments, saving the priceless _____ of our planet.

B. Word Analysis

*Divide these words into their parts. Some of them include Latin or greek parts: **vit** = Latin for* life, **vis** = Latin for *see,* **micro** = Latin for *small,* **astro** = Latin for *star, and* **anti-** = Latin for *against,* **proto** = Greek for *first/before. What do the following words mean as a whole? What does each part contribute?*

1. revitalize (¶1) _____

2. invisible (¶3) _____

3. microorganisms (¶6) _____

4. astronomical (¶8) _____

5. anticoagulant (¶8) _____

6. transplants (¶8) _____

7. prototype (¶9) _____

8. underutilization (¶11) _____

Text Analysis

A. Figurative Language

Wilson expresses several important ideas through similes and metaphors.
1. How are wildlands like a magic well? (¶1)
2. How is poverty like a mill? (¶3)
3. What does Wilson suggest is happening to the Earth when he says we need to "stanch the hemorrhaging of biological wealth"? (¶15)

B. Text Organization

Suppose this excerpt from Wilson's book were going to be reprinted in a magazine. An editor has requested that you and a partner divide it into sections and give each section an appropriate heading that reflects its content. How many headings would you need? What would you suggest they be? Where would you put them?

Writing Task

1. Write a one-paragraph summary of this selection using the headings you created in Text Analysis B above as a guide. Include appropriate examples from the selection to illustrate the points you choose to include.
2. Forest land in your area is going to be cleared for a shopping center. Write a letter to the editor of a newspaper arguing against this project. Before beginning to write, list the reasons for your position, and put them in a logical order (most to least important or vice versa). Remember, you want to convince the public to agree with your position. Exchange letters with a partner; read each other's writing and determine if the reasons are clear, convincing, and where possible, supported by facts. If not, revise accordingly.

SELECTION FOUR

Before Reading

Forrest Carter was orphaned at five years of age and went to live with his Cherokee grandparents in the mountains of Tennessee. "The Way" is a chapter in his autobiographical book about his boyhood, *The Education of Little Tree*.

What do you know about Native American ideas about the relationship of humans to the Earth?

The Way

by Forrest Carter

1   IT HAD TAKEN GRANMA, sitting in the rocker that creaked with her slight weight as she worked and hummed, while the pine knots spluttered in the fireplace, a week of evenings to make the boot moccasins. With a hook knife, she had cut the deer leather and made the strips that she wove around the edges. When she had finished, she soaked the moccasins in water and I put them on wet and walked them dry, back and forth across the floor, until they fitted soft and giving, light as air.

2   This morning I slipped the moccasins on last, after I had jumped into my coveralls and buttoned my jacket. It was dark and cold—too early even for the morning whisper wind to stir the trees.

3   Granpa had said I could go with him on the high trail, if I got up, and he had said he would not wake me.

4   "A man rises of his own will in the morning," he had spoken down to me and he did not smile. But Granpa had made many noises in his rising, bumping the wall of my room and talking uncommonly loud to Granma, and so I had heard, and I was first out, waiting with the hounds in the darkness.

5   "So. Ye're[1] here," Granpa sounded surprised.

6   "Yes, sir," I said, and kept the proud out of my voice.

7   Granpa pointed his finger at the hounds jumping and prancing around us. "Ye'll stay," he ordered, and they tucked in their tails and whined and begged and ol' Maud set up a howl. But they didn't follow us. They stood, all together in a hopeless little bunch, and watched us leave the clearing.[2]

---

[1] ye're   you are

[2] clearing   open area in the forest

8   I had been up the low trail that followed the bank of the spring branch,[3] twisting and turning with the hollow[4] until it broke out into a meadow where Granpa had his barn and kept his mule and cow. But this was the high trail that forked off to the right and took to the side of the mountain, sloping always upward as it traveled along the hollow. I trotted behind Granpa and I could feel the upward slant of the trail.

9   I could feel something more, as Granma said I would. Mon-o-lah, the earth mother, came to me through my moccasins. I could feel her push and swell here, and sway and give there…and the roots that veined her body and the life of the water-blood, deep inside her. She was warm and springy and bounced me on her breast, as Granma said she would.

10   The cold air steamed my breath in clouds and the spring branch fell far below us. Bare tree branches dripped water from ice prongs that teethed their sides, and as we walked higher there was ice on the trail. Gray light eased the darkness away.

11   Granpa stopped and pointed by the side of the trail. "There she is—turkey run[5]—see?" I dropped to my hands and knees and saw the tracks: little sticklike impressions coming out from a center hub.

12   "Now, "Granpa said, "we'll fix the trap." And he moved off the trail until he found a stump hole.

13   We cleaned it out, first the leaves, and then Granpa pulled out his long knife and cut into the spongy ground and we scooped up the dirt, scattering it among the leaves. When the hole was deep, so that I couldn't see over the rim, Granpa pulled me out and we dragged tree branches to cover it and, over these, spread armfuls of leaves. Then, with his long knife, Granpa dug a trail sloping downward into the hole and back toward the turkey run. He took the grains of red Indian corn from his pocket and scattered them down the trail, and threw a handful into the hole.

14   "Now we will go," he said, and set off again up the high trail. Ice, spewed from the earth like frosting, crackled under our feet. The mountain opposite us moved closer as the hollow far below became a narrow slit, showing the spring branch like the edge of a steel knife, sunk in the bottom of its cleavage.

15   We sat down in the leaves, off the trail, just as the first sun touched the top of the mountain across the hollow. From his pocket, Granpa pulled out a sour biscuit and deer meat for me, and we watched the mountain while we ate.

16   The sun hit the top like an explosion, sending showers of glitter and sparkle into the air. The sparkling of the icy trees hurt the eyes to look, and it moved down the mountain like a wave as the sun backed the night shadow down and down. A crow scout[6] sent three hard calls through the air, warning we were there.

17   And now the mountain popped and gave breathing sighs that sent little puffs of steam into the air. She pinged and murmured as the sun released the trees from their death armor of ice.

18   Granpa watched, same as me, and listened as the sounds grew with the morning wind that set up a low whistle in the trees.

---

3 spring branch   division or part of a river, probably near a spring (source of water)

4 hollow   valley or low-lying area

5 turkey run   marks left by passage of wild turkeys

6 crow scout   one crow, watching out for the other birds

19   "She's coming alive," he said, soft and low, without taking his eyes from the mountain.

20   "Yes, sir," I said, "she's coming alive." And I knew right then that me and Granpa had us an understanding that most folks didn't know.

21   The night shadow backed down and across a little meadow, heavy with grass and shining in the sun bath. The meadow was set into the side of the mountain. Granpa pointed. There was quail[7] fluttering and jumping in the grass, feeding on the seeds. Then he pointed up toward the icy blue sky.

22   There were no clouds but at first I didn't see the speck that came over the rim. It grew larger. Facing into the sun, so that the shadow did not go before him, the bird sped down the side of the mountain; a skier on the treetops, wings half-folded…like a brown bullet…faster and faster, toward the quail.

23   Granpa chuckled. "It's ol' Tal-con, the hawk,"[8]

24   The quail rose in a rush and sped into the trees—but one was slow. The hawk hit. Feathers flew into the air and then the birds were on the ground; the hawk's head rising and falling with the death blows. In a moment he rose with the dead quail clutched in his claws, back up the side of the mountain and over the rim.

25   I didn't cry, but I knew I looked sad, because Granpa said, "Don't feel sad, Little Tree. It is The Way. Tal-con caught the slow and so the slow will raise no children who are also slow. Tal-con eats a thousand ground rats who eat the eggs of the quail—both the quick and the slow eggs—and so Tal-con lives by The Way. He helps the quail."

26   Granpa dug a sweet root from the ground with his knife and peeled it so that it dripped with its juicy winter cache of life. He cut it in half and handed me the heavy end.

27   "It is The Way," he said softly. "Take only what ye need. When ye take the deer, do not take the best. Take the smaller and the slower and then the deer will grow stronger and always give you meat. Pa-koh, the panther, knows and so must ye."

28   And he laughed, "Only Ti-bi, the bee, stores more than he can use... and so he is robbed by the bear, and the 'coon[9]….and the Cherokee. It is so with people who store and fat themselves with more than their share. They will have it taken from them. And there will be wars over it…and they will make long talks, trying to hold more than their share. They will say a flag stands for their right to do this… and men will die because of the words and the flag…but they will not change the rules of The Way."

29   We went back down the trail, and the sun was high over us when we reached the turkey trap. We could hear them before we saw the trap. They were in there, gobbling and making loud whistles of alarm.

30   "Ain't[10] no closing over the door, Granpa," I said. "Why don't they just lower their heads and come out?"

---

7 quail   small bird, often hunted and eaten by humans

8 hawk   a bird that eats other birds and small animals, catching them in sharp talons or claws

9 'coon   shortened form of raccoon; small forest animal with white patches on eyes and black rings on the tail

10 ain't   isn't

31 Granpa stretched full length into the hole and pulled out a big squawking turkey, tied his legs with a thong and grinned up at me.

32 "Ol' Tel-qui is like some people. Since he knows everything, he won't never look down to see what's around him. Got his head stuck up in the air too high to learn anything."

33 "Like the bus driver"?[11] I asked. I couldn't forget the bus driver fussing at Granpa.

34 "The bus driver?" Granpa looked puzzled, then he laughed, and kept laughing while he stuck his head back in the hole, pulling out another turkey.

35 "I reckin,"[12] he chuckled, "like the bus driver. He did kind of gobble now, come to think of it. But that's a burden fer him to tote around, Little Tree. Nothing fer us to burden our heads about."

36 Granpa laid them out on the ground, legs tied. There were six of them, and now he pointed down at them. "They're all about the same age...ye can tell by the thickness of the combs.[13] We only need three so now ye choose, Little Tree."

37 I walked around them, flopping on the ground. I squatted and studied them, and walked around them again. I had to be careful. I got down on my hands and knees and crawled among them, until I had pulled out the three smallest I could find.

38 Granpa said nothing. He pulled the thongs from the legs of the others and they took to wing, beating down the side of the mountain. He slung two of the turkeys over his shoulder.

39 "Can ye carry the other?" he asked.

40 "Yes, sir," I said, not sure that I had done right. A slow grin broke Granpa's bony face. "If ye was not Little Tree...I would call ye Little Hawk."

41 I followed Granpa down the trail. The turkey was heavy, but it felt good over my shoulder. The sun had tilted toward the farther mountain and drifted through the branches of the trees beside the trail, making burnt gold patterns where we walked. The wind had died in that late afternoon of winter, and I heard Granpa, ahead of me, humming a tune. I would have liked to live that time forever...for I knew I had pleased Granpa. I had learned The Way.

---

[11] the bus driver   Little Tree cannot forget the bus driver who gave an obnoxious imitation of Cherokee speech when he and his grandfather got on the bus to go home after his mother's funeral. Granpa is confused because he doesn't understand how Little Tree connects the comment about people who think they know everything with the bus driver.

[12] I reckin (reckon)   I guess/believe

[13] combs   the red growth of flesh on the head of domestic fowl and other birds

Comprehension Check

1. When does the narrative begin? Where are Little Tree and Granpa going?
2. Does Granpa want to go alone? How do you know?
3. How does Little Tree feel about getting up to go with his grandfather? Why?
4. How did Granpa and Little Tree set the trap for turkeys?
5. What happened between the hawk and the quail? What lesson does Granpa teach with it?
6. How does Granpa know that Little Tree has learned the lesson?

Sharing Your Thoughts

1. Carter suggests that Native Americans view the natural world as a living being. Find examples of this view in the story.
2. According to the story, what is the place of hunting and killing in the natural world?
3. What connections does Granpa see between animal and human behavior?
4. What does this story have to say to people in the modern world?
5. What, if anything, does the story teach us about sustainable economic growth?
6. This selection comes from an autobiographical work. Do you think it is a long anecdote or a nonfiction story? Explain.

Vocabulary

Content Vocabulary

Complete the following statements about the story with words from the list. Use each word only once. Change the form of verbs if the grammar of the sentence requires it.

bare	**branches**	**come alive**
dig	**dirt**	**scatter**
share	**sparkle**	**stump**
trail	**trap**	

1. Grandpa and Little Tree set out one morning to catch some turkeys. They walked along a _____ that followed the river to the turkey run where they built a _____ to catch turkeys.

2. Grandpa _____ a hole in the ground with his knife where the _____ of a dead tree had been.

3. Little Tree helped take out the _____. They covered the hole with _____ and spread leaves on top to hide the hole.

4. Finally Grandpa cut a trail from the turkey run to the hole and _____ corn along it to attract the turkeys to the hole.

5. Then they sat and watched the sun rise and _____ on the ice on the _____ branches of the trees. In the early morning, they felt the world _____.

6. Grandpa was very happy when Little Tree selected the three smallest turkeys they found in the trap. He knew that Little Tree had learned the lesson—take only what you need; do not take more than your _____.

Text Analysis

Figurative Language

Reread the paragraphs mentioned in the exercise below. What images, similes, metaphors, and examples of personification do you find in them? Describe in your own words the pictures and feelings that Carter creates for the reader. If you are artistic, draw a picture of an aspect of one of these passages.

1. the picture or feeling of the morning (¶2, ¶10)
2. the view from the high trail (¶14)
3. daybreak and the effect of the rising sun (¶15–¶18)
4. the picture of the hawk hunting quail (¶21–¶24)
5. the return home (¶41)

Writing Task

1. Write two or more paragraphs in which you explain what Granpa taught Little Tree and what that lesson has to say to people in the modern world. Write a paragraph for each teaching and what it says to us today. If you want, add an introduction and conclusion to turn it into a composition.

2. Write a conversation between Granpa and a developer who wants to cut down trees in his area to put in a large poultry farm. Each person should speak at least five times in the conversation.

SELECTION FIVE

Before Reading

"Prayer for the Great Family" appeared in *Turtle Island*, the collection that won the Pulitzer Prize for poetry in 1975. The poem is based on a Native American prayer from the Mohawk tribe.

1. What kinds of prayers do people say?
2. Who might the Great Family be? What kind of prayer could this be?

Prayer for the Great Family

by Gary Snyder

1   Gratitude to Mother Earth, sailing through night and day—
and to her soil: rich, rare, and sweet
in our minds so be it.[1]

2   Gratitude to Plants, the sun-facing light-changing leaf
and fine root-hairs; standing still through wind
and rain; their dance is in the flowing spiral grain
in our minds so be it.

3   Gratitude to Air, bearing the soaring Swift[2] and the silent
Owl at dawn. Breath of our song
clear spirit breeze
in our minds so be it.

4   Gratitude to Wild Beings, our brothers, teaching secrets,
freedoms, and ways; who share with us their milk;
self-complete, brave, and aware
in our minds so be it.

---

[1] **so be it**   like amen, a typical ending for a prayer

[2] **Swift**   a type of bird, related to the hummingbird

5   Gratitude to Water: clouds, lakes, rivers, glaciers;
    holding or releasing; streaming through all
    our bodies salty seas
    in our minds so be it.

6   Gratitude to the Sun: blinding pulsing light through
    trunks of trees, through mists, warming caves where
    bears and snakes sleep—he who wakes us—
    in our minds so be it.

7   Gratitude to the Great Sky
    who holds billions of stars—and goes yet beyond that—
    beyond all powers, and thoughts
    and yet is within us—
    Grandfather Space.
    The Mind is his Wife.

    so be it.

                                (*after a Mohawk prayer*)

Comprehension Check

1. What aspect of the environment is dealt with in each stanza?
2. What details about each aspect of the environment does the poet mention? What images do they create? What senses do they appeal to?

Sharing Your Thoughts

1. Find evidence in stanzas 4 and 5 of a connection between humans and Mother Earth.
2. What connection is suggested in stanza 7 between humans and the Great Sky?
3. What connections do you see between the world view in this poem and Granpa's world view in Selection Four?
4. What characteristics of animals are expressed in this poem? What connections do you see to ideas from the unit on humans and animals?
5. What do you think Snyder means by "the Great Family"?

Text Analysis

A. Writing Conventions

What words does Snyder capitalize in this poem that are not normally capitalized? Why do you think he does this?

B. Stanzas

Notice the ordering of the stanzas. Do you think there is any special reason they are in this order? Explain.

C. Repetition

Imagine how this poem would sound if read aloud to an audience. Now have a student read it aloud. What is the effect of the repetition in this poem?

Writing Task

1. Write at least one paragraph describing your reaction to this poem. Is there something about it you particularly liked? Explain.
2. Consider what you noticed in Text Analysis C; write a prayerlike piece that reflects your philosophy or view of something important.

A FINAL LOOK

Discussion

1. Work with a partner, in a small group, or as a whole class. Drawing on all five selections in this unit, and the quote on the introductory page, discuss the focus questions.

2. What is the difference between damage to the environment that occurred in previous centuries and the damage we are inflicting now? Compare causes and effects of the damage then and now. What can be done about the damage we are now inflicting on the planet?

3. In your opinion, is it possible to follow "The Way" today? Why or why not? How do you think Edward O. Wilson would answer this question?

4. What have you noticed about the relationship between human societies and the natural world? Give examples of how people's actions, good or bad, have consequences on other people, animals, or the natural world.

   EXAMPLE:

   If we stop consuming so much beef, that could have a positive effect on forests. But then maybe some ranchers would go out of business.

5. How can you relate ideas in this unit to those in previous units in this book?

   EXAMPLE:

   Granpa and Little Tree remind us of the role parents play in teaching values to children. Those values should include taking care of the environment.

Writing

1. Choose one of the topics and main ideas below. Modify the main idea if you want to.

   a. the interconnectedness of everything

   Idea: When we invent something new or change our behavior in some way, we don't always know what the effects of our actions will be.

   b. environment and education

   Idea: Education is the key to changing the way people treat the environment.

   c. environment and population

   Idea: Stabilizing population is the key to protecting the environment.

   d. environment and industrialization

   Idea: Industrialization can be both good and bad for an area.

   e. environment and international agreements

   Idea: Protecting the environment requires international agreements.

List specific examples you could use to illustrate the idea you choose. Examples can come from selections in this unit, from other reading you have done, or your personal experience.

Draft a three- to five-paragraph composition in which you explain and illustrate the idea you choose. Remember to give proper credit to the authors whose examples you use. You will probably find the IBC pattern useful in organizing your writing.

Have another student read your composition and ask you questions when they do not understand something. Write a second draft of the composition, clarifying the parts that the reader could not understand.

2. Freewrite about what nature means to you or about your place in the natural world in order to generate ideas for a three- to five-paragraph composition. Select the idea you want to develop and support it by describing particular experiences you have had with nature. Discuss how your views are similar to or different from one or more of the authors of the selections in this unit. When you use other people's ideas, remember to give proper credit.

ANSWER KEY

STUDENT'S INTRODUCTION
Basic Abilities of Efficient Readers

VOCABULARY

A. Content Vocabulary

1. literate; handle
2. up-to-date
3. captions; take advantage
4. held accountable; mistaken
5. figure out
6. agree; disagree
7. pleasure
8. take the plunge

B. Recognizing Definitions

2. preview: "read the entire first two paragraphs... organization of the material before they begin.
3. background knowledge: what they already know about the topic
4. skim: They read quickly, looking for key words and sentences to give them the general idea.
5. hypotheses: tentative ideas
6. monitoring comprehension: the whole paragraph beginning with "Research shows...."
7. infer: guess
8. paraphrase: Put them (ideas) into your own words.

UNIT 1: FRIENDSHIP

1. The Fabric of Friendship

VOCABULARY

A. Content Vocabulary

Verb Forms:
assist
confide in
enjoy
respect
trust
understand

1. enjoy
2. assistance
3. understand
4. respect
5. acceptance
6. trust
7. confide

B. Idioms and Phrasal Verbs

1. b
2. a
3. a
4. b
5. b
6. a

2. All Kinds of Friends

VOCABULARY

A. Content Vocabulary

1. close
2. dormant
3. share; in common
4. exchange
5. allow
6. enrich
7. broaden our horizons
8. matters

B. Word Analysis

1. broad/-en	make broader or wider
-en	changes adjective to verb; means to cause to be/have; to become *shorten, fatten*
2. en-/rich	improve, make richer
en-	changes nouns and adjectives to verbs, also used with verbs; means to cause to be, to put into *enlarge, enforce, encode, endanger, enclose*
3. regular/-ly	at regular time intervals, consistently
-ly	changes adjectives to adverbs that answer the questions *how?* or *how often?*) *quickly, occasionally*
4. girl/-hood	period of youth for a female
-hood	changes nouns to other nouns with a related meaning; means state or time of being *childhood, boyhood*
5. straight/-en	make straight (as in #1)
6. mother/-hood	state of being a mother (as in #4)
7. un-/equal	not equal
un-	means *not*, also negates the action of a verb *unhappy, unsuccessful, undo, untie*
8. en-/liv/-en	make more active, spirited, cheerful; make more alive
en-	as in #2
-en	as in #1
9. un-/connected	not connected
un-	as in #7
10. frequent/-ly	often
-ly	as in #3

3. The Barber

VOCABULARY

A. Content Vocabulary

1. stages; odd
2. roles
3. discussed
4. joked
5. argued
6. loss
7. realize

B. Idioms and Phrasal Verbs

1. b
2. b
3. a
4. a
5. a
6. b

TEXT ANALYSIS

Text Organization

¶1–2	b
¶3	e
¶4	a
¶5	c
¶6–7	f
¶8	d

4. The First Day of School

VOCABULARY

Content Vocabulary

1. died; frightened
2. way; wished
3. proud
4. try him out; got along
5. funny
6. on the way
7. amazed
8. delighted

UNIT 2: PARENTS AND CHILDREN

1. Mother Was Really Something

VOCABULARY

A. Content Vocabulary

1. complained
2. raise
3. praise
4. chores
5. mentor; reach; success
6. managed; proud; achieved

B. Grammatical Function

1. V; N
2. N; V
3. N; A
4. V; N
5. V; N
6. A; N
7. N; V
8. N; V
9. N; V

C. Inferring Meaning from Context

¶8

quit	stopped or left "and gave herself to her family"
commuted	traveled He moved to a farm 40 miles from his business in Chicago.
run	manage from the context of "business"

¶29

shivering	shaking from the cold They were wearing thin sweaters. It was a cold day.
stared	looked, with desire of some sort
greedily	The children were apparently poor, and therefore probably hungry. Therefore, they looked at the hot soup with desire.
steaming	*hot* from the context of soup in a pot (presumably on the stove)

D. Word Analysis

1. medical-school: school where one studies medicine in order to become a doctor
2. ice cream: cream that has been made into ice (frozen)
3. rail\road: road of rails (long pieces of steel) that trains run on
4. wind\blown: blown by the wind
5. hit-and-run accident: an accident in which one driver hit another and ran away (fled from the scene of the accident)
6. farm\house: the main house on a farm
7. home\made: made at home
8. flash card: a card for flashing information (showing it quickly); used in teaching the multiplication tables for example. One side of the card has *3 x 4*; the other *12*.
9. book\case: a case (box in which goods can be stored) made to hold books
10. dining room: a room for dining (formal eating)
11. paint-by-number: pictures (in outline) with numbered spaces to be painted; each number represents a different color
12. home\work: school work to be done at home
13. report card: a card that reports elementary and high school students' grades
14. record player: a machine for playing records
15. sleepy-eyed: with eyes that look sleepy

2. The Problem of Fathers and Sons

VOCABULARY

A. Content Vocabulary

1. articulate; accurately; fascinating
2. beyond his grasp
3. aware; illiterate; ignorance
4. humble; painstaking; quit

B. Inferring Meaning from Context

1. a
2. f
3. c
4. g
5. e
6. b
7. d

TEXT ANALYSIS

Text Organization

¶1–8	c
¶9	d
¶10–15	a
¶16	b

3. *Untitled*

VOCABULARY

A. Content Vocabulary

1. amusing; run away
2. sobbing; trade (him) in; tucked (him) in
3. crumpled; incoherent
4. hated; failure
5. been through

B. Idioms and Phrasal Verbs

1. find
2. vomit
3. enter, sit down in
4. become an adult
5. rebel, leave with a kick or fight
6. return

4. *Love, Your Only Mother*

VOCABULARY

Content Vocabulary

1. wandered
2. brief
3. wonders; vowed
4. faithful
5. come back; bolt upright; terrified

UNIT 3: COPING WITH STRESS

1. *Plain Talk about Handling Stress*

VOCABULARY

A. Content Vocabulary

1. impact; challenge; tension; overwhelmed
2. sources; respond
3. avoid; signs; irritable

B. Word Analysis

1. un-/exciting	not exciting
excite/-ing	causing excitement
2. well-being	personal and bodily comfort, esp. good health; being well (in good condition)
3. stress-filled world	world filled with stress
4. stress/-ful	causing stress -ful changes nouns and verbs to adjectives; means *full of*
5. harm/-ful	dangerous -ful changes nouns and verbs to adjectives; means *full of*

6. rush-hour traffic	heavy traffic in the early morning and late afternoon when people are in a hurry (rush) to get to work or get home
7. irrit/-able	tending to get angry at small things irrit- related to irritate (to make angry) -able changes verbs to adjectives; means able or needing to be or likely to suffer the stated action
8. give and take	flexibility; give something and get (take) something
9. over-the-counter medication	medication that can be sold directly to the customer without a doctor's prescription
10. habit-forming	addictive; can create customary or habitual behavior

C. Grammatical Function

Adjectives ending in *-ing* describe that which causes a feeling. Adjectives ending in *-ed* describe the person or thing affected.

D. Synonyms and Paraphrases

1. unexciting
2. handle, deal with
3. distress
4. relaxing, having fun
5. nervous

2. *Energy Walks*

VOCABULARY

A. Content Vocabulary

1. alert; anxiety; fatigue
2. brisk; mood
3. pick-me-up; boost; tip

B. Idioms and Phrasal Verbs

1. approaching; coming soon
2. in rather good physical condition
3. continued (to be true)
4. appear
5. in progress
6. reduce
7. start to smoke; light the cigarette
8. immediately

3. *The Stress-Resistant Person*

VOCABULARY

A. Content Vocabulary

1. demanding; vulnerable
2. anxiety
3. engage; seek out; committed
4. attitude; strategy

B. Word Analysis

1. stress-resistant people — people able to resist stress
2. walk-in clinic — a clinic which takes care of people without appointments; they walk in when they need the services
3. full-time jobs — jobs that require eight hours of work five days a week
4. night-school students — students who take classes at night
5. problem solvers — people who can solve problems well
6. stone-age habits — habits or customs of people who lived in the Stone Age

4. The Dinner Party

VOCABULARY

Content Vocabulary

1. frighten; outgrown
2. warning; commotion; bait
3. crisis

UNIT 4: FORMATION OF GENDER ROLES

1. It Begins at the Beginning

VOCABULARY

A. Content Vocabulary

1. grow up; peers
2. accustomed
3. hierarchically; resists; argue
4. status; boasting; concerned; intimacy

B. Vocabulary of Contrast

1. boys and girls grow up in the same neighborhood, block, house / they grow up in different worlds of words
2. some boys' and girls' activities are similar / their favorite games and ways they use language in games are different
3. some girls more skilled than others / girls are expected not to boast or show they think they are better
4. boys and girls grow up in the same family / they play in different ways and learn different styles of communication
5. boys say "Gimme that!!" etc. / girls say "Let's do this" etc.
6. boys tend to play outside in large groups / girls are more accustomed to playing indoors with one or two friends
7. boys play in large groups that are hierarchically structured (¶2 Tannen) / girls play in small groups or in pairs
8. boys' groups have a leader and followers / girls' groups appear more democratically structured
9. status is important in boys' groups / girls are concerned with having close friends, intimacy is important

¶1–4: focus on something which contrasts with what is expected

¶5–9: show direct opposition

2. Hidden Lessons

VOCABULARY

A. Content Vocabulary

1. treat
2. called on; bias
3. catch up; declined; rose; hindered
4. crucial

B. Grammatical Function

	Verb	Noun	Adjective	Adverb
1.	achieve	achievement		
2.		awareness	aware	
3.	differ	difference	different	differently
4.	expect	expectation		
5.	remedy	remedy	remedial	
6.	succeed	success	successful	successfully
7.	treat	treatment		
8.	vary	variety	various	

1. remedial; remedy
2. aware; awareness
3. expectations; expect
4. successful; succeed
5. achieve
6. vary; variety
7. treatment
8. differently

C. Word Analysis

1. out-/number — be more of; be larger in number
   out- (more than, to a greater degree) + number
2. un-/intention/-al — accidental, not intended or planned
   not + intention + -al adjective suffix
   intend + -tion noun suffix
3. non-/sex/-ist — not showing bias toward one sex or the other
   non (not) + sex + -ist (having certain ideas, about sex in this case)
4. better-paying jobs — jobs with higher salaries (that pay better)
5. pre-/school — in the years before starting school
   pre- (before) + school
6. other/-wise — if not, in different conditions
   other (different) + -wise (older form of "ways") would not be helpful to students, but they can learn to use partial help

3. Understanding Gender Differences

VOCABULARY

A. Content Vocabulary

1. sex; gender
2. genuine
3. accurate; supports
4. gap, show up
5. sources; appropriate
6. raise

B. Idioms and Phrasal Verbs

1. a lot of research; research piled high like mountains (literally thousands of studies)
2. remember; keep in mind (*bear* meaning "carry")
3. fictitious; like a myth, not real
4. expect and accept without thinking about it or questioning its correctness
5. make a special effort
6. conform to, make it similar to

C. Qualifying/Limiting Statements

1. *on the average* (not all females, limits statement to the typical female)
   somewhat (not a lot)
2. *tend to* (not all children or not all the time)
3. *rather* (not small but moderately small)
4. *suggest* (conclusion not very strong, not proved)
   may (possible but not sure)
5. *often* (but not always)
6. *likely to* (probable but not sure)

4. X

VOCABULARY

A. Content Vocabulary

1. no matter; promised; consult
2. treat; plenty of
3. weird; cheer X up
4. give up; imitate
5. influence; mixed up

B. Connotations

As the author of this story uses these words, they have the following connotations:
active masculine
brave masculine
cute feminine or neutral though author uses it with feminine connotation
dainty feminine
handsome masculine
husky masculine
nice feminine or neutral though author uses it with feminine connotation
strong masculine
sweet feminine
tiny neutral

The word *brave* is used once with the expected masculine connotation (¶34); in ¶32 Gould uses it to modify *princess*, to suggest that there is no reason females cannot be brave too.

UNIT 5: CULTURES IN CONTACT

1. Culture

VOCABULARY

A. Content Vocabulary

1. acquire; conform
2. notions; familiar
3. aware; share
4. aversion
5. background

B. Word Analysis

1. con-/scio/-ous — with awareness, understanding that one is learning
   with + know + adjective suffix
2. un-/conscious — without awareness, learning without knowing one is learning
3. inter-/act/-tion — action between two or more things
   between + act + noun suffix
4. internal/-ize — make part of one's self (especially a principle or pattern of behavior)
   inside + make
5. in-/corpor-/ate — make part of one's self
   in (Lat. prefix = into) + body + verb suffix
6. trans-mit-ted — send or pass from one person/place to another
   across + send + past participle
7. back/ground — information necessary for the understanding of something
   back (previous) + ground (surface of the earth, hence a foundation)
8. high/lands — a mountainous area

C. Grammatical Function

Verb	Noun	Adjective	Adverb
1. believe	belief	believable	believably
2.	culture	cultural	culturally
3. diversify	diversity	diverse	
4. modify	modification		
5. prefer	preference	preferable	preferably
6. socialize	socialization	social	socially
	society		
7. tolerate	tolerance	tolerant	tolerantly
		tolerable	tolerably

1. diverse
2. culturally
3. preference
4. tolerance; tolerate
5. social
6. modify
7. beliefs

2. Touching

VOCABULARY

A. Content Vocabulary

1. avoid
2. collide; misconstrue; sign
3. realize; uproar
4. faintest
5. warn

B. Grammatical Function

1. V
2. N
3. N
4. V
5. V
6. startled
7. complain; crowded
8. steely
9. contradiction

3. Don't Misread My Signals

VOCABULARY

A. Content Vocabulary

1. surveillance; lectured
2. flashy; suitable
3. misinterpreted; signal
4. amused
5. misconceptions; replace

B. Inferring Meaning from Context

1. new, recently arrived
   Knowing what a pub is and how the man behaved help you infer the meaning.
2. a little self-contained world, representing a larger reality
   Knowing *micro-* (small) helps. My parents designed our life as a (small version) of their *casas* on the island (Puerto Rico).
3. flashy, bright
   colors
4. criticized
   for wearing "everything at once" —meaning too much jewelry and too many accessories, implying they were not appropriately dressed
5. principal
   Knowing *main* (principal) is enough.
6. sexually exciting, provocative
   Hot Tamale, sexual
   Knowing *fire* can help too.
7. too fast, excited, passionate
   painfully sloppy, kiss, when I didn't respond with sufficient passion (The young man expected passion, so he was probably passionate too.)
   over-, prefix meaning *too great, too much*
8. song
   sing
9. sophisticated, knowledgeable about the world
   corporate executive
   Knowing *world* can help.

4. Assembly Line

VOCABULARY

Content Vocabulary

1. accomplished; gathers; dyes; weaves
2. exquisite; tax; bargain; cheat
3. stock
4. willing; deal
5. profit(s); get on his feet
6. grasp

UNIT 6: HUMANS AND OTHER ANIMALS

1. People and Other Animals

VOCABULARY

A. Content Vocabulary

1. impact; reduce; boost
2. catalyst; handicapped; expectancy
3. empathy; thrive; isolated

B. Word Analysis

1. over-/medic-/ given too much medication,
   ate/-ed   over- (more than, above) + medicine + verb suffix + past participle

2. un-/precedent/ never having happened before
   -ed   precedent (a former action or case used to guide present decisions)
            Knowing *pre-* (before) can help.
3. home/-bound   unable to leave the home
            home + limited to, kept in
            Knowing *home* can help.
4. bed/ridden   unable to leave a bed because of illness or old age
            Knowing *bed* can help.
5. out-/casts   persons forced from their home or without friends
            cast out (thrown out)
6. un-/condition/ not limited by any conditions
   -al/-ly   not + condition + adjective suffix + adverb suffix
7. un-/self-/   not thinking of self
   conscious   not + self + aware of
8. primat-/   person who studies primates
   -ologist   (monkeys, gorillas, etc.)
            primate + person who studies

2. Food for Thought

VOCABULARY

A. Content Vocabulary

1. cages; pens; calves; anemic
2. ailments; feed
3. warn; beyond
4. threat; wreak havoc
5. prone

B. Word Analysis

1. fatt/-en/-ed   made fat
            fat + verb suffix (make) + past participle
2. slaughter/   building where animals are
   house   killed for meat
            slaughter (kill) + house
3. new/born   recently or just born
4. wide/spread   found in many places, common covering a large (wide)
            space/range + spread (extended)
5. common/place ordinary, usual
            Knowing *common* can help.
6. count/-less   very many, too many to be counted
            count + adjective suffix (without)
7. over-/crowd/   putting too many animals in a
   -ing   cage or pen
            over- + crowd + noun suffix (present participle as noun)
8. live/stock   animals kept on a farm
            living + stock (goods for sale)
9. over-/use   excessive use of
            over- (more than, above) + use
10. life/saving   able to save lives
            life + save + present participle
11. in-/discrimi- careless
    nate   not + choosing carefully
12. un-/treat/   not possible to treat
    -able   not + treat + adjective suffix
13. mis-/use   wrong use
            mis- (wrong or bad) + use
14. in-/abil/-ity lack of power or skill
            not + able + noun suffix
15. agri-/business farming, on a large business scale
            agri (from agriculture) + business

3. A Plea for the Chimps

VOCABULARY

A. Content Vocabulary

1. justified; brought up; resemblance
2. bonds
3. confined; bleak
4. callous; condone
5. insane
6. alleviate

B. Word Analysis

1. care/take/-er   person who takes care of something
2. motion/-less   still, without motion
3. over-/emphas-/   to give too much emphasis
     -ize   or importance to
4. out-/stretch/   spread, extended
     -ed   Knowing *out* can help.
5. power/-less   weak, unable, without power
6. hand/ful   a small number
      a number that would fit in your hand
7. bear/-able   tolerable, able to be borne or suffered

4. The Pig Who Loved People

VOCABULARY

Content Vocabulary

1. triggered
2. creature
3. reluctantly; get rid of
4. dread
5. mimic; reward
6. edgy; face
7. handle

UNIT 7: HUMANS AND THEIR ENVIRONMENT

1. Ten Major Threats to the Environment

VOCABULARY

A. Providing Definitions

1. disrupt: bring, throw into disorder
2. ecosystem: plants, animals, people and environment functioning as a unit
3. famine: very serious lack of food
4. emit, emissions: put/send out; something put/sent out
5. ozone layer: region of upper atmosphere, 15-30 km high, with high levels of ozone
6. deteriorating: becoming worse
7. release: set free, let go
8. deplete, depletion: lessen greatly in quantity, contents, power, value; reduction
9. source: place from which something comes, origin
10. contaminate, contaminants: make impure or bad by mixing in/with impure, dirty, poisonous matter; the impure, dirty or poisonous matter
11. rely on, reliance on; depend on; dependence on
12. dump: drop or unload, get rid of
13. sewage: waste material and water carried in sewers
14. runoff: eliminated liquid waste
15. waste: used, damaged, unwanted materials

16. pollution, polluted: act, process, or result of contaminating soil, water, or air with harmful substances; contaminated (This word is generally used in the context of *environment,* that is *environmental pollution. Contamination* is more common in the context of specific chemicals, as in *nitrate contamination* in Section 4.)
17. toxic: poisonous
18. hazardous: dangerous
19. dispose of, disposable: get rid of, throw away; intended to be used once and thrown away
20. landfill: place where solid waste is buried
21. burial: put under ground; putting under ground
22. trash: waste material to be thrown away, garbage
23. recycling: take useful materials from waste and return them to the production process
24. diversity: variety
25. sustainable: maintainable, that which can be kept in existence
26. species: group of plants or animals of the same kind (can breed together)
27. endangered: put in danger
28. topsoil: upper level of earth where most plants have their roots
29. erosion: action or result of eroding, the wearing away of something from sun, wind, rain.
30. replenish: fill up again
31. habitat destruction: destruction of the environment where an animal/plant usually lives
32. degradation: lower in quality
33. food reserves: food supplies, stored for future use
34. resources: possessions (esp. of a country) in the form of wealth and goods

B. Content Vocabulary

1. pollution; erosion
2. emissions; hazardous; landfills; sewage
3. endangered; habitats
4. deteriorate; resources

2. The Destruction of the Rain Forests

VOCABULARY

A. Content Vocabulary

1. shrinking; clearing; delicate; support
2. demand; profit; compacts; runs off
3. climate; desert; destruction; sustainable

B. Inferring Meaning from Context

1. impress us (without educating us)
People will try to prove anything with statistics.
2. communicate (writers try to ... problems)
3. give, write, supply (numbers)
4. deal with, understand, calculate
5. places where we can walk in a forest, paths
6. go down (boots needed because walker's feet sink several inches in the mud)
7. a big part, most (although the lion's share has already been cleared, what remains)
(Presumably, lions eat most of the meat of their prey; then smaller animals eat what remains.)
8. great (variety)
9. gives food to (Sunlight filters to mid levels where it nurtures palm trees.)
10. having (plants sporting exotic flowers)
11. has a lot of (anthill teems with life)
12. looks, views (eye can catch glimpses of birds)

3. Unmined Riches

VOCABULARY

A. Content Vocabulary

1. wilderness; priceless
2. preserve
3. poverty; make a living
4. income
5. derived; available
6. restoration; biodiversity

B. Word Analysis

1. re-/vit-/-al/-ize — bring back to life
   re- (back) + life + adjective suffix + verb suffix (make)
2. in-/vis-/-ible — cannot be seen
   not + see + variation of -able
3. micro-/organ-ism/-s — living creatures too small to be seen without a microscope
   micro- (small) + organism (living being) + plural
4. astronom(y) -ical — a very large number/amount
   astronomy (study of of stars) + adjective suffix

5. anti-/coagul-/-ant — substance that prevents a liquid, most commonly blood, from coagulating (becoming a solid)
   anti- (against) + coagul (solidify) + -ant (person/thing that causes a stated effect)
6. trans-/plants — grafts, moving of skin from one part of the body to another
   trans- (across) + plant
7. proto-/type — the first form of anything, from which all later forms develop proto- (first in time or order) + type (kind)
8. under-/util-/-ize/-ation — use below potential under- (less than) + util- (use) + -ize (verb suffix) + -ation (noun suffix)

4. The Way

VOCABULARY

Content Vocabulary

1. trail; trap
2. dug; stump
3. dirt; branches
4. scattered
5. sparkle; bare; come alive
6. share

CREDITS

TEXT CREDITS

UNIT 1

1. "The Fabric of Friendship" – Reprinted with permission from *Psychology Today* Magazine. Copyright © 1985 (Sussex Publishers, Inc.)

2. "All Kinds of Friends" –- from *Necessary Losses*, by Judith Viorst. Copyright by Judith Viorst: reprinted by permission of Simon & Schuster, Inc.

3. "The Barber" – from *All I Need To Know I Learned in Kindergarten*, by Robert Fulghum. Copyright © 1986, 1988 by Robert Fulghum. Reprinted by permission of Villard Books, a division of Random House, Inc.

4. "The First Day of School" – Reprinted with the permission of the William Saroyan Foundation.

5. "Encounter" – by Marie-Thérèse Colimon; English translation by Elizabeth "Betty" Wilson. Used by permission of the author and translator.

UNIT 2

1. "Mother Was Really Something" – by Joseph N. Michelotti, MD. Reprinted with permission of Carla Michelotti, Esq.

2. "The Problem of Fathers and Sons" – by Enrique Hank López; reprinted from *Reading on Purpose*, Addison-Wesley, 1987.

3. "Untitled" – from *It Was on Fire When I Lay Down on It*, by Robert Fulghum, copyright © 1988, 1989 by Robert Fulghum. Reprinted by permission of Villard Books, a division of Random House, Inc. UK and Commonwealth permission by HarperCollins Publishers, Limited.

4. "Love, Your Only Mother" – by David Michael Kaplan, from *Comfort* © 1987 by David Michael Kaplan. Reprinted by permission of Brandt & Brandt Literary Agents, Inc.

5. "Those Winter Sundays" – is reprinted from *Angle of Ascent*, New and Selected Poems, by Robert Hayden, copyright © 1975, 1972, 1970, 1966 by Robert Hayden. Reprinted by permission of Liveright Publishing Corporation.

UNIT 3

1. "Plain Talk about Handling Stress" – by Louis E. Kopolow, MD. From the U.S. Department of Health and Human Services, DHHS Pub. # (ADM) 91-502; printed 1977, revised 1983, reprinted 1985, 1987, 1991.

2. "Energy Walks" – by Robert E. Thayer, reprinted from *Psychology Today* Magazine. Copyright © 1988 (Sussex Publishers, Inc.)

3. "The Stress-Resistant Person" – by Dr. Raymond B. Flannery, Jr. Excerpted from the February 1989 issue of the *Harvard Health Letter*, copyright © 1989, President and Fellows of Harvard College.

4. "The Dinner Party" – by Mona Gardner, from the January 31, 1942, *Saturday Review*. Reprinted by permission of the *Saturday Review*.

5. "Washing Dishes" – from *Peace Is Every Step* by Thich Nhat Hahn. copyright © 1991 by Thich Nhat Hahn. Used by permission of Bantam Books, a division of Bantam Doubleday Dell Publishing Group, Inc.

UNIT 4

1. "It Begins in the Beginning" – from *You Just Don't Understand* by Deborah Tannen, Ph.D. Published by Virago Press, 1992. Copyright © by Deborah Tannen, 1990. Used by permission of William Morrow & Company, Inc.

2. "Hidden Lessons" – by Claire Safran - reprinted from *Parade* Magazine, October 9, 1983. Copyright © 1983 by Claire Safran.

3. "Understanding Gender Differences" – Adapted from *Psychology: Themes and Variations*, 2nd edition, by Wayne Weiten. Copyright © 1992, 1989 by Wadsworth, Inc. Adapted by permission of Brooks/Cole Publishing Company, Pacific Grove, CA 93950.

4. "X" – by Lois Gould. Copyright © by Lois Gould.

5. "Black Woman" – by Ini Statia. Used by permission of the author.

UNIT 5

1. "Culture" – by Conrad Phillip Kottack. Excerpted from *Anthropology: The Exploration of Human Diversity*, 5e, copyright © 1991 McGraw-Hill Inc. Reproduced with permission of McGraw-Hill.

"Reflections" from *A Light in the Attic* by Shel Silverstein. Copyright © 1981 by Evil Eye Music, Inc. Reprinted by permission of the Edite Kroll Literary Agency.

2. "Touching" – from *Gestures! The Do's and Taboos of Body Language Around The World*, by Roger E. Axtell, copyright 1991. Reprinted with the permission of John Wiley & Sons, Inc.

3. "Don't Misread My Signals" – from *The Latin Deli: Prose and Poetry* by Judith Ortiz Cofer. Copyright © 1993 by Judith Ortiz Cofer. Reprinted by permission of the publisher, the University of Georgia Press.

4. "Assembly Line" – from *The Night Visitor and Other Stories* by B. Traven. Copyright © 1986 by B. Traven. Reprinted by permission of Hill and Wang, a division of Farrar, Straus & Giroux, Inc.

5. "Yuba City School" – by Chitra Banerjee Divakaruni, copyright © by Chitra Banerjee Divakaruni, is reprinted from *Black Candle* (Calyx Books, 1991) by permission of the publisher.

UNIT 6

1. "People and Other Animals" – from *Revolution from Within* by Gloria Steinem. Copyright © 1992 by Gloria Steinem. By permission of Little, Brown and Company.

2. "Food for Thought" – adapted from *The Dangers of Factory Farming*, published by the Humane Farming Association. Used by permission of the publisher.

3. "A Plea for the Chimps" – by Jane Goodall, from the May 17, 1987 *New York Times Magazine*. Copyright © 1987, by the New York Times Company. Reprinted by permission.

4. "The Pig Who Loved People" – by Jo Coudert, reprinted from the April, 1992, *Reader's Digest*. Reprinted with the permission of the author.

5. "Snake" – by D. H. Lawrence, from *The Complete Poems of D. H. Lawrence* by D. H. Lawrence, edited by V. de Sola Pinto & F. W. Roberts. Copyright © 1964, 1971 by Angelo Ravagli and C. M. Weekley, Executors of the Estate of Frieda Lawrence Ravagli. Used by permission of Viking Penguin, a division of Penguin Books USA Inc.

UNIT 7

1. "Ten Major Threats to the Environment" – by Jeremy Iggers. Reprinted with the permission of the publisher, the *Minneapolis St. Paul, Star Tribune*.

"How Do Trees Benefit the Urban Environment?" Reprinted with the permission of Fideicomiso de Conservación de Puerto Rico.

2. "The Destruction of the Rain Forests" – from *Diet for a Gentle World* by Les Inglis. Copyright © Avery Publishing Group, Inc. Reprinted with the permission of the publisher.

3. "Unmined Riches" – from *The Diversity of Life* by Dr. Edward O. Wilson. Copyright © 1992 by the Belknap Press. Published with the permission of the publisher.

4. "The Way" – from T*he Education of Little Tree* by Forrest Carter, published by the University of New Mexico Press. Reprinted by arrangement with Eleanor Friede Books, Inc. Copyright © 1976 by Forrest Carter. All rights reserved.

5. "A Prayer for the Great Family" — from *Turtle Island* by Gary Snyder. Copyright © 1969 by New Directions Publishing Corp. Reprinted with the permission of the publisher.

PHOTO CREDITS

ACKNOWLEDGMENTS

Many people have helped and encouraged us while we were working on this book. We would like to thank the numerous colleagues and friends who suggested material for inclusion in the book and were otherwise supportive of our effort: Alena Alberani, Juanita Baumgartner, Sonia Crespo, Pierre Cudmore, Elizabeth Dayton, Sheila Dunstan, John Green, Anthony Hunt, José Irizarry, Mary Leonard, Mary Martin, Ann Murdaugh, Ellen Pratt, Sandra Ríos, Ismael Rivera, Robert Sherwin, Robert W. Smith, Barbara Strodt, and Rita Davila, Carmen Pérez, and Scott Ware at the *San Juan Star* among others. The ways in which our nuclear and extended families have helped, supported, and tolerated us could never be enumerated. Special thanks are due to numerous staff at Addison-Wesley/Longman (Allen Ascher, Mary Carson, Joanne Dresner, Polli Heyden, Françoise Leffler, Laura McCormick, Jessica Miller, and Liza Pleva) and to our developmental editor, Randee Falk. We gratefully acknowledge the writers whose work constitutes the core of this book, especially those who granted permission to reprint without cost. Finally, special thanks to our students who have proven to us the benefit of learning from sets of related readings. We hope that many other students around the world will benefit in a similar way.